Letters of Light

Letters of Light

Passages from *Ma'or* va-*shemesh*

consisting of the homilies of

Kalonymus Kalman
Epstein of Kraków

translated with notes
and comments by

Aryeh Wineman

☙PICKWICK *Publications* · Eugene, Oregon

LETTERS OF LIGHT
Passages from *Ma'or va-shemesh*

Copyright © 2015 Aryeh Wineman. All rights reserved. Except for brief quotations in critical publications or reviews, no part of this book may be reproduced in any manner without prior written permission from the publisher. Write: Permissions. Wipf and Stock Publishers, 199 W. 8th Ave., Suite 3, Eugene, OR 97401.

Pickwick Publications
An Imprint of Wipf and Stock Publishers
199 W. 8th Ave., Suite 3
Eugene, OR 97401

www.wipfandstock.com

ISBN 13: 978-1-62564-883-9

Cataloguing-in-Publication Data

Wineman, Aryeh

    Letters of light : passages from *Ma'or va-shemesh* / consisting of homilies of Kalonymus Kalman Epstein of Kraków, translated with notes and comments by Aryeh Wineman

    X + Y p. ; 23 cm. Includes bibliographical references.

    ISBN 13: 978-1-62564-883-9

    1. Epstein, Kalonymus Kalman, –1823. 2. Bible. Pentateuch—Criticism, interpretations, etc., Jewish. 3. Hasidim. 4. Ma'or va-Shemesh. I. Epstein, Kalonymus Kalman, –1823. II. Title.

BS1225.52 W46 2015

Manufactured in the U.S.A.   01/14/2015

Translation of biblical texts are reproduced from the TANAKH : THE HOLY SCRIPTURES by permission of the University of Nebraska Press. Copyright 1985 by the Jewish Publication Society, Philadelphia.

In memory

of

Dorothy

Table of Contents

List of Abbreviations | xiii
Introduction | xvii

1   On the First Book of the Torah (*B'rei'shit* / Genesis)
    B'rei'shit
        The need to go beyond the literal sense of the Torah | 3
        The Hidden Light | 6
        The surface meaning of the Torah and the Torah's innerness | 8
        A longing permeating all existence | 11
        Two modes of Torah-study | 14
        The function of Shabbat | 16
        Humility and the world's sustainability | 20
        When one person judges another | 21
    No'aḥ
        Noah repaired the animals | 23
    Lekh-l'kha
        Go forth!—"Go to you!" | 26
        Purity and impurity of motivation | 28
        As the stars that shine by their own light | 29
    Vayera
        The pearl of healing | 31
        The element of physical desire in intercourse | 33
        The poles of mercy and justice | 34
    Ḥayyei Sarah
        A person's coming to the *tzaddik* (holy man) | 37
    Tol'dot
        The lure and cooling of appetite | 40

Vayetzei
    Jacob's dream-episode | 42
    The letters within all that exists | 45

Vayishlah
    Angels | 49
    The *tzaddik*: solitude and community | 51

Vayeishev
    The two poles that one must avoid | 53

Miketz
    The *tzaddik* is oblivious to fame | 57

Vayiggash
    Submission | 59

Vay'ḥi
    Jacob's final testament and failure | 61

2   On the Second Book of the Torah (*Sh'mot* / Exodus)

Sh'mot
    Torah and time | 67
    True worship requires joy | 68
    The descent of the Divine | 69
    Moses' fear of losing his humility | 70
    The bush aflame | 71
    The infinite Names of God | 72

Va'era
    The basis of Moses' hesitation | 76

Bo
    Humility renewed | 79
    The meaning of *matza* (unleavened bread) | 80

B'shallaḥ
    The miracle at the Sea | 83
    Miriam and the dance at the Sea | 88
    The meaning of manna | 91

Yitro
    Why did Yitro journey to Moses? | 94
    A portrait of Moses as a judge | 96
    The status of the Sinaitic event in context | 98
    The gate of humility and its recurrence | 100

Mishpatim
    Justice and worship | 104
T'rumah
    Moses as a model of the Tabernacle | 107
    From each only according to his ability | 109
    Repentance before and after study | 111
T'tzavveh
    Fellowship and mutuality | 113
Ki tissa
    The Seventh Day as a day of renewed existential connection | 115
    For each soul to know its initial location | 118
    The veil over Moses' radiant face | 120
Vayakhel
    Exploring the parallel between Creation and the Tabernacle | 124
    The joy of giving | 126
    Bezalel and humility | 129
P'kudei
    An accountant of the spirit | 130

3 On the Third Book of the Torah (*Vayikra* / Leviticus)
Vayikra
    The implications of humankind's uniqueness | 135
    Every person is as the First Man | 136
Tzav
    The fire to be kept burning upon the altar | 138
Sh'mini
    The inner experience at the core of a cultic act | 140
Tazri'a
    On laws of purity and impurity | 144
    The affliction of pride and false piety | 147
    The danger caused by deception | 149
M'tzora
    The sadness that leads to joy and healing | 151
Aḥare mot
    Concerning those with whom we share a higher soul-root | 153

K'doshim
: The paradoxical relationship between solitude and community | 157

'Emor
: The inner meaning of the calendar | 161

B'har
: Satiety | 164

B'ḥukkotai
: The world's benefit from Torah-learning | 167

4   On the Fourth Book of the Torah (*B'midbar* / Numbers)

B'midbar
: The need for both Torah-study and prayer | 171

Naso
: Blessing requires love | 173

B'ha'alotkha
: Sadness and the craving for food | 175

Sh'laḥ l'kha
: God's mercy overrides His anger | 180

Koraḥ
: Aaron, as high priest, maintains his humility | 183

Ḥukkat
: To each his own: the uniqueness of each person | 186
: The significance of song | 188

Balak
: The danger in one's imitating another's path | 191

Pinḥas
: The longing for the sublime Light that can be fulfilled only with death | 194

Mattot
: Defining one's motivation | 199

Mas'ei
: Cities of Refuge as Cities of Repentance | 202

5   On the Fifth Book of the Torah (*D'varim* / Deuteronomy)

D'varim
: As the stars of the heavens | 209

Va'ethannan
    The background of Moses' death | 212
    Prayer in community and solitude | 215
'Eikev
    The nature of manna | 217
R'eih
    Fellowship as the path to God | 219
    The need to overcome, and sometimes to strengthen, a sense of self | 221
    The call to unseat pride within the self | 222
Shoftim
    To judge oneself: internal judges | 225
    Altars of pride and routine | 226
Ki tetzei
    The beginning of the year: *Rosh ha-shanah* | 229
    Amalek | 231
Ki tavo
    The bringing of the first-fruits: thanksgiving must precede fulfillment of appetite | 234
Nitzavim
    What comprises a community in its entirety? | 236
    The paradox of religious expression | 238
Vayeilekh
    The limits of relying upon one's leader | 241
Ha'azinu
    Fallen, unripe fruit of a tree | 244
Zot ha-b'rakhah and *Rimze Simḥat Torah*
    Our Torah is copied from a supernal Torah | 246
    Continuity transcending death | 247

Glossary of terms | 249
Bibliography | 253

List of Abbreviations

Biblical books:

Gen	Genesis
Exod	Exodus
Lev	Leviticus
Num	Numbers
Deut	Deuteronomy
Josh	Joshua
Judg	Judges
1 Sam	I Samuel
2 Sam	II Samuel
1 Kgs	I Kings
2 Kgs	II Kings
Isa	Isaiah
Jer	Jeremiah
Ezek	Ezekiel
Hos	Hosea
Mic	Micah
Nah	Nahum
Hab	Habakuk
Zeph	Zephaniah
Hag	Haggai
Zech	Zachariah
Mal	Malachi
Ps. / Pss.	Psalm(s)
Prov	Proverbs

Song	Song of Songs
Lam	Lamentations
Eccl	Ecclesiastes
Esth	Esther
Dan	Daniel
Neh	Nehemiah
1 Chr	I Chronicles
2 Chr	II Chronicles
tg	(Aramaic) translation of the Bible or parts thereof
Tg Ps-J	Pseudo-Jonathan translation
m.	Mishna
b.	Babylonian Talmud
y.	Yerushalmi (Palestinian Talmud}

Talmudic tractates:

ʼAbod. Zar	Avodah zarah
ʼArak.	Arukhin
B. Bat.	Bava Batra
B. Meṣiʼa	Bava metziʼa
B. Qam	Bava Kamma
Ber.	Berakhot
Bikk.	Bikkurim
ʻErub.	Eruvin
Ed.	Eduyyot
Ḥag.	Hagigah
Ḥal.	Hallal
Ḥul.	Hullin
Ketub.	Ketubbot
Kil.	Kilʼayin
Mak.	Makkot
Meg.	Megillah
Menaḥ.	Menahot
Mid.	Middot

Mo'ed	*Mo'ed*
Mo'ed Qat.	*Mo'ed Katan*
Naz.	*Nazir*
Ned.	*Nedarim*
Nid.	*Niddah*
Pe'ah	*Pe'ah*
Pesaḥ	*Pesahim*
Qidd.	*Kiddushin*
Roš.Haš.	*Rosh ha-shannah*
Šabb.	*Shabbat*
Sanh.	*Sanhedrin*
Ta'an	*Ta'anit*
Yebam.	*Yevamot*

Other rabbinic texts:

'Abot	*Pirkei Avot*
'Avot R. Nat.	*Avot deRabbi Natan*
Meh.	*M'khilta*
MHG	*Midrash ha-gadol*
midr.	*Midrash*
midr. Gen.	*B'rei'shit rabbah*
midr. Exod	*Sh'mot rabbah*
midr. Lev.	*Vayikra rabbah*
midr. Num	*B'midbar rabbah*
midr. Deut	*D'varim rabbah*
midr. Lam	*Ekhah rabbah*
midr. Pss.	*Midrash T'hillim.*
Pesiq. Rab Kah.	*Pesikta deRav Kahana*
Pirqe R. El	*Pirke deRabbi Eliezer*
Sipra	*Sifra*
Sipre	*Sifre*
Tanḥ.	*Midrash Tanhuma*
Yalqut	*Yalkut*

Introduction

Hasidism, the Hasidic Homily, and Kalonymus Kalman Epstein

THIS BOOK IS A journey through another book that was first printed in 1842 and was afterward reprinted numerous times. It includes material from homilies delivered by Kalonymus Kalman haLevi Epstein who lived in Kraków, Poland and was first printed some nineteen years after his death in 1823. The literal meaning of the title of the book, *Ma'or va-shemesh*, would translate into English as "Light (or Luminary) and Sun."

Words expressing light are prominent in Hasidism and in the older tradition of Kabbalah in which it has its roots. The central literary masterpiece of medieval Kabbalah is the Zohar, the title-word meaning "radiance" or "brilliant light." Light is a metaphor for the Divine and also for the Torah, grasped as a manifestation of the light of the Divine. The readings of verses from the Torah comprising *Ma'or va-shemesh* grew out of a conception that viewed the very letters of the Torah-text as forms reflecting a Light that itself transcends the more limited meaning of the words they comprise. It is in that sense that this collection of passages from *Ma'or va-shemesh*, along with its running commentary, is entitled "Letters of Light," which would approximate the actual sense of the original Hebrew title.

The preacher, whose words we will meet, came, quite early in life, to identify with a stream of Jewish religious life known as Hasidism. The word *ḥasid*, a word with a long history, can perhaps best be translated for practical purposes as "pietist," and the term "Hasidism" came to refer specifically to a pietistic stream that emerged in eighteenth-century Eastern Europe. Historians view it as a transmutation of an earlier pietism, highly ascetic in nature, which was significantly transformed by the teachings attributed to the Baal Shem Tov (Israel ben Eliezer, d. 1760, known as the *Besht*) and which parted from that older asceticism in favor of an emphasis and even a requirement of serving God in joy.

Though the *Besht* did not write any books, he succeeded in gathering around him a circle of associates and followers. During the decade following his death, the *Maggid*, Dov Baer of Mezherich (d. 1772), went far to develop and crystallize a worldview based upon teachings ascribed to the *Besht*, as Hasidism began gradually to draw an increasingly larger following among Jews in certain areas of Eastern Europe. Though Hasidism emerged within the world of Jewish tradition as it had developed over many centuries, based upon talmudic law and learning, it took exception to the attitude that regarded talmudic study *in itself* as the supreme value in Jewish religious life. Hasidism evolved in a direction that came to express itself in a different type of religious leadership, that of the *tzaddik* or the *rebbe*, a holy man touched by spiritual illumination, rather than the traditional *rav* devoted primarily to study and known for his legal decisions.

Allowing for a considerably broader frame-of-reference, one might grasp Hasidism as an example within Jewish tradition of an inclination and ideological bent that is present also in the history of other religious traditions. Those traditions, too, experienced a temperamental split as some followers were drawn more to emotional experience than to intellectual formulations and creedal statements and sought attunement to a deeper level of the self. Sufism, in Islam, and medieval Christian mysticism are pronounced examples, and one might mention also the pietistic revolt that emerged within German Protestantism in the seventeenth and eighteenth centuries.[1] And though Kalonymus Kalman haLevi Epstein of Kraków, like other Hasidic masters, was firmly and deeply rooted in the world of traditional Jewish texts and practices, certain tendencies evident in his homilies might well suggest an affinity with voices within other traditions that related to their own very different roots in terms of some of the same general inclinations.

Ma'or va-shemesh is just one example of a type of literature that voiced the teachings associated with Hasidism. Beginning in 1780, just two decades following the death of the Baal Shem Tov, a stream of books began to appear containing homilies or homiletical notes of the teachers of Hasidism. With rare exception, the Hasidic worldview and its ideas

---

1. See Stoeffler, *The Rise of Evangelical Pietism*.

and themes were communicated principally in the form of sermonic discussions on the weekly Torah-portions, in itself a highly traditional form, even while the content of those same homilies might suggest, in various ways, a radically innovative understanding of the tradition.[2]

As a written statement of oral presentations the printed homilies might comprise an imperfect record of the sermonic discussions themselves; in addition, such texts were not the most widely printed and disseminated within the population influenced by Hasidism and, in terms of Hasidism's growth, were likely less significant than legendary traditions of a very different character.[3] The homily-texts, nevertheless, serve as the indispensable key to our understanding the religious thought of the Hasidic stream during its earlier period. Taken together, the Hasidic homily-texts might be approached as a highly creative reading of the Torah (the Pentateuch), the basic Jewish sacred text which is read in the synagogue and is also studied and discussed in more informal settings, especially on the Shabbat on which any particular Torah-portion is read.

Beyond its role as a vehicle of communication on the part of the teacher and preacher, the Hasidic homily reveals how the Torah-text lived within the consciousness of the Hasidic Masters and what they heard or overheard in it. Not only the meaning, but the very texture of the Torah-text underwent transformation in the Hasidic homily. Even as they utilized traditions of interpretation inherited from much earlier periods, the Hasidic Masters and teachers would expound a passage or verse from the Torah in the light of their own specific complex of values, revolving largely around the importance of *p'nimi'ut*—the innerness and depth-dimension of the self, of a holy deed, of the Torah or any particular legislation included in the Torah, and of existence itself.

In expounding the text of the Torah, the Hasidic preacher tended to grasp the more ultimate setting and reference of any particular passage from the Torah to be the Jew's inner life as it confronts both the complexity of the human make-up and the unique soulfulness present at the deepest level of a person's psyche. Hasidism defies definition; it is many things that might even contradict one another and must be studied in relation to an entire complex of historical and social factors and inherited

---

2. Dan, *Sifrut ha-musar v'had'rush*, 267.

3. Gries, *Sefer, sofer vesippur*, 27–30, 47–68; *The Book in the Jewish World 1700–1900*, 85–87.

ideas, but central to the homily-literature of its teachers is this core theme and quality of *innerness* and *interiority*.[4]

In the Hasidic homily, what in the Torah-text itself would appear to relate to what is out there in the objective world is frequently read as an allusion to what occurs within the self. While a passage from the Torah might convey details of a particular type of institution or cultic or judicial practice, the Hasidic homilist overheard in the same text a call for *inner* transformation, for a happening and drama that transpires within a person's own inner self. And furthermore, any passage from the Torah, irrespective of subject-matter, when sifted through the interpretative process of the Hasidic homily, tends to acquire a devotional character. This "character-change" in the texture of the Torah-text suggests an implicit understanding, to the homilist's mind, that the tone of his homily reflects the real and more ultimate character of the Torah itself which addresses a person's inner life and the need to serve and worship God in the most comprehensive sense. Though often bypassing the textual context of any particular passage in the Torah, the Hasidic homilist read even single words or phrases as keys that open the listener or reader to introspective insight, reading such elements as existential comments upon human life, emotions, conflicts, and growth in spiritual awareness.

What the text of the Torah would seem to present as a record of the past is read in the Hasidic homily more commonly as an allusion to states of mind and to changes within the self, with the result that specific moments in the "sacred history" recounted in the Torah become archetypal events that might radiate any person's life at any time. Words which, in the Torah-text, have a precise context in the life of a particular individual or even in the historical experience of the people of Israel are read by the homilist in a way to apply to every person at any time. One might express that tendency in the claim that the Hasidic homily aspired to read the Torah in the present (or "ever-present") tense, as a narrative that is constantly occurring.[5]

Already in *Toldot Ya'akov Yosef*, the very first printed Hasidic book, Ya'akov Yosef, the preacher of Polonnoye, repeatedly insisted that the true meaning of any element in the Torah must have validity and relevance concerning all persons and all times. The most relevant meaning of a verse—the homilist assumed—is one that applies to *all* time, not

---

4. See Margolin, *Mikdash 'adam*.
5. Wineman, "How the Hasidic Masters Read the Torah."

exclusively to a single point-of-time in the past or limited to a specific occasion during the course of the year. In this light, Kalonymus Kalman, like others, explained that though something in the Torah-text may have been occasioned by a one-time happening or circumstance, it nevertheless contains a message that is not time-bound but rather speaks to all persons and to all of time. And accordingly, for example, the Kraków master, like some others, would interpret *matza* (unleavened bread associated with the exodus from Egypt) and manna (the wondrous food that descended for the Israelites during their wanderings in the wilderness) as having a meaning quite independent of the larger biblical narrative in which they appear in the Torah.

The mode of interpretation permeating the classical Hasidic homily-texts presumes that the surface-level of the Torah comprises a garment of the Torah's deeper, inner character. Every letter in that garment is significant, even while the Torah, in its present form with which we are familiar, is a translation of that inner and more sublime state of the Torah to our own level of being in order to accommodate the nature of our own physical and finite reality, a theme of significance repeatedly brought out in *Ma'or va-shemesh*. That radical recognition, echoing some much older sources, echoes in the way the Hasidic homilists tend to go beyond the surface meaning (*p'shat*) as they read the text of the Torah as a network of allusions and overtones suggesting a deeper and more inner meaning. The Hasidic homily sought to understand the garment in the light of that more sublime core.[6]

Hasidism emerged in the small towns and villages of the Ukraine and Podolia, spreading afterward to other areas of Eastern Europe. Only closer to the onset of the nineteenth-century did Hasidism begin to make inroads in Poland. Kalonymus Kalman Epstein, who came to Kraków at a rather tender age, became a central figure in Hasidism's emergence in Kraków, the second largest city in Poland.

The young Kalonymus Kalman once went to hear Elimelekh of Lyzhansk (d. 1772) when the latter was speaking in Kraków and was much moved by the words of that noted Hasidic master, himself a student of the Maggid, Dov Baer of Mezherich. In the homilies collected in *Ma'or va-shemesh*, Kalonymus Kalman frequently refers to statements of Elimelekh. Identifying himself as a follower of Elimelekh, he would have had to stand his ground against the leadership of the local community at

---

6. Note *S'fat 'emet*, IV, 3b (*B'midbar*).

a time when the conflict between the followers of Hasidism and their Opponents often resulted in various accusations and counter-accusations which were sometimes brought to the governmental authorities. At that time Kraków Jewry, which continued to live in the shadow of the memory of the reknown sixteenth-century rabbinic scholar, Moses Isserles, was not hospitable to efforts to introduce Hasidism in that city. In 1785 for example, the rabbinate in Kraków proclaimed a ban on adherents of Hasidism, and a dozen years later a similar ban was proclaimed there against reading Hasidic texts.[7]

While Kalonymus drew a following, only after his death did those followers succeed in establishing their own synagogue in the city, and he never established a Hasidic dynasty that would continue after him. Neither he nor his sons succeeded in building any kind of enduring movement that looked to Kalonymus Kalman as its forebearer. His real legacy is that collection of homilies that outlived him. In referring to him in this work as one of the Hasidic Masters, the term does not connote any official position of leadership in a Hasidic community (a *tzaddik*) but rather an exponent of Hasidic teaching.

Even when touching upon complex topics in his homilies, Kalonymus Kalman tended to speak in rather simple terms. And he employed a conversational tone, a trait that may have accounted for the popularity of that collection of his homilies. Together with that simplicity, however, the reader cannot but appreciate the artistry involved in the preacher's reading a sacred text often clearly against its very grain to derive a startling, unexpected interpretation. Far from reiterating the obvious, he tended to draw from a biblical verse some insight exceedingly remote from what would appear to be conveyed in the source itself. That art of transformation with all its subtleties, along with the preacher's occasional ability to unearth a precious note of paradox in earlier texts and teachings, assigns to the collection of his homilies a place among significant Jewish literary texts.

Upon analysis, the most memorable homilies of Kalonymus Kalman Epstein reveal aspects of an anatomy of the Hasidic homily in which a biblical passage or law is severed from some significant aspect of its own context. That context might be the larger narrative to which it belongs or a detail clearly intrinsic to the biblical passage. And when a verse or narrative-fragment or law is severed from its more obvious context, the homilist connects it to a different context. That new context might be a

---

7. Hundert, *Jews in Poland-Lithuania*, 180, 196.

specific value or theme found in Jewish tradition or in Hasidic teaching or a more unexpected theme. The reader can note that kind of substitution of a new context in the more impressive and striking homilies in *Maʾor va-shemesh*, homilies in which the preacher emerges as a true artist. And the artistry of Kalonymus Kalman is revealed most clearly when the master substitutes a significantly more sublime context for what appears as a rather prosaic passage from the Torah.

The volume, printed almost two decades after the death of Kalonymus Kalman Epstein, is structured as a continuous running commentary on the (Written) Torah as read in the synagogue over the course of a year and is composed of homilies or material from homilies, presumably delivered in a prayer-room in the residence of the preacher himself. *Maʾor va-shemesh* is a decidedly Hasidic reading of the Torah, but it also reflects the thinking of a particular person and the ongoing tensions within his own mind and consciousness.

Beyond questions of authorship and editing and beyond the preacher's literary strategies, a text of this nature reveals the master's personal understanding of the Torah itself and of its very nature and character. Throughout history and extending to the present day in any tradition, a sacred text is read in a way that mirrors something of the mind and the values, the sensitivities and inner wrestlings of the person engaged in reading it. Every example of transformation of meaning in *Maʾor va-shemesh* represents his reading the Torah in a manner consonant with the stirrings of his own soul, and in that sense *Maʾor va-shemesh* is a kind of profile of Kalonymus Kalman Epstein himself. While he drew in large measure from the literature of traditional Jewish lore, including Midrash, in his homilies—as in those of his Hasidic peers—homily itself becomes a kind of midrash as the master's pietistic and mystic values are grounded in a creative reading of the Torah and of later texts.

His sensitivities include a powerful sense of the uniqueness of each person—and even the uniqueness of every blade of grass. They include, as well, a recoiling from thinking of the Divine as an agent of punishment. Kalonymus Kalman went to great lengths, for example, to retell the biblical account of the drowning of the Egyptians at the Sea of Reeds in a way that separates the fate of the Egyptians from any intentional divine, punitive action. And an emphasis on compassion and forgiveness colors even his readings of episodes in the Torah that themselves would clearly seem to exemplify judgment and wrath. In a remarkable stroke of transformation, the Kraków master, with recourse to *g'matria* (an interpretative strategy based upon the numerical value of letters), read the command in the Torah to obliterate the very memory of Amalek, a desert tribe associated with the extremes of cruelty and inhumanity, as a code to transform egotism and arrogance into love and into a sense of the all-pervading divine Oneness.

The homilies disclose the preacher's ongoing inner tensions as he wrestled with the relationship between the innerness of the Torah and the "revealed" Torah, including both its surface-meaning and the tradition of interpretation and rabbinic law that it engendered. Similarly, he struggled, without resolution, but in highly interesting ways, with the question of the primacy of the group versus that of the individual, the values of the inner life in solitude vis-à-vis those of the community. The Kraków preacher's insights into that polarity might prefigure some very contemporary discussion and issues arising specifically in our own time.

The very title given to the collection, *Ma'or va-shemesh*, points to an emphasis upon light. Identifying the Torah and its very letters as manifestations of divine Light, Kalonymus Kalman was instinctively driven to interpret any and every element in the text of the Torah in a way that he felt expresses and exemplifies that Light. And though Kalonymus Kalman Epstein was certainly a child and product of his time, significant elements of that collection of his homilies might also suggest some more modern sensitivities and can serve as a source of spiritual illumination to those living in our own hour of time.

NOTE: In the 1877 printing of *Ma'or va-shemesh*, from which the passages in this collection were translated, the homilies generally opened with a quotation from the appropriate Torah-portion, often in very abbreviated form with the assumption that the reader would easily and immediately associate the brief quotation with its larger textual context and its link with the homily. This edition has often expanded those very brief passages or fragments for the purpose of enabling the reader to grasp the actual connection between the quotation and the homily. Such additions are generally placed in parentheses, and certain explanatory additions, quite indispensable for grasping the precise meaning of the biblical text in terms of its relevance to the homily, are placed in square brackets. And when the particular nuance in the way the homilist read a biblical verse differs from the JTS translation, the homilist's emphasis appears in parentheses within the translation.

1

On the First Book of the Torah (*B'rei'shit* / Genesis)

B'rei'shit
The Need to Go beyond the Literal Sense of the Torah[1]

The first verse of the Torah, introducing an account of creation, consists of seven Hebrew words, and the combined numerical value (*g'matria*) of the first letter of each of those words adds up to twenty-two, the number of letters of the Hebrew alphabet, an allusion suggesting that all the worlds were created through those twenty-two letters of the Torah.

[According to *g'matria*, each letter of the alphabet has a numerical value. Hence it is possible to add up the numerical values of all the letters of a word and deduce meaning in terms of the equivalence of that word with another word having the same total numerical value. *G'matria* served as an interpretative strategy already in the rabbinic period and not infrequently served the same function in the Hasidic homily-literature. The mathematical observation mentioned above reinforced the concept that the Torah preceded the world and that God created the world(s) on the basis of the Torah and its letters, which served as a blueprint of creation.[2]]

Onkelos [who translated the Torah from Hebrew to Aramaic in the second century, C.E.] translated the first three words as "In the beginning / created / God," but one must understand, as Rashi [acronym for *Rabbi Shlomo ben Yitshak*, the foremost medieval commentator of both the Torah and the Babylonian Talmud] explained, that grammatically it is not possible to interpret the first word, *B'rei'shit*, simply as indicating "In the beginning." It would appear, rather, that the words and their order intimate that God's own Self is beyond the reach of comprehension, as no idea or thought is at all capable of grasping God. The words convey

---

1. *Ma'or va-shemesh* (Warsaw, 1877), I, 2b.
2. b. Ber. 55a and Menaḥ. 29b, Midr.Gen 1.9 and y. Ḥag. 77c; Ginzberg, *Legends*, 5:56, n. 10.

that all thoughts necessarily fail to grasp God's own essence and selfhood, which remains hidden beyond the reach of any idea. In the holy books this conception is referred to as "the Light that is unknowable."

Even those heavenly creatures who bear the divine Throne (referring to the vision in Ezek 1) and who hallow Him each day as they declare, "The Lord of Hosts! His presence fills all the earth!" (Isa 6:3), still find it necessary to ask, "Where is the place of His Presence?" (Ezek 3:12). His Oneness, which fills all the worlds, is not subject to any limit or qualification, and His very Self cannot be likened to any image. When the thought to create the world arose within Him, God contracted His infinite Divinity and prepared an empty space (vacuum, *ḥalal panui*) for the worlds, and that contraction (*Tzimtzum*) then allowed for the appearance of the worlds.

This is what the *tanna* [generic name for the rabbinic sages of the period culminating with the editing of the Mishna, around 220 C.E.] Shmu'el bar Nahman said, "The blessed Holy One clad Himself with light and created the world."[3] Of course, due to the vast brightness of the Divine, within the very course of this contraction the vessels containing the Light lacked the sufficient strength to bear that Light, and so the vessels themselves could not endure but were shattered due to the infinitely greater brightness of the Primordial Light. [In this homily, the preacher refers not to the Primordial Light which, according to a midrashic interpretation, was later removed from the world as a result of the sin the First Man, but rather to the intrinsic Light of God's infinite state itself.][4]

Consequently the world was left formless, leaving it without any possibility to endure, and so the Emanator (the Divine in its infinite state) had further to contract its Divinity so that the vessels might then be able to bear that Light. And through the second Contraction, they were able, in some small measure, to contain the Primordial Light, and the World of Repair (*'olam ha-tikkun*) came into being in which the vessels, holding that Light, might endure.

And from this conception, we are able to grasp those first three words of the Torah, which Onkelos had translated as "In the beginning / created / God," in terms of the contraction that occurred so that there might be an empty space for the worlds. The very name *'Elohim* ("God"),

---

3. *Midr. Gen* 3.4; *Pirqe R. El*, ch. 3.
4. Note Zohar I, 1b-2a, and Scholem, *Major Trends*, 220–21.

as is known, connotes limitation and infers such contraction of the Light. [Hence, the name became associated with judgment.][5]

But unable to bear that Light due to its intense and powerful brightness, the initial existence of the vessels was annulled by the Light's very presence, and the world turned to chaos ("The earth being unformed and void," Gen 1: 2). And God said, 'Let there be light,' and there was light" (Gen 1:3), signifying that following that chaos, the World of Repair emerged. The words, "Let there be light, and there was light," refer to that second contraction.

As a consequence, the much more limited Light was such that the vessels were able to contain it [and it came at least within the periphery of what the mind and language can attempt to express], though in a higher respect that Light itself remains on a level of "darkness," as that which is utterly beyond the reach of mind and language is referred to as "darkness," as is written, "He made darkness His screen . . ." (Ps 18:12). This is conveyed in the words, "And God separated the light from the darkness" (Gen 1:4)—the blessed Holy One made a division between the Light which came into being through the second contraction, that Light which is attainable to some degree, and between the Primordial Light, which is called "darkness" in that it remained utterly beyond reach. . . .

Comment: This opening discussion in *Ma'or va-shemesh* makes the case that the account of creation found at the very beginning of the Torah is both not to be understood literally and unable to be understood literally and, furthermore, that the biblical text itself clearly indicates that such is not its purpose.

Drawing from the legacy of kabbalistic teaching upon which his worldview was rooted, the biblical text was read in quite a metaphorical sense, and virtually every word or element of that text came to be interpreted symbolically. Kalonymus Kalman clearly understood various verses and elements in the account of creation, which opens the Torah, as allusions to the worldview of Lurianic Kabbalah, the teachings of Rabbi Isaac Luria (1534–1572), which revolutionized the earlier body of kabbalistic thought, and in large measure he viewed the biblical creation-text as a kind of code for the much more complex Lurianic explanation of how the world or worlds came into existence. That pattern, based upon Lurianic teaching, centers largely around the basic principles of Contraction (*Tzimtzum*), the

---

5. *Midr. Exod.* 3:6 (*Sh'mot*), perhaps on basis of Ps 82:8.

Shattering of the Vessels (*Sh'virah*) and Repair (*Tikkun*). Reference to the building-blocks of Lurianic cosmology recurs at various places within the homilies of *Ma'or va-shemesh* and of kindred Hasidic homily-texts. In this homily on the very opening verse of the Torah (Pentateuch), the preacher fused his very brief synopsis of the Lurianic cosmology with the much earlier motif of the Primordial Light, subject of the following passage, perhaps causing some confusion in the process.

In his discourse on various passages from the Torah, the preacher's ruling out a literal reading creates an enlarged space for his homiletical interpretation which, by its very nature, goes beyond the simpler, surface meaning of the biblical text.

The Hidden Light[6]

The Sages said that with that Light (of the six days of creation) man could see from one end of the world to the other, but, seeing that the world is not worthy of utilizing that Light, God removed it and hid it for the righteous (*tzaddikim*) of a future time. The righteous of our time have taught that the Light is hidden within the Torah, and the righteous who purify themselves and study Torah for its own sake (not for any personal benefit) succeed in finding that Light.

Comment: The theme of the Primordial Light that was later hidden has its source in that the creation-account that opens the Torah speaks of light as created on the First Day of creation (Gen 1:3), while further on in that same account, the sun and the moon and stars are all said to have been created on the Fourth Day (Gen 1:16). This apparent discrepancy gave birth to the aggadic motif that the much greater original Light created on the First Day was later hidden by God when He realized that man (created on the Sixth Day) would gravely disappoint Him. The Primordial Light was looked upon as being spiritual rather than physical or solely physical in nature. Rabbinic statements of that theme express the idea that the Primordial Light was removed and hidden for the righteous in the World-to-Come (*'olam ha-ba*), where, following their death, the righteous would bask in its light.[7]

---

6. *Ma'or va-shemesh*, I, 2b-3a.
7. b. Ḥag. 12a, *Midr. Gen* 3.6, *Midr. Exod.* 35.1, and *Midr. Num.* 13.5.

The above excerpt from *Ma'or va-shemesh* represents a transmutation in that it speaks of that Light as being hidden for the righteous (*tzaddikim*), not necessarily in the World-to-Come, but rather throughout the generations, in the sense that they would be able to draw upon that greater spiritual Light and understanding in their own respective times. That general re-interpretation of the older agada is heard already in *Degel mahaneh 'Efrayim* (*B'rei'shit*) and also in *No'am 'Elimelekh* (*B'rei'shit*), which consists of homiletical notes of Kalonymus Kalman's own teacher, Elimelekh of Lyzhansk.

The theme that God hid the Light within the Torah is attributed to the Baal Shem Tov, the central figure of early Hasidism.[8] In this way, the Light came to be associated not with its being hidden, but rather with its presence and availability, as it is accessible to those who make the effort to seek it by going beyond the surface-level of the Torah's text to its richer, experiential nature. The more pessimistic nuance of the hidden Light was transposed in the process to the much more positive possibility of being able to pierce its hiddenness and to discover it within the Torah as well as within all of existence. The Light, in that sense, has become virtually synonymous with the Divine, which, though hidden, is yet paradoxically present within all that is.

The more positive understanding of the theme of the Hidden Light is evident already in the Zohar, which voices the claim that were that Light to be completely hidden, nothing would be able to exist, as existence itself is dependent upon that hidden but-not-totally-hidden Light.[9] The view presented in the Zohar represents a shift from emphasis upon the Light's absence, its having been withdrawn, to that of its continued presence. The position of the Zohar can be explained in light of the fact that while the motif of the *Hidden* Light is a distinctively midrashic motif, that of the *Primordial* Light, found in many traditions in ancient and medieval times including Neo-Platonism, viewed that light as underlying all existence and as present within all that exists. In addition, the view attributed to the *Besht* that the Light is hidden in the Torah might interestingly parallel an Islamic identification of the Primordial Light with Muhammad[10] and the much earlier Christian identification of that Light with Jesus.[11]

---

8. See *Ba'al shem tov 'al ha-torah*, 1:48–49 (#32–35). Also *Shivḥei ha-Besht, In Praise of the Baal Shem Tov*, 49 (#33), and 89 (#69).

9. Zohar II, 148b–149a.

10. Schimmel, *Mystical Dimensions of Islam*, 214–15 and *Muhammad is His Messenger*, 130.

11. John 1:1, 9; also The Apostalic Fathers, 1:51 (Second Epistle of Clement to the Corinthians, #14).

The Surface Meaning of the Torah and the Torah's Innerness[12]

> "God said, 'Let there be an expanse in the midst of the water, that it may separate water from water.' God made the expanse, and it separated the water which was below the expanse from the water which was above the expanse. . . . God said, 'Let the water below the sky be gathered into one area, that the dry land may appear.'" (Gen 1:6–9)

It is important to note that the waters are not included in the list of created objects; there is no verb indicating their being created. . . .

And God created the world with the Torah (as its blueprint). The Torah, however, assumes different manifestations appropriate to the various levels of existence. At the very highest level (*'Atzilut*), it is completely beyond our grasp, and concerning the Torah at that level it is said, "I was with Him as an infant, a source of delight every day, rejoicing before Him at all times" (Prov 8:30), two thousand years prior to creation.[13] On another level (*B'ri'ah*), it exists as the innerness of the Torah, while at our level, appropriate to our world (*'Asiyah*), it assumes the form of the simple surface meaning of the Torah. Accordingly, the plain, simple meaning was given to us while the Torah's innerness is concealed from us, for if not, we would inflict damage upon the Torah's innerness, God forbid, just as did the early generations who knew the Torah's innerness and severely damaged it.

For this reason, only the simple level of the Torah was given to us; however, through our study of that plain surface level of the Torah and our engaging with it in discourse and observing it (being faithful to its commandments), we will come to grasp its innerness.

The very core-principle of *'avodah*, the service/worship of God, is to attain a sense of presence of God and to attach oneself to the blessed *'Ein-sof* (the Infinite state of the Divine), sublime beyond all the heights, something that not every person is able to experience. And in what way can one arrive at that understanding? Our Sages determined that one is to recite the *Sh'ma*, "Hear, Israel, . . . God is One," (Deut 6:4) morning and evening with the intention of recognizing the majesty of the blessed Holy One both above and below and extending in all directions. And in

---

12. *Ma'or va-shemesh*, I, 3a.
13. *Midr. Gen* 8:2.

reciting this verse morning and evening with this inner intent and with great longing and yearning for God, it will be possible to attach oneself to God every day and every night.

But the person who has not yet adequately repaired his qualities and who has not shattered the force of his physical desires will be unable to recite this verse and to proclaim the word "One" (*'eḥad*) with clear and flawless intention. This is because alien, disturbing thoughts still prevail within him to confuse him, and in reciting the *Sh'ma*, one ascribes kingship to God according to the extent that the person has attained a degree of oneness and unity within the self.

In order to recite the word "One" properly as is required, in a way that such foreign thoughts will not confuse him, he is advised, before praying, to devote considerable time to the study of Mishna and Gemara and the Zohar with this intention in mind. [The Mishna and Gemara are the two layers comprising the Talmud, the Gemara consisting of discussions on the Mishna, and the Zohar became the central text in medieval Kabbalah.] In that case, one will certainly be able to affirm and reify God's reign over all the higher and lower worlds, providing the person proves his diligence and devotes considerable time to study and does not trespass the time of prayer, God forbid. [The leaders and followers of Hasidism were accused by those who opposed the new stream of reciting traditional daily prayers when they were so moved, even long after their proper time, and in this comment the preacher voices his own opposition to taking such liberties. The various prayer-services connect with different times of the day: *Shaḥarit* after the first sign of dawn, *Minḥah* prior to sundown, and *Ma'ariv* (*'Aravit*) after sundown.]

It is known that the Torah is called water [*mayyim*,[14] based on Isa 55:1, "Ho, all who are thirsty, come for water . . . ." As the prophet speaks of water metaphorically, that metaphor provided Kalonymus Kalman with a key to reading a verse from the toraitic creation-account in a way that transcends its much simpler surface meaning]. And from these points we can clarify what is written, "And God said, 'Let there be an expanse in the midst of the water, that it may separate water from water'" (Gen 1:6). With the understanding that Torah is called "water," we can grasp that water is not included in the list of created things for the reason that the Torah preceded the world by two-thousand years. But the verse points to something very necessary: "Let there be an expanse in the midst

---

14. *b. Bava Qam.* 17a.

of the water," meaning that a curtain is spread between the innerness of the Torah and its plain meaning. For the Torah's innerness must be concealed; not everyone should have access to that innerness of the Torah lest that person inflict damage upon it, God forbid, as did those early generations (prior to Abraham's time). [This theme might have its source in the Zohar, I, 176a in reference to the "secrets of wisdom" given to those early generations who utilized them for evil purposes.]

The pronouncement of the King, "God made the expanse," serves as counsel to humankind who would be moved to see that innerness of the Torah. With the words, "And God said, 'Let the water beneath the sky be gathered into one area'" (Gen 1:9), one is advised to study the simple level of the Torah, which is beneath the heavens, in our own level of existence, with great intent. Doing so, a person thereby accepts upon himself the yoke of the Kingdom of God and crowns the blessed Holy One in the heavens and everywhere on earth, including all the corners of the earth, as he recites the *Sh'ma*, which includes the word *'eḥad* ("One"). And in that way it will be possible to attain the Innerness of the Torah.

And the verse continues, "that the dry land appear," signaling that in reciting the word, *'eḥad* ("One"), one will be able to grasp whether that person's uttering that word is something dry and lifeless or whether it contains the vitality of holiness. For according to the level of one's own self-purification, a person will be able to accept upon himself the yoke of the Kingdom of God while reciting the *Sh'ma*. And understand.

Comment: In his discussion of verses from the Torah's creation-account, the concern of the Kraków preacher is remote from the actual phenomenon of waters, above and below. Rather, building upon the metaphorical significance of water itself, as evident in that verse from the book of Isaiah (55:1, and delineated at length in *Midrash Shir ha-Shirim rabbah* 1.19 on the opening verse of the Song of Songs), Kalonymus Kalman overheard in those verses from the creation-account a key-issue concerning conflicting senses of Torah itself, an issue with which the Kraków master engaged and wrestled in several of his discourses. This homily is built upon the premise that the more sublime essence of the Torah, its depth and innerness, transcends its surface-meaning, the manifestation and character that the Torah assumes in our finite, physical world. And accordingly, the homily raises the question: how do we then relate to that simpler meaning of the Torah which includes also a body of law that might be felt to occupy even a vast distance from the Torah's innerness?

That Innerness is hidden from us, and our path to find it, the preacher insists, must bring us through the Torah's surface meaning with all that is contained in it. There is no shortcut to a grasp of the Torah's innerness. Building upon the biblical and rabbinic use of water as a metaphor for Torah, the master went on to read the verses concerning the division of waters as an allusion to those two dimensions of Torah.

In one respect, he subscribed to a consciousness anchored to the recognition of a higher and inner meaning of all that is written in the basic Jewish sacred text, while in another respect he remained fully loyal and insistent upon the importance of the tradition as a whole which developed around the written Torah-text. He viewed that necessary relationship with the Torah's simple meaning, however, not as an end in itself, but rather as a means and as the keys with which to attain a sense of the Torah's Innerness.

In this sense, he was, at one and the same time, both radical and conservative. He advised his fellows to study and direct their lives according to that surface-dimension of the Torah and its traditional rabbinic understanding, while also maintaining that through doing so, they might be able to reach that deeper, more sublime, and even mystic grasp of the Torah identified with its guarded innerness.

The dual-emphasis in this passage is sounded in any number of homilies in which the preacher continued to wrestle with a potential paradox in his understanding of the central Jewish sacred text.

A Longing Permeating All Existence[15]

When the thought of creating the worlds arose in God's highest and most essential will, God contracted His Divinity from its heights and the worlds evolved and the blessed Light of Infinity glistened through all the worlds from the most sublime to this very lowest, physical world. The Light of Divinity could then be experienced in the higher realms of existence, while in the lower realms it appears hidden, even though there is no created object in the world in which the Light of the Infinite (*'Or 'ein-sof*) does not glisten. This is noted in *'Or ha-Ḥayyim*, which explained the verse, "The heavens and the earth were finished and all their

---

15. *Ma'or va-shemesh*, I, 3b.

array" (Gen 2:1), reading the word, *vaykhulu* (literally, "were finished") as conveying longing, as in the expression, *kalta nafshi* ("I long, I yearn ... my soul longs," Ps 84:3). This same interpretation is found also in the teachings of the *Ar'i* (Rabbi Isaac Luria) who understood plants' growing upward from the ground as indicative of the ascent of the worlds (to their sublime Source).

The Midrash mentions that each blade of grass here below has an angel from above who strikes it and commands it to grow.[16] [The midrashic source actually refers to a *mazal*, a star or constellation, striking the blade of grass, while the preacher refers instead to an angel, avoiding the astrological overtones of crediting a *mazal*.] This comment can be understood only with the realization that the blessed Holy One created all the worlds with the twenty-two letters of the Torah together with the Torah's vowel-points and cantillation signs, through the combinations of names in a way that the Ineffable Name joins with every single letter. And if that is so, there is nothing in the world that does not have a part in some letter or vowel-point of the Torah (which in itself, on a more sublime level, is a manifestation of the Divine). And as every letter or vowel-point is a part of the Ineffable Name, all the plants and trees naturally seek to ascend to their Root.

The writings of the *Ar'i* refer to such combinations of letters as "an act of striking," specifically striking one letter with another and joining one letter together with another. And it is in this light that we can grasp that each blade of grass has an angel from above who strikes it and tells it to grow, meaning that the angel illuminates the combination belonging to that specific blade of grass. Every single blade of grass has its own combination of letters by means of which it has a portion in the blessed Ineffable Name.

And how do they awaken to ascend to their Root? They awaken by means of the *tzaddik* (holy man) who studies Torah purely for its own sake to unite the blessed Holy One with the *Sh'khinah* (acting to unify the world of the *s'firot* which underlies and permeates all existence) and who attaches himself to the letters of the Torah and to the combinations of names and connects with the *'Ein sof* (the infinite state of the Divine). In this way, such a person provides divine energy (*ḥiyyut*) and awakening to all created things, whether they be inert or plants or (zoological) living beings or humans (literally, having the gift of speech and language) to the

---

16. *Midr. Gen* 10:6.

end that they all long to ascend to their divine Root. For in the combinations and permutations of their names, all these have some part of the letters of the Torah.

And by means of the *tzaddik*'s awakening the lower world, he attaches himself to the holy patriarchs and draws down lovingkindness upon the community of Israel (*Knesset Yisra'el*). [The image of "feminine waters" conveys an awakening initiated by action of the lower world which effects what is above.] In this light, Rashi explained the verse, "When no shrub of the field was yet on earth and no grasses of the field had yet sprouted . . . and there was no man to till the soil" (Gen 2:5), in that these grew when a human emerged and prayed for the vegetation of the field. Everything depends upon the prayer of the *tzaddik*, and in particular upon his acts of unification (*yiḥuddim*) . . . .

From this we come to the explanation of the verse, "And God said, 'Let the earth sprout vegetation . . .'" (Gen 1:11), meaning that the *tzaddik* will unite the lower worlds with the higher worlds. And via the *tzaddik*'s awakening, he is able to awaken the feminine waters (the lower worlds) and unify the worlds through bringing all created things to long to ascend to their Root . . . .

Comment: Like the earlier Hayyim ben-Attar, author of *'Or ha-ḥayyim*, also Kalonymus Kalman Epstein sensed in all of nature, including even inert nature, a longing for the divine Root of all existence. Everything created has within it a longing to ascend to its higher, divine Root and, furthermore, that longing which is, in turn, awakened by the longing of the *tzaddik* (holy man), serves to unite all the realms of being. This homily expresses a remarkable poetic intuition and opens for the reader an essential aspect of how the master and preacher, a city-dweller who nevertheless lived with a sense of cosmic longing, experienced the natural world.

He explained the source of such cosmic longing in the sense that everything that exists, even every blade of grass, shares in the Torah—which he grasped as much more than a conglomeration of words. And he went on to connect his sublime sense of the nature of being to what was for him the highest human ideal. A *tzaddik*, means literally, a "righteous person," though the word came to suggest more essentially a *holy man*, and the same term, *tzaddik*, came to signify, more particularly, the holy man who served as the leader and center of a Hasidic community and who embodied its spiritual ethos. Here, the role of the *tzaddik* is defined as one of awakening such longing not only in one's human associates but in all the cosmos. One might overhear in this conception an echo and reflection of sensitivities associated with European romanticism.

A glimpse into the homilist's own consciousness is revealed in his interpreting the glistening which he experienced in the plant-world as a sign of connection with Divinity, a connection explained in that the letters of the Torah are stamped on each particular plant or blade of grass. Not only is each such specimen in the world of vegetation a living sign of the Divine, but he viewed each such specimen as a *unique* living sign of the Divine. The master's sense of the uniqueness of each person, emphasized in various ways in this collection of homilies, is grounded in this broader vision of being which recognizes the uniqueness even of every single botanical specimen.

While the Kraków sage more often presented his interpretations within the framework of basic concepts of Lurianic Kabbalah, this homily might signify that his particular spiritual temperament is closer to that of Moses Cordovoro (the *Rama"k*) in granting greater importance to immanence and the experiential, a legacy of still earlier "ecstatic kabbalah."[17]

Two Modes of Torah-study[18]

> "God created the great sea monsters and all the living creatures of every kind that creep . . ." (Gen 1:21).

The word *t'ninim* (sea monsters, a plural word) is derived from *t'nina*, which means "study" and thus indicates that God created different types of study. For there are two ways of study: one is the way of life and of the good, namely study of Torah for its own sake (*torah lishmah*), while the second is study not for its own purpose (*torah shelo lishmah*), but for an evil purpose, God forbid. Both types of students can become great in Torah in their own way, though the one engages in Torah for its true, legitimate purpose, to experience the divine sweetness, while the other chooses an evil path, as his motivation derives from his quest for position and material benefit and uses Torah "as a spade with which to dig."[19] "The one no less than the other was God's doing . . ." (Eccl 7:14).

---

17. Idel, *Hasidism—Between Ecstasy and Magic*, 53–65.
18. *Ma'or va-shemesh*, I, 3b–4a.
19. *m. 'Abot* 4:7.

And this is alluded in what our Sages relayed in their saying that the Creator chilled the male, meaning the one who studies Torah for its own purpose; this is associated with the male and is necessitated to an extent lest one would cease to exist in the face of the enormous delight in his engaging in Torah-study for its own sake, leaving him no possibility of existence. [The sexist overtones typify the attitudes largely prevalent in the preacher's environment and in much of prior tradition. The male is described here as driven by such an all-powerful love of Torah-study that he could easily die in the course of pursuing that love.] And God killed the female, connoting the person who studies not for the sake of the Torah itself, killing and weakening that person's strength lest the world be destroyed as a consequence of his mode of study.[20] [In the talmudic agada, which refers to the danger of the sea monsters' mating, as with their boundless appetite their offspring could consume the entire world, the male is castrated and chilled and preserved to serve as a feast for the righteous in the World-to-Come.]

And the text concludes, "and all the living creatures of every kind that creep . . . and all the winged birds of every kind" (Gen 1:21), referring to the young ones—and there are many of them—who only limitedly study Torah for its own sake, each one according to the person's own aspect and level. For "Torah-learning for its own sake" assumes many faces, just as there are also many varieties of "Torah-learning not for its own sake." And fortunate is the person who chooses the good, thereby coming to experience the pleasantness of God.

Comment: In a society with few intellectual outlets other than the study of sacred text and the discourse relating to it, the issue at the center of this homily becomes very real. Does one's mental endeavor, in such a situation, respect the nature of the subject of his study?

While the concepts of *torah lishmah* and *torah shelo lishmah* (studying out of sincere motivations or out of self-centered pragmatic motivations such as position, prestige, or reputation) are found already in talmudic literature (conveying that whereas *torah shelo lishmah* is a death-potion, *torah lishmah* is a potion for life),[21] the contrast between those two modes bore a special and more particular relevance in the polemics between the Hasidim and their opponents (*Mitnagdim*). Hasidic homilists accused their opposition,

20. *b. B. Bat.* 74b.
21. *b. Ta'an.* 7a.

specifically those devoted to the intense talmudic study of the academies (y'shivot), of often being driven by very impious, self-centered motivations, while the opponents of Hasidism, in turn, accused the Hasidim both of ignorance in terms of the level of their talmudic knowledge and of disrespectfully denigrating the scholar-class and talmudic learning itself.

Kalonymus Kalman claimed to find an allusion in the rabbinic agada of the two sea monsters to those two modes of study which differed in terms of their motivations. The one monster represents all-too-this-worldly considerations, while the other might be drawn to a life beyond the grave as he prefers death for the sake of a more complete sense of God's presence.

The reader, however, can hear in his discussion a more conciliatory position according to which both modes, carried to an extreme, represent dangers to the world. The totally unblemished ideal of *torah lishmah* can remove its practitioners from this world through their total cleaving to the Divine in a way that could evoke a negative attitude toward life. And the blatent examples of *torah shelo lishmah* endanger the very existence of the world by the falsity masked in their study itself.

Realizing the pitfalls of both modes, the Creator placed both those modes themselves beyond the pale of reality, something the preacher felt to be symbolized in that much earlier agada of the two sea monsters.

The rabbinic agada itself, which would appear to echo ancient myths of a primeval sea monster (such as Tiamat),[22] would not interest Kalonymus Kalman in its own terms, but he utilized that agada to engage an issue that acquired special importance in his own time and experience. His more complex reading of this cultural or spiritual conflict into that agada of a mythological character is an expression both of his creativity and of his ongoing struggling with the polarities involved.

The Function of Shabbat[23]

> "And God saw all that He had made and found it very good. . . . On the seventh day God finished the work which He had been doing, and He ceased on the seventh day (from all the work which He had done." (Gen 1:31—2:2)

---

22. Fishbane, *Biblical Myth and Rabbinic Mythmaking*, 112–23.
23. *Ma'or va-shemesh*, I, 4b–5a.

Rashi explained that a person of flesh and blood, not knowing his hours and minutes in all their preciseness, must add from the profane (weekday) to the holy [as a precaution, one must begin a holy day, such as the *Shabbat*, at least somewhat earlier than required lest he might be violating the holy day], whereas the blessed Holy One, knowing His times and minutes, enters into a holy day at the precise split second, with the accuracy of a hair-breadth.[24]

That, however, still doesn't suffice to explain, for God nevertheless completed His work on the Sixth Day and not on the Seventh Day. And a rabbinic reading maintains that the demons were created at dusk just before the *Shabbat*, and though there was need yet to create bodies for them, nevertheless the Creator hallowed the Day and refrained from creating bodies for them.[25]

... For the sake of choice and will, in order that the Israelites who accepted upon themselves the yoke/commitment of His Kingship might receive a reward for their good deeds, God contracted His Divinity in stages, from world to world, and made partitions and a screen separating one world from another. They limit the Light of God's Divinity and holiness through a series of contractions culminating with the physical world, doing so, however, in a way that nothing exists even in this lower, material world in which the Light of God's holiness does not glisten, for otherwise this lower world could not even exist.... And the person who accepts upon himself the yoke of God's kingdom and comes to attach himself to one's Root must remove all the partitions until one can experience the pleasantness of God, the sublime Light, the blessed Infinite One.

And concerning the quality of *Malkhut* [royalty, reign; the lowest of the *s'firot*], it is said "Her feet go down to death" (Prov 5:5, in reference to the strange, forbidden woman), meaning that it is the level closest to the realm of the *ḥitzonim* [demonic agents, the very word signifying "external"] and if, God forbid, the world would become materialized to any greater degree, then due to the thickness of the physicality of things, it would no longer be possible for man to turn to attach himself to the sublime Light. But certainly the merciful God who, desiring mercy, does not wish that anyone be banished (*leval yidaḥ mimenu nidaḥ*, a composite of words from Mic 7:18 and 2 Sam 14:14).

---

24. *Midr. Gen* 10:9.
25. *Midr. Gen* 7:5.

And accordingly, God said to the world "Enough" (*dai*),²⁶ lest it undergo further materialization, so that even considering the contractions and evolving of the worlds, it might still be possible for God's created ones both to attain a sense of Divinity and to raise up the holy Sparks from this material world to the higher levels of being. And for this very reason bodies were not created for the demons, lest the world become materialized to any greater extent.

And even now, it is necessary for each person to be careful to seek quickly to repair what he has damaged, because no person is able to grasp to what extent he has distanced himself from what is holy. It is concerning this that our wise ones intimated that God hallowed the Day and the bodies of the demons were not created, in order that the world would ascend and not become further materialized.

And this is the interpretation of the verse, "on the Seventh Day God finished . . .": that with the Seventh Day, the holiness of *Shabbat*, God completed His work in the sense that it would not continue further. And as Rashi alluded, the blessed Holy One, knowing precisely His times and moments, entered into the Seventh Day as a hairbreadth, setting a very precise limit to the contraction, even to the extent of a hairbreath, and bringing down the holiness of *Shabbat* in order to halt the world's process toward materialization. The divine Wisdom decreed that the world might assume physical character up to that precise point, but not beyond it. . . .

Comment: The master and preacher latched on to a rabbinic agada which explains the divine Name, *'El Shaddai*, in terms of its last syllable, *dai* ("enough"), signifying God's halting the expansion of the world immediately following the days of creation. The preacher, however, did not simply repeat a much older bit of cosmological lore.

He understood that motif in terms of a context gleaned from Lurianic Kabbalah which delineated the physical world's evolving from the infinite state of the Divine. The vessels brought into being were unable to contain the Light, the manifestations of divine energy, and hence they collapsed. This cosmic scheme speaks in terms of a complex and uncertain relationship between forms and what they contain, presented almost on a mechanical level. The Kraków master, however, read both that example of rabbinic lore and its Lurianic interpretation in terms of the effect of such

---

26. *b. Ḥag.* 12a.

contractions on human consciousness and even on a broader consciousness pervading all of existence.

In Kalonymus Kalman's reading of that agada in the context of Lurianic teaching, all that is spiritual in nature could have acquired a very precarious state-of-being. Hence, a critical need to halt the further expansion of the created world was crucial, lest it continue to acquire a more and more material, physical character to the point that it could fail to allow for any awareness of its more ultimate spiritual moorings.

A delicate balance between the material and the spiritual was in danger of being violated, and only a definite halt to the expansion of materialization could preserve that balance. The timing contributes a meaning to the Seventh Day as a way of preventing man's drowning in his materialistic orientation and understanding of himself, something that could forever close the door to humankind's reaching upward to its Root in the divine. *Shabbat* (the Seventh Day) preserves a sense of connection with a deeper spiritual reality, a connection that, however, continues to stand in danger of being conclusively lost. And the world hangs in the balance.

That sense of balance is heard and overheard in various passages in the collection of Kalonymus Kalman's homilies. Furthermore, it will become evident that the balance is one that works in more than one direction as it guarantees that neither physicality nor spirituality would completely demolish the other, as only a proper balance between the two can truly allow for the world's continued existence.

This homily refers also to another rabbinic agada, this time having to do with the *ḥitzonim*, demonic agents, for which bodies were never created due to the entrance of the Seventh Day following the days of creation. The very name *ḥitzonim* indicates their externality and their opposition to all that is holy. Reflecting Hasidic teaching's emphasis upon interior meaning and the inner life, the name *ḥitzonim* defined those demonic forces as the antithesis of Hasidism's own value-system. It would follow that understanding the world and life and humans and the Torah itself solely in terms of their external character brings in its wake something that is in itself potentially demonic in nature.

Humility and the World's Sustainability[27]

> "Such is the story of heaven and earth when they were created...." (Gen 2:4)

As it appears in the Torah-text, the word *b'hibar'am* ("when they were created") contains one letter, *hei*, written very small, an occurrence which has been explained in various ways including reading that word as *b'Avraham* (through the merit of Abraham, simply situating the same letters in a different order).[28]

... When the worlds evolved one from the other, down to this physical world, its inhabitants forgot God's Divinity and came to think that they have no Lord or ruler over them. Each person said, "I shall rule," and consequently they were destroyed.

The important point is the need to know that God is the master and ruler and the Root of all the worlds[29] and to be humble before Him, like Abraham who said, "I who am but dust and ashes" (Gen 18:27). And through the merit of such a person, the world is sustained. And this is *b'hibar'am: b'Avraham* (through Abraham), continuing in the way of the quality of Abraham which is one of humility before God, unlike that of the early generations, each one of whom said, "I shall rule" and, accordingly, were destroyed. And the small letter *hei* alludes to his humility; conveying that each person should consider himself small and lowly before God, and in this way the world can continue to exist.

Comment: In the Torah's opening chapters Abraham emerges as a figure who stands in rather sharp contrast to the generations that preceded him. While all else conveys a picture of consistent and repeated human failure, only Abraham stands out in a positive way against that background. In that one word, *b'hibar'am*, that rabbinic midrash claimed to locate a somewhat concealed reference to Abraham already in the Torah's account of creation; the letters of that word, given a different order, could read as *b'Avraham*, conveying that the world was created for the sake of Abraham and those like him.

---

27. *Ma'or va-shemesh*, I, 5a.
28. *Midr. Gen* 12:9.
29. *Zohar*, I, 11b (Int.).

That thought in itself might be interpreted in terms of various qualities or actions of Abraham, but Kalonymus Kalman, in the above passage, focuses on one particular quality, namely Abraham's humility. The homilist here viewed Abraham's humility as his distinguishing trait. And in the context of Hasidic teaching, humility represents the antithesis of egotism which is itself understood as taking seriously something that lacks any true place in existence itself. Humility, in this sense, is a recognition of truth and a rejection of distorted self-centered perceptions of oneself in comparison with others.

When One Person Judges Another[30]

> "(Of every tree of the garden you are free to eat;) but as for the tree of knowledge of good and bad, you must not eat of it . . . ."
> (Gen 2:16–17)

The person who comes to serve God must be careful not even to look at the fault of his fellow, and not to consider himself wise and capable of understanding his fellow and his way. "Man sees only what is visible, but the Lord sees into the heart" (1 Sam 16:7). The person who looks upon the faults of his fellow does so out of one's own arrogance, whereas if that person were humble, recognizing his own shortcomings, he would have a more favorable picture of his fellow and would not come to any awareness of the latter's shortcomings. It is only due to a person's sense of self-importance that his fellow's words and ways fail to meet his approval. In contrast, our father Jacob, may he rest in peace, who was a mild man (Gen 25:27) did not look upon himself as a person of wisdom capable of judging the ways of others.

This thought connects with the verse, "but as for the tree of knowledge of good and bad, you must not eat of it . . . " For if you do, pride and the Evil Inclination will enter into you, and because you perceive yourself to be a person of wisdom, your heart will be drawn to discern the ways of your fellows and to consider whether they are good or evil. And this was the claim of the serpent, "And you will be like divine beings who know good and bad" (Gen 3:5), for by eating of the tree you make yourself wise (in your own eyes), believing that you know how to evaluate the ways

---

30. *Ma'or va-shemesh*, I, 5b.

of your fellow and to know whether they are good or evil. And you will reach a conclusion that you would not have arrived at otherwise.

And this is heard in the words, "And they perceived that they were naked" (*'arumim*, Gen 3:7), which connects with the words, "Now the serpent was the shrewdest, *eirom* (of all the wild beasts that the Lord God had made," Gen 3:1). For as a consequence of their eating from the tree, they opened themselves to the Evil Inclination and to arrogance, and in their guile they attributed to themselves wisdom. And this connects also with the man's saying, "And I was afraid because I was naked (*'arum*)..." (Gen 3:10)—I fear because I see that my heart arrogantly puffs up within me saying, I am shrewd and wise. And we should be very fearful of that.

Comment: In this homily, the Kraków master offered his interpretation of the Tree of Knowledge of Good and Evil in a way that amazingly brings that theme very much down-to-earth. While statements concerning the effects and consequences of eating from that tree have included very far-reaching and complex implications, for Kalonymus Kalman in this brief homily, the meaning of the sin of the First Man has to do with something extraordinarily commonplace: the tendency of people to be judgmental concerning others and the self-importance involved in a person's viewing others critically. A rare beauty is displayed in the very simplicity of the master's interpretation.

No'ah

Noah Repaired the Animals[31]

The First Man repaired all the beasts and the animals by assigning names to them, as is written, "(And the Lord God formed out of the earth all the wild beasts and all the birds of the sky,) and brought them to the man to see what he would call them; (and whatever the man called each living creature, that would be its name. And the man gave names to all the cattle and to the birds of the sky and to all the wild beasts . . ." Gen 2:19–20).

And so following his fall and failure, although he later repented and on the holy Shabbat even sang the Psalm for the *Shabbat*[32] [Psalm 92, understanding the infinitive *l'hodot* in the second verse of the Psalm not as "to praise," but rather as "to confess"] and repaired everything and was forgiven for everything, that act of repair (*tikkun*) did not essentially effect the beasts and the animals. And it was for this reason that it was initially forbidden to eat meat (Gen 2:16), something that became permissible only in connection with Noah (Gen 9:3).

It is written in the holy Zohar that "Noah and the ark are one" [interpreting Noah's entering the ark as representing union between the masculine and feminine *s'firot*[33]]. These words convey, in brief, that the ark of Noah included also the Tablets of the Decalogue and the Ark of the Covenant, as the *tzaddik*, as is known, is required to bring all that is outside within the realm of the holy. And Noah made the ark, which included all things belonging to this world, inert phenomena and plant-life along with animals, and he brought these into what is holy. This is the meaning of the "building of the ark," which refers actually to the Ark of

---

31. *Ma'or va-shemesh*, I, 6b.
32. *Midr. Pss.* 92:4, 5, 7; *Pirqe R. El.*, ch. 18.
33. Zohar, I, 59b.

the Covenant: Noah entered into the ark and took everything with him, for the human being, as is known, includes all that exists—all the created things, all that is inert along with plant-life and animals and humankind [literally, "that which speaks," possessing language]; he took everything with him into the ark and repaired them by means of his own repentance. . . . He took them with him, as is known that a human is called a microcosm. [The conception of man as a microcosm, found in 'Avot deRabbi Natan (recension B, ch. 31) and present also in various ancient Greek philosophical texts, entered into the writings of medieval Jewish figures such as Saadya Gaon, Moses Maimonides, Isaac Israeli, Abraham Ibn Ezra, and Bahya ibn Pakudah.[34]]

For this reason Noah, unlike Adam, was permitted to eat the flesh of living things because Noah took all the created things with him and repented [of his earlier indifference to the fate of all living things], as we learn in the Midrash.[35] And in this manner he repaired everything—all that is inert and the plants and animals and humankind—and therefore Noah and his sons were permitted to eat animal-flesh. The First Man, it is true, repaired them in the sense of giving them names. But he did not "take them with him" to repair them (on a deeper level). And so when he sinned and all the creatures fell with him, though he repented and recited the *Shabbat* Psalm, the creatures themselves were not truly repaired until the time of Noah and his sons when Noah repaired and brought everything with them into the ark. Noah brought into the realm of the holy all the Fallen Sparks found within all that is inert and all that is found in plants and animals and human beings, and everything became unified as it is written (in the Zohar) "that Noah and the ark became one."

Comment: In Hasidic texts, Noah often emerges in quite a negative light. He is contrasted to Abraham who pleaded with God on behalf of the cities of the plain (Gen 18:22–33), whereas regarding Noah, the biblical account itself includes no mention of his protesting God's bringing a flood to destroy the rest of life on earth (Gen 6:11–22). But *Ma'or va-shemesh*, following a precedent in the Zohar, compared Noah, instead, to Adam, and

---

34. *Tanḥ* (P'kudei), #3. See Altmann, *Studies in Religious Philosophy and Mysticism*, 19–28.

35. *Tanḥ-Yelamdenu*, 52 (on Gen 6:14); *Zohar hadash* (No'aḥ), 29a; Ginzberg, *Legends*, I, 165, V, 186, n. 49.

consequently Noah emerges not only as a significantly more positive figure, but as one with mythic connotations.

In this homily, both Adam and Noah engaged in *tikkun* (repair). Kalonymus Kalman viewed Adam's act of *tikkun* in regard to animals as much more superficial in nature, as it was accomplished simply by Adam's assigning names to all the various animals (Gen 2:19–20). Noah, in contrast, took the animals with him into the ark. And the homilist explained that it is for this reason that Noah and his descendents, unlike the earlier generations, were permitted to eat the flesh of animals.

Noah's taking his assortment of animals and birds and the like into the ark which he had built acquires also a symbolic dimension, that of bringing everything that comprises the world within the realm of the holy. This is viewed, in the passage, as Noah's work of cosmic repair. And in its view of man as containing within himself all that is in the world, the homily reflects, in its own way, the conception of man as a microcosm, a miniature replica of the entire world.

Kalonymus Kalman echoed this concept in that through man's repentance, all is repaired; the fallen Sparks within all aspects of reality are lifted up and redeemed, allowing for a unification of all that exists. That conception expresses a sense of the complexity of the human being who is understood as including all levels of the larger reality in which he lives, including inert nature and plant and animal-life—all these are viewed as being part of the human being. (Although the Kraków master and those whose interpretations influenced him had no awareness of the theory of evolution, the reader might overhear an implication of evolution in this conception.) Hence, Noah's coming into the ark together with the animals both symbolizes and exemplifies his bringing all of earthly existence into the realm of the holy.

The homily views the biblical portrait of Noah through the lens of a kabbalistic worldview in a way that makes of Noah a supreme spiritual hero. And beyond that, the use of the word *tzaddik* ("righteous") in reference to Noah (Gen 6:9) invites the homilist to perceive in Noah a kind of prototype of the Hasidic holy man striving for the repair of existence precisely by bringing the totality of life within the realm of the holy.

The reader can easily hear in this homily an intrinsic human connection with the entire world of life and even with inert matter.

Lekh l'kha

Go Forth!—Go to You![36]

> "The Lord said to Abram, 'Go forth from your native land and from your father's house to the land that I will show you . . .' Abram went forth . . . ." (Gen 12:1–4)

All the commentators already related to the expression, "Go forth" (*Lekh l'kha*) (an idiom which, hyperliterally, would read, 'Go to you'). It is known from holy books that Abraham investigated and sought God in order to serve Him. In the beginning he explored the possibility that the sun is God and then that the moon and the stars were divine rulers and he examined their character. Then he considered the world of the angels, in which each angel is appointed over a certain aspect of the world, and he concluded that they are not God. Then, upon coming to the land of Israel, he continued to investigate and determined that there is a ruler who is beyond our reach, for in the land of Israel God Himself acts in a providential way, as it is written, "It is a land which the Lord your God looks after, on which the Lord your God always keeps His eye . . ." (Deut 11:12), and he understood that this Ruler is above all the other forces and that He alone is the true God who is worthy of worship, and he served Him with all his heart.

But he then thought that he had already attained all that it is possible to comprehend and that one cannot advance beyond that point, that having already reached the goal and purpose of such service he needn't endeavor to go beyond that level of understanding. But in truth he was only at the very opening of the gate at which the truly righteous (holy men) ask of God, "Open for me the gates of righteousness" (Ps 118:19). And it is explained in the holy book, *No 'am 'Elimelekh*[37] concerning this

---

36. *Ma'or va-shemesh*, I, 8b-9a.
37. *No 'am 'Elimelekh* (*Lekh-l'kha*).

verse that it is the way of the truly righteous ones to constantly examine their deeds with humility every single day, for in their own eyes they have not yet satisfactorily fulfilled their duty in respect to religious devotion, and with that recognition and striving it is possible for them to reach the place of their Root from which their souls were hewn.

And for this purpose God said to him, "Go forth" (go to you), meaning that you must go to your deeper self, for you have not yet reached the Root of your soul. And you must further humble yourself, in the way of the truly righteous, to realize that you are still situated only at the very opening of the gate and have not attained all that is possible. And you must engage in further effort to "go to yourself"—meaning to the very Root of your soul. . . .

And Abram went as the Lord had spoken to him, ascending higher levels, as God directed him. And this is understood in the holy Zohar[38] on this verse as his need to go forth from his present level. Though he had already proceeded to explore and investigate the existence of the Divine, only now did he proceed further to go forth from one level of understanding to another.

Comment: While in the narrative context of the command to Abraham as it appears in the Torah one would understand the wording of the command as calling for a change of location, the Zohar read that command in a way that alluded to Abram's need to know his deeper and truer self and to become aware of his real nature. Elimelekh of Lyzhansk, Kalonymus Kalman's own mentor, and also the author(s) of the Zohar similarly overheard in that verse a command involving more than a change of geographical location.

In this passage, Kalonymus Kalman drew from earlier lore concerning Abram's own religious searchings in his youngest years.[39] Transcending the spirit of those tales, however, to the mind of the preacher the searchings of young Abraham went beyond a cognitive, mental or intellectual level as they required a depth of humility along with a deepening of the quality of devotion.

Abraham's "going forth" is read here in a way that extends beyond both physical relocation itself and beyond his successfully crossing a line in rejecting polytheistic paganism in favor of a monotheistic worldview.

38. Zohar, I, 78b.
39. See *Sefer ha-yashar*, ed. Dan, 68; also Ginzberg, *Legends*, 5:210, n. 16.

In that sense, the Kraków preacher clearly transcended and deepened the nature of the aggadic tale of Abraham's mental investigations. Abram goes forth, the homily makes clear, not in a single move either of body or mind, but rather in continuing to deepen his spiritual understanding also after having adopted a monotheistic view. The call to go to a deeper place within oneself is a continual command and challenge. Elimelekh of Lyzhansk explained concerning those very words that the essence of spiritual devotion and quest is to know that it is never complete.[40] And to the mind of the homilist, in Abraham's continuing to ascend from one level of understanding to another, he becomes a mystic.

Purity and Impurity of Motivation[41]

> "Abram went forth as the Lord had commanded him, and Lot went with him." (Gen 12:4)

One must analyze why the text made a point of reporting that "Lot went with him." To what do those words allude? It would appear to make clear that the principal desire and motivation of our father, Abraham, may he rest in peace, was to do God's will, and even though the blessed Holy One promised him material blessings, he was moved to go to the land of Israel solely in order to fulfill the command of his Creator and not at all by the promise of (physical) blessings; he went simply because God commanded him.

But concerning Lot, why did he hasten (to join his uncle)? He joined Abraham only because he had heard that the blessed Holy One had promised Abraham blessings in the form of wealth, children and fame, and he was moved by the expectation that he would similarly be blessed. And so it was that he was blessed for the sake of Abraham.

"Abram went forth as the Lord spoke to him"—he went for the purpose of fulfilling the command of his Creator, while Lot simply "went with him," in order to acquire wealth and share in what was promised to Abram.

---

40. *Likkutei shoshanah* (affixed to *No'am 'Elimelekh*), beginning.
41. *Ma'or va-shemesh*, I, 9a.

Comment: The distinction between one's acting in a certain way for the sake of God as one fulfills a divine command and between one's being motivated by the possibility of worldly reward is sounded in much earlier sources. Echoing talmudic comments, the contrast between these two types of motivations is defined clearly, for example, in the code of Maimonides in the distinction between *ʿavodah mi-yirʾah* (serving or obeying God either from fear of punishment or from expectation of reward) and *ʿavodah meiʾahavah* (serving God purely out of love without any consideration of reward).[42]

That distinction, however, was further accentuated in Hasidic teaching with its emphatic focus upon the purity or impurity of a person's inner intent. The Torah, in various places, makes the point that following the commands of God will bring material reward. While the Hasidic masters did not negate that aspect in principle, they went out of their way to emphasize that doing any *mitzvah* for the purpose or consideration of reward impugns the integrity of one's very deed. It is this distinction that the homilist located in the wording of a single verse within the episode relating to Abraham and Lot.

As the Stars That Shine by Their Own Light[43]

God brought Abram outdoors and said to him, "Count the stars," and he told him "So shall your offspring be" (Gen 15:5), meaning that they will be similar to the stars which are intelligent beings, as it is written "And the knowledgeable will be radiant (like the bright expense of the sky, and those who lead the many to righteousness will be like the stars forever and ever," Dan 12:3). For the stars do not receive brightness one from another; rather, each one shines by itself, by its own light, and therefore the light of one star is not similar to that of another. And God promised him, "So shall your offspring be," in that each one of them will serve God according to that person's own intelligence (and inner lights), and their *mitzvot* will not be in the manner of something that one person learns from another. Rather, all will be true (springing from an inner truth of the person). And understand.

---

42. Maimonides, *Mishneh torah, Hilkhot teshuvah*, ch. 10.
43. *Maʾor va-shemesh*, I, 11a.

Comment: Just as, echoing the Zohar, Kalonymus Kalman provided a meaning to the words *Lekh-l'kha*, which directed the listener's understanding in quite an unexpected direction, so he similarly provided an unexpected suggestion for the reference to the stars in connection with God's words to Abraham. This is the case even though the Torah-text makes it quite clear that the implication is numerical in nature: Abraham's descendents will be too numerous to be counted.

Kalonymus Kalman heard in that reference to the stars something very different—not their vast number, but rather the idea that "each star shines by its own light." To the Kraków preacher, the stars are to serve as a model for the individual. One should not seek to be a carbon copy of anyone else. Rather each person has to reach deep within himself to find the gateway to understanding. That image of "shining by one's own light" is reflected in a number of the preacher's other homilies and serves as one of the principal thrusts and concerns of the homilist. In his turning to the stars as a model of true community, Kalonymus Kalman was perhaps inspired by an early rabbinic source which taught that "just as among the stars there is no hatred or envy or rivalry, so it is the case among the righteous, and just as among the stars the light of one is not similar to that of another, so it will be among the righteous."[44]

---

44. *Sipre: 'Ekev*, 83a, #47, on Deut 11:21.

Vayera

The Pearl of Healing[45]

"The Lord appeared (to him) . . . ." (Gen 18:1)

On the basis of a talmudic source,[46] Rashi explained that the Lord did so "to visit the sick." But one notes that Rashi's words *et ha-ḥoleh* ("the sick one" as the object of the verb) are superfluous, as the commentator could more easily have said "to visit *him*." The Gemara relates that a pearl was suspended from Abraham's neck, and any ill person who saw it was immediately healed.[47]

But that very idea would seem to convey that there are different levels of holy men (*tzaddikim*). There are those who draw down healing for the ill through their own actions; they actually bless the ill with their hands and by that means the person is healed. And there are those who bring healing simply through the holy man's seeing the ill person. And still higher is the level of the *tzaddik* that an ill person who sees him is immediately cured, insofar as something of the holy essence of God is present with the *tzaddik*. When the ill person sees the holy man, simply seeing him awakens in him a thought of *t'shuvah* (repentance) and he subjects his heart to his Father in heaven, and this brings on his healing. As is found in the Talmud,[48] whenever Israel subjected their hearts to God, immediately they were cured. [In the toraitic accounts of the battle with Amalek, the Israelites triumphed only when Moses' hands were held high (Num 17:11–12), and a plague of serpents was overcome by constructing a copper serpent (Num. 21:8); the Mishna, however, clarified that in

---

45. *Ma'or va-shemesh*, I, 12b.
46. *b. Sotah* 14a.
47. *b. B. Bat.* 16b.
48. *m. Roš. Haš.* 3:8.

both of those episodes, the only determinative factor was the Israelite's subjecting their hearts to God.]

And this is alluded in the Gemara in reference to the pearl hanging from the neck of our father, Abraham, in that any ill person who would see it was immediately healed, meaning that the sick person was cured through the presence of the Divine situated with the patriarch. And that is the good pearl which alludes to God's presence.

… And the verse concludes, "… he was sitting at the entrance of the tent as the day grew hot" (Gen 18:1), meaning that though Abraham was in a state of inner warmth and exalted enthusiasm, he nevertheless felt very humble in the presence of the blessed Holy One. It always seemed to Abraham that he was situated only at the very opening of the tent and had not entered further to any extent at all.

Comment: The above passage is interesting in light of the fact that the figure of the Hasidic *tzaddik* or *rebbe* came, early on, to be associated in the folk-mind with a belief in the latter's healing powers and with similar miraculous abilities that loomed important in the tales and lore associated with the Hasidic *tzaddikim*. While that theme is not totally absent in the homilies of Kalonymus Kalman, in *Ma'or va-shemesh* as in various other Hasidic homily-texts there is relatively little attention directed to that theme of the *tzaddik* as a healer. That distinction has been pointed out as an example of the ways in which Hasidism would address very different sectors of their population of followers and their particular interests in quite different ways.[49]

In the above homiletical excerpt, one notes how the preacher transformed the motif of the pearl of healing. The rabbinic agada itself, as quoted above, typifies a large group of tales from various locations and cultures involving a magic artifact.[50]

In the transformation of the talmudic passage at the hands of the Kraków master, however, the purely magical element gives way to a different kind of theme, namely the effect of *t'shuvah* (repentance). The cure occurs not via some kind of magic object, but rather as the effect of an awakening of thoughts of repentance which begin to stir within the person's consciousness.

---

49. Gries, *Sefer, sofer vesippur*, 35–39; *The Book, 1700–1900*, 85–87.

50. Thompson, *Motif-Index of Folk-Literature*, D800–1699, Magic Objects. Note: D1071, Magic jewel, D1342, Magic object gives health, D1500.1.2, Sacred healing stone. Also D2161, Magic healing power, D1900.1.9, Magic jewel cures disease.

(Of course, that implies that a person's illness results from some fault of the ill person or reflects a spiritual stagnancy on the person's part.)

The reader or listener feels that Abraham, referred to in the passage as a *tzaddik,* calls to mind the Hasidic holy man, who was similarly felt to convey a sense of the divine Presence and who is associated, in much of more popular Hasidic lore, with the power to heal. In the above passage, however, the pearl itself is understood only symbolically.

The concluding note in the above passage, which builds upon the detail that Abraham was sitting in the opening of his tent, is found also in *No'am 'Elimelekh,* the collection of interpretations by Elimelekh of Lyzhansk whom Kolonymus Kalman had considered to be his own teacher and master. Whereas a tent, in traditional interpretation, came to symbolize Torah-study, Elimelekh read the tent as symbolizing a life of true reverence, and he read the patriarch's "sitting at the opening of the tent" (Gen 18:1) as indicating that in Abraham's own eyes, he had not yet even entered the tent of the life of reverence, but had attained only the very opening steps toward that spiritual ideal.[51] Following in the steps of Elimelekh's interpretation, Kolonymus Kalman went further to suggest that it was precisely Abraham's essential humility in his spiritual journey that made him a force for healing.

The Element of Physical Desire in Intercourse[52]

> "Now Abraham and Sarah were old, advanced in years; Sarah had stopped having the periods of women. (And Sarah laughed to herself, saying, 'Now that I am withered, am I to have enjoyment—with my husband so old?' Then the Lord said to Abraham, 'Why did Sarah laugh, saying, "Shall I in truth bear a child, old as I am?" Is anything too wondrous for the Lord?) I will return to you at the time that life is due, and Sarah shall have a son.'" (Gen 18:11–14)

It is important to grasp how our mother, Sarah, was so lacking in faith that she could not believe in the wonders of the blessed Creator who is able to give her seed even in her old age. And we will attempt to explain. It is known that sexual intercourse requires a pronounced aura of holiness and purity. However, with that alone it is not possible to draw

---

51. *No'am 'Elimelekh* (*Vayera*).
52. *Ma'or va-shemesh,* I, 12b.

down a pure soul from the high world to bring it into this lowly and physical world except by means of its fusing, even to some small extent, with physical delight in intercourse, even when it takes place in holiness and purity. For the body comes about through the physical aspect of intercourse, and without that bodily act it is impossible to give birth. And to do so the body requires at least some small measure of physical desire and pleasure.

Comment: The reader might well connect this passage with a rather implicit theme found within one of the passages found above, "The Function of Shabbat," on *parashat B'rei'shit*. It becomes obvious that to the mind of the Kraków master, a desirable balance between materiality and physicality, on one hand, and spirituality, on the other, is required, a delicate balance allowing a place for both. Just as the very possibility of spiritual consciousness and awareness can be devastated by the world's becoming materialized beyond a certain point, so here the birth of a child requires that spirituality include a necessary space for physical desire and pleasure. Both poles must be accommodated. This sense of balance is one of the implied underlying themes that typify *Ma'or va-shemesh*.

The Poles of Mercy and Justice[53]

It is known that the essential quality of our father Abraham was lovingkindness (*ḥesed*), and his principal intention was to draw down lovingkindness to benefit all that was created. In addition, the angels who were sent to punish the men of Sodom (Gen 19) were really angels of mercy, as is made clear also in the Midrash,[54] and they tarried somewhat to allow for the possibility that the wicked people might turn from their evil way, hence allowing the quality of justice to be transformed to compassion, sparing them from annihilation.

Accordingly, the Lord said, "Shall I hide from Abraham (from what I am about to do?" Gen 18:17), for Abraham is the personification of mercy, and perhaps he will draw down heavenly lovingkindness upon them, sparing them from destruction. The Blessed and Exulted One desires lovingkindness, for lovingkindness can allow for a sweetening of the

53. *Ma'or va-shemesh*, I, 13a.
54. *Midr. Gen.* 50:1.

judgments. And so it is said (concerning Abraham), "For I have singled him out, that he may instruct his children and his posterity to keep the way of the Lord by doing what is just and right, in order that the Lord may bring about for Abraham what He has promised him" (Gen 18:19).

Now, the word *dibbur* (spoke), wherever it occurs, alludes to harsh judgment, as is known.[55] Its meaning in this verse is that perhaps through Abraham, who is the source of lovingkindness, the judgments might be included in mercy and be sweetened at their root. And so even though it is written, "The men set out from there and looked down toward Sodom . . ." (Gen 18:16), afterward it is said, "The men went on from there to Sodom" (Gen 18:22). Even though they had already gone, they returned and waited a while, for perhaps Abraham had spoken on behalf of the people of the cities of the plain. In other words, after they were already in Sodom, and "Abraham remained standing before the Lord" (Gen 18:22), they returned and saw Abraham who had continued standing before the Lord to awaken mercy, for perhaps he was able to extend heavenly lovingkindness upon the inhabitants for the purpose of averting their destruction.

And the Midrash alludes to this as it understood the men's turning (*vayifnu*) from there to infer that angels lack brazenness (associated with *'oref*, "the back of the neck")[56] as they lack any inclination for judgment and punishment. For they are angels of compassion who do not hurriedly execute vengeance but rather wait patiently, for perhaps the people of Sodom might repent or Abraham might bring about mercy for them.[57]

Comment: Kalonymus Kalman constructed this passage upon various threads that the Midrash had woven together to emphasize the attribute of compassion both in regard to Abraham and to the very angels sent to destroy the cities. The preacher did not introduce innovative interpretations as much as impress upon his flock the tone of some interesting midrashic readings on this biblical episode.

The tone of this passage is in accord with emphases found elsewhere in *Ma'or va-shemesh*. For example, in his homilies on *Lekh l'kha*, he related to the saying in *Mishna 'Avot* that God created the world with Ten Utterances[58] (Gen 1, rather than with a single utterance) in order to increase

---

55. *Sipre* (*B'ha'alotkha*) #99, on Num 12:1.
56. *Midr. Gen* 49:7.
57. *Midr. Gen* 50:1.
58. *m. Abot* 5:1.

both the reward for the righteous and the punishment for the wicked who might respectively sustain or destroy the world. But in his interpretation of that statement, Kalonymus Kalman associated the Ten Utterances with the contractions and garments involved in creation that made it more difficult to know God, hence providing a justification for evil-doers which could allow for greater leniency toward them.

In *Ma'or va-shemesh*, the homilies on this portion, perhaps conveniently, omit any treatment of the 'Akedah (the binding of Isaac) with its very problematic aspects. But elsewhere in the same volume,[59] the preacher related to that episode in a distinctly allegorical manner, drawing upon earlier interpretations in which Abraham represents the quality of *ḥesed* (lovingkindness) while Isaac represents that of *din* (judgment, punishment). In his treatment of the subject, the very command of the 'Akedah is read symbolically as the triumph of lovingkindness and mercy over strict judgment: judgment is bound and hence made subservient to mercy.

---

59. *Ma'or va-shemesh (Rimze Rosh hashanah)*, V, 32b.

Hayyei Sarah

A Person Coming to the *Tzaddik* (Holy Man)[60]

> "Raising her eyes, Rebekah saw Isaac. (She alighted from the camel and said to the servant, 'Who is that man walking in the field toward us?' And the servant said, 'That is my master.') So she took her veil and covered herself." (Gen 24:64–65)

And Rashi commented, "Rebekah saw Isaac"—she saw him as splendid and awe-inspiring.

The words require clarification. And it would seem to allude to the effect on the person who journeys to the *tzaddikim*. It is normal for every person to view himself as upright, and specifically one who studies Torah and engages in prayer and devotion will feel in his heart that he is already on the level of a *tzaddik*. However, in approaching the *tzaddik*, one becomes fearful and is given to awe, and he sees that his deeds are really nothing at all. He descends from his level in his own eyes in that though he had considered himself a *tzaddik* and a person of moral and spiritual rank, he now comes to the level of *t'shuvah* (repentance) as he examines his deeds and perceives that they are not as they should be. And as he notes the very high devotion of the *tzaddik*, he feels shame in his own deeds and qualities and grasps the need to repair them and to serve God on a higher level with greater energy. This is brought about by his journey to the *tzaddik*. And it is known that Isaac both personified the quality of awe (*yir'ah*), connected with the world of repentance, and directed his contemporaries to strive to improve their actions.

This is inferred from the verse, "Raising her eyes, Rebekah saw Isaac. She alighted from the camel . . . ." The word camel (*gamal*) is related to the root *gemul* (*gemilut ḥasadim*, engaging in acts of lovingkindness and charity), for she fell from her former level (in her own eyes), realizing

---

60. *Ma'or va-shemesh*, I, 15b.

now that she hadn't really performed good deeds at all in the world. She lowered herself from her former self-estimation and came to the world of *t'shuvah*, exemplifying the effect on persons as they come to the *tzaddik*. Rashi alluded to this in explaining that she saw Isaac as majestic and awe-inspiring: she now perceived his wholeness of repentance and, amazed at the deficiency of her own deeds up to that time, was determined to repair them. And she came to the world of *t'shuvah*, the world of *Binah* (the *s'firah*, "Understanding"), from which the fifty gates of Understanding branch out, realizing the need to repair all of them.

For there are five levels of every soul: *nefesh*, *ru'aḥ*, *n'shamah*, *ḥayah*, and *y'ḥidah* [the first three of which are naturally found in each person, while the latter two, of a higher nature, must be earned and acquired during the course of one's life], and the repentant must repair all of them in terms of those fifty gates. Now five multiplied by fifty adds up to 250, a number having the numerical equivalence (in terms of *g'matria*) of the word *tz'aif* (scarf or veil), conveying that she repaired all five parts of her soul, each having fifty gates. And "she covered herself," for through engagement in *t'shuvah*, one receives a garment which protects a person from all the accusing agents.

Comment: With the establishment of Hasidic courts came the practice of a follower's making a periodic journey to his *tzaddik*, sometimes on holy-days and special occasions or at other times as well. Though Kalonymus Kalman, it appears, never actually assumed the role of a *rebbe*, the preacher, on more than this occasion, strove to dissect the inner meaning of such a journey to a *tzaddik*.

In the above homily, Rebecca, who has journeyed from her prior location in Haran to Isaac's location in Canaan to become his wife, is thought to exemplify the role of a follower journeying to the *tzaddik*, the Hasidic holy man, and Isaac, in that sense, is portrayed as a *tzaddik*.

With her first actual sighting of Isaac, Rebecca is thought here to undergo the transformation that Kalonymus Kalman ascribes to the followers in their viewing the *tzaddik* and experiencing his presence, namely a realization of the gulf separating them from the holy man, the gulf between a person's self-estimation and the ideal that far transcends that reality. So Rebecca, in her very initial impression of Isaac, goes beyond her more common norm of devotion and lovingkindness. Though she had been described as an exemplar of lovingkindness in not only consenting

Hayyei Sarah

to draw water for a stranger at the well but, in addition, in her offering to draw water also for his animals (Gen 24:15–20), with the very sight or sign of presence of the *tzaddik*-figure the homily presents her as challenged by Isaac's incredibly higher norm and level.

That transformation is a movement from a person's sense of spiritual self-satisfaction in the direction of *t'shuvah*. It is clear, however, that *t'shuvah*, normally translated as "repentance," is not necessarily a matter of repenting for some kind of negative behavior. It is rather a questioning of the quality of one's deeds in light of a perpetually higher standard of holiness. This definition colors all mention of *t'shuvah* in this collection of homilies.

A more subtle suggestion underlies this homily: the perpetual danger of spiritual smugness. Any degree of self-satisfaction is a hurdle in the way of that person's real spiritual growth. It blinds oneself to one's own blemishes and fosters in a person an unreal self-image. Kalonymus Kalman's spiritual guide, Elimelekh of Lyzhansk, who so accentuated the role of the *tzaddik* in his teachings, explained that a true *tzaddik* does not see himself as such; if he does, that is a sign that he is not a *tzaddik* and has far to go to reach that level.[61]

In this passage, Kalonymus Kalman recast an episode in the account of the biblical foreparents in terms of the social reality of Hasidism with the figure of the *tzaddik* and the practice of pilgrimage to the *tzaddik*, and the subject of this homily focuses on the relationship between the Hasidic holy man and his followers. In that sense, the preacher leaped over the tremendous gulf separating the patriarchal biblical period from Jewish life in Eastern Europe. This homily hence clearly illustrates quite emphatically the common tendency of a commentator to read the past in terms of one's present.

---

61. *No'am 'Elimelekh* (*No'aḥ*) 23.

Tol'dot

The Lure and Cooling of Appetite[62]

> "And the Lord said to her (to Rebecca), 'Two nations (*goyim*) are in your womb.'" (Gen 25:23)

[On the basis of sound-similarity], Rashi [63] explained this verse in reference to two persons of lofty rank (*gei'im*), Antigonus [a high Roman official in Palestine] and Rabbi [Rabbi Yehuda ha-Nasi, the rabbinic sage who edited the Mishna in the early third century, C.E.] on whose tables neither radish (*tz'non*) nor horseradish (*ḥazeret*) were ever absent. His words allude to the saying of our Sages of blessed memory that now [in the absence of the altar in the Temple which had been destroyed], our eating-table serves as a means of atonement.[64]

The words would seem to convey that the righteous walk in the ways of the Torah of God and do not pursue (material and gastronomical) desires, eating only what is necessary for the maintenance of the body which enables them to engage in the service of God. Eating at their table, they abstain, even in the middle of a meal, and even when their inclination burns to tempt them to continue with some tasty food or sweet drink, they cool off their inclination to eat or drink more. And they even worry and engage in repentance (*t'shuvah*) concerning what they have already eaten, lest they ate or drank more than was necessary. This is overheard in the words *ts'non* and *ḥazeret*, for they cool off (*miston'nim*) their inclination (and desire) and repent (*ḥozrim bit'shuvah*) concerning what they had done.

This contrasts with the way of the wicked. For even if they had engaged in some *mitzvah* with enthusiasm and great desire, the wicked cool

---

62. *Ma'or va-shemesh*, I, 17a.
63. Based on Rashi's comment on *b. 'Abod. Zar.* 11a.
64. *b. Ber.* 55a.

off that spiritual enthusiasm and turn from it due to their stronger desire for additional food and drink.

The same pattern [of cooling off and repenting, linguistically symbolized by the radish and the horseradish] characterizes both the righteous and the wicked, though in diametrically opposite directions.

Comment: The talmudic passage on which this brief discourse is based, a statement of Rabbi Yehudah in the name of Rav, read the two nations (*goyim*), mentioned in a verse from the Torah-reading, as indicating two persons of lofty rank (*gei'im*), namely Antigonus and his contemporary, Rabbi Yehudah haNasi ("Rabbi"). Rashi, in his comment on that source, explained that the former was a descendent of Esau (Edom/Rome) while the latter was a descendent of Jacob.

The talmudic passage states that lettuce, radish, and cucumbers were always to be found on Rabbi's table for reasons having to do with how their respective medicinal properties effect the body. That kind of statement might indeed interest those curious about ancient medicine. The passage as re-stated in *Ma'or va-shemesh*, however, understands radishes and horseradish-root symbolically in terms of the letters and sounds comprising those words and brings the listener into a very different world of concern—not physical health-measures, but rather two distinct types of persons with very different value-systems and dispositions. The "righteous" (represented by Rabbi) regard food as a requirement of bodily survival which, in turn, is viewed as necessary in order to serve God in life, while the "wicked" (represented by Antigonus) eat out of a boundless desire for food and drink. The first emphasize the spiritual dimension of life, while for the second group the lust for food, beyond any health-considerations, takes precedence.

In addition to the liberty the preacher has allowed himself in arriving at what he claims to be the real contrast between the two men, he added what might be a humorous nuance in locating a shared formula at work in terms of each of the two groups: each follows the same basic formula, one which, however, is interpreted in terms of distinctly opposing sets of values.

Vayetze
Jacob's Dream-Episode[65]

> "(Jacob) came upon a certain place and stopped there for the night.... Taking one of the stones of that place, he put it under his head (and lay down in that place)." (Gen 28:11).

Rashi explained that the stones began to argue with one another (each seeking to serve as Jacob's pillow) and the Blessed Holy One immediately made of them a single stone, and hence "Jacob took *the* stone . . ." (Gen 28:18). [Two rabbinic texts,[66] providing different backgrounds, explained that the twelve stones were merged into a single stone.]

But one might interpret Rashi's words as intimating a deeper thought....

Our holy Torah comes to teach us the ways of the worship of God as we are to praise Him through Torah (study) and prayer. And in doing so, it is important not to corporealize any word or letter of the Torah or prayer, thinking that these are understandable simply according to their surface-meaning.

Rather, when one is standing in prayer, it is necessary to remember that the very existence and life-energy of thousands upon thousands of worlds depend upon the holiness of the letters and upon every word and letter and even upon a small dot in the Torah-text. This is alluded in the saying of our blessed Sages that God "is the place (*makom*) of the world,"[67] [rather than the world being God's place; the comment in the Midrash refers to Ps 90:1, "O Lord, You have been our dwelling-place (*ma'on*) in every generation," as a prooftext] and that the Torah is entirely one with the Blessed Holy One. Failing to realize this, one might corporealize

---

65. *Ma'or va-shemesh*, I, 21ab.
66. b. Ḥul. 91b, and *Midr. Gen* 68:11.
67. *Midr. Gen* 68:9.

his prayer, which in that case is not a prayer of *tzaddikim*. For the core principle of prayer lies in one's attaching himself to the spirituality of the letters which can awaken higher realms.

"He had a dream; a stairway was set on the ground and its top reached to the sky . . . . Jacob awoke from his sleep (*mi-sheinato*), and he said, 'Surely the Lord is present in this place (and I did not know it). Shaken, he said, 'How awesome is this place! This is none other than the abode of God, and that is the gateway to heaven" (Gen 28:12–17).

The Midrash strangely explained that Jacob awoke from his study (*mi-mishnato*).[68]

The Midrash would seem, however, to suggest that the core and goal of human prayer is the fullness of perfection in the worship of the Blessed One as a person grasps God's blessed Divinity through Torah-study *and* prayer. This cannot be achieved by one without the other, because "An unlearned person (*'am ha'aretz*) cannot be devout,"[69] and through Torah-study alone one cannot cultivate his soul to attain a state of wholeness, as our Sages said, "Anyone who says he has nothing but Torah does not even have Torah."[70] [Deeds are also necessary.]

Certainly through engaging in Torah for its own sake, one comes to a pronounced state of holiness and attaches himself, in the three basic levels of the soul, *nefesh*, *ruaḥ* and *n'shamah*, to the letters of the Torah. However, even so he cannot fully attain the quality of awe and love and thirst and longing for serving God and cannot attain a true sense of Divinity other than through praying with devotion and enthusiasm, as is said in all the holy books.

Our Sages explained Jacob's "coming upon a certain place" as his instituting the evening prayer (*'aravit/ma'ariv*).[71] Until then he did not know the greatness of prayer. While we find that Jacob had previously sought refuge in the Academy of Shem and Ever where he studied Torah,[72] and so he certainly came to know the mystery of prayer, nevertheless he did not actually experience a revelation of Divinity until that moment when he truly grasped the mystic significance of prayer.

---

68. *Midr. Gen* 69:7.
69. *m. 'Abot* 2:6.
70. *b. Yebam.* 109b.
71. *b. Ber.* 26b, quoted in Rashi's comment on Gen 28:11.
72. *Midr. Gen* 63:10; 68:11, also *b. Mak.* 23b.

And this is the interpretation offered in the Midrash: "Jacob awoke from his sleep"—from his Torah-study. Through this prayer he grasped that he had not attained what he did through Torah alone. And he said, "Surely the Lord is present in this place," indicating that through this prayer he was able more completely to understand how God revealed Himself through his study, "And I did not know" this secret. "This is none other than the abode of God"—meaning that precisely through prayer in a state of inner awakening and enthusiasm, one is able to experience awe of God's exulted state.... For prayer is of the nature of the gate of heaven, the attainment of a sense of Divinity and awe of God.

Comment: Like other Hasidic teachers, Kolonymus Kalman grasped episodes from the Torah essentially not as narrative, but rather as a *code*, as exercises in need of deciphering. The end-product focuses not upon Jacob and his particular happenings and situation but is nothing less than a vision of being itself. And accordingly, the story revolving around Jacob's famous dream is deciphered as a statement of a deeper truth.

The motif of the stones fusing together to comprise a single stone, based upon midrashic readings of that episode, invited the preacher to ponder the nature of oneness. Going beyond the midrashic motif of twelve stones, symbolizing the twelve tribes of Israel which emerged through Jacob's own twelve sons and their becoming a single people, the homily directed his attention to the theme of the innerness of the very words and letters of the Torah itself which is understood, in some more ultimate sense, as a manifestation of the Divine. In accord with that sense, one's understanding of the Torah-text must go beyond the level of its simpler meaning.

The discourse on Jacob's dream-episode goes on to echo rabbinic statements concerning the role of deeds that must accompany Torah-study. Study itself, unaccompanied by deeds, is insufficient.[73] In the Kraków master's homily, however, the basic contrast is not one between study and deeds, but rather between study and prayer. Building upon a rabbinic tradition that Jacob had studied in a prototypical academy, the Academy of Shem and Ever, the homily attributes to Jacob's dream a realization on his part that study alone is insufficient without a devotional dimension expressed in prayer (*t'filah*). The preacher re-carved the account of Jacob's dream to voice a critique of a total and exclusive emphasis upon study to the exclusion of any real emphasis upon that devotional dimension.

73. *m.'Abot* 1:17.

The Letters within All That Exists[74]

> "And the mound was called *Mitzpah*, because Laban said, 'May the Lord watch between you and me when we are out of sight of one another.'" (Gen 31:49)

On the level of its plain meaning, this verse is not understandable. But we might interpret it in terms of what it intimates, namely that while it is impossible to attain a sense of the essence of the blessed Creator, one can obtain a sense of God's existence on the basis of His actions. The Will of the Emanator was that His existence might so be revealed, allowing His creations to attain a sense of His Divinity, and to this end the worlds evolved, one world from another, continuing even to the depths of the earth. And His Divinity is present within them, for without that presence the world could not exist, as is said in Scripture, "There is nothing but You," [actually words from the liturgy for Shabbat morning following the call-to-prayer (*Borkhu*), before the *piyyut*, *ʾEl ʾAdon*; the phrase in the liturgy echoes Isa 45:6 and 14, also Deut 4:35] as without God no created being or object could exist. Created things have existence solely through the Light of Divinity that is present within them.

And all created beings together serve as a garment for the innerness of God's Divinity present within them and giving them life. Through the actions of created things, of humans and beasts and animals and all other things having life-energy (*ḥiyyut*), we can conclude that the Divine is present within all that exists, bestowing upon all of them life and being. And in this way we grasp God's blessed Divinity.

It follows that all physical bodies serve as garments for the light of God's Divinity that dwells within them. And similarly in all the higher worlds, the spirituality of every world is like a garment of the particular level of being just above it, *ʿAsiyah* to *Y'tzirah*, and *Y'tzirah* to *B'riʾah* [among the four levels of existence in the kabbalistic world-picture] and similarly until we come to the blessed *ʾEin Sof* (the Divine in its totally infinite sense). The difference is simply that in the higher realms, the garments are emphatically thinner and so they differ from the external character of those worlds in which physical bodies comprise the garments of the Light of divine-energy which radiates them, making for a contrast between what is physical and spiritual in character. In the higher spheres

---

74. *Maʾor va-shemesh*, 23b.

even the garments serve as souls for the next lower world, as is clarified in the holy books and alluded in the Gemara.

We learn that the blessed Holy One created the world by cladding Himself in light,[75] as it is said, "Wrapped in a robe of light, You spread the heavens like a tent cloth" (Ps 104:2). The higher garments are actually lights, and what are the lights?—letters of the Torah, as our Sages said in B'rei'shit rabbah, "With the Torah the blessed Holy One created the world."[76] [This theme was developed further in the Zohar, I, 5a.] God clad Himself in the letters and their innerness and created everything, both external reality and its innerness, the Light of the letters which gives life and existence to all its aspects.

It follows from our words that there is absolutely nothing in the world, even in the lowest point in this lower stratum, in which the holiness of God's blessed Divinity is not present as its innerness, bestowing being to it. And similarly this is true of the higher worlds; each world is a garment of the inner light of the next higher world which gives light and being to it. And this is the core aspect of the Israelites' service ('avodah) in Torah and prayer and in fulfilling the *mitzvot*: to purify even the material character and to know that in every material entity there is something of a spiritual nature within it, giving it existence.

It is necessary to elevate everything to its Root, the light of God's blessed holiness, the source of life and being of all that is. Through this means, one may realize the reality of God's Divinity which gives being to everything, realizing that this light too is merely a garment of the higher worlds, and extending on and on as far as the ultimate level, the blessed Infinite One, the '*Ein-sof*.

And in this way one can attain deep attachment and understanding. The very goal of creation itself was that through the garments we might attain a sense of the inner Light. That is God's great delight, and this revelation and realization can come about only through a purification of what is external in character.

But this does not occur with the wicked who perceive only the external reality, failing to consider that beyond it is that innerness of the Light which gives being to all that is. Consequently, they are like dead bodies devoid of real life, and it seems to them that the world functions in its own particularly materialistic manner. It is this that distinguishes the

---

75. *Midr. Gen* 3:4.
76. *Midr. Gen* 1:1, referring to Prov 8:30, and *m. 'Abot* 3:14.

people, Israel, a people brought close to God, from the nations and that distinguishes the righteous from the wicked.

And these verses intimate this view: the mound (*mitzpah*) comes from the word *malbush* (garment), as "and he overlaid it" (as Bezalel "overlaid the incense ark with pure gold," Exod 37:26). In all the worlds created by divine Utterance, the innerness is clad within what is external.

"The Lord will watch between me and you" (Laban's statement concerning the mound, Gen 31:49)—this is the screen separating us, in that Jacob and his sons believed and pondered that even within every material thing is the spiritual light that gives it being. In this way they attach themselves to the innerness of everything and purify everything to draw it close to its Root, the inner Light that is within it.

Not so the wicked son [mentioned in the *Haggadah* of *Pesaḥ*, the text read and discussed at the Seder, which refers to four sons, each of a different character or inclination, and suggests how the head of the family should respond to a question asked, or not asked, by each one of them] and his faction who consider only what is external in nature and hence are unable to understand the level of Jacob who cleaves to the holiness of God's blessed Divinity. And as a consequence, one person becomes hidden from the sight of his fellow [in the sense that the one is unable to understand the mind of the other].

Comment: The above passage, commenting upon a final meeting of Jacob and Laban some two decades after the earlier dream-episode, revolves around the word, *mitzpah*, a mound which Laban built in order to separate his household from that of Jacob, who had married his two daughters. That word, as indicated in the verse, would mean "to look over, watch," the mound serving as a look-out point. But the homilist read the word, *mitzpah* as meaning "to overlay, to cover over," hence serving as an intimation concerning the true nature of all physical reality: the physical, empirical world in its totality is a garment placed over—covering, overlaying—the deeper reality, which is the Divine.

Spelling out this thought in terms of a kabbalistic conception of many worlds or levels of being, the preacher stated perhaps the core Hasidic conception of the cosmos as just such a garment which draws its very existence from what it covers and conceals, namely the presence of the Divine which is the innerness of all that exists. This view neither negates nor ignores physical, external reality, but instead conveys the need to purify and lift up that external reality to the level of its own true innerness.

The mound in this passage was constructed to separate Laban and Jacob, and that note of separation in the homily is then read as a separation between the people of Israel and the other nations of the world in terms of a basic contrast between each population's consciousness and conception of existence. In that sense, it reflects attitudes that predate any sense of mutual understanding and appreciation among different religious traditions and any sense of what they might share.

Vayishlaḥ
Angels[77]

> "Jacob sent messengers ahead (to his brother Esau)." (Gen 32:4)
> [The word, *mal'akh,* could indicate either "angel" or "messenger."]

Rashi maintained that they were really angels. And one must consider the precise meaning of *lefanav* ("ahead of him"), which would seem to be superfluous. In addition, it is difficult to grasp how the wicked Esau would be able to see angels sent from on high. Did we not find that Rashi commented on the verse "(to see your face is) like seeing the face of God" (or "the face of angels," Gen 33:10), as Jacob's informing Esau that he saw angels in order to make his brother fearful. From this it would appear that to perceive angels was something threatening to Esau, and now Jacob himself sent angels to Esau!

But one might first consider something found in the Zohar as well as in other holy books: anything of a spiritual nature that comes from a higher realm to this lower world must assume a physical character to a degree through a garment (*malbush*) in order that this world might be able to bear it. And even when God gave our holy Torah to Israel for the lower world, it was necessary that the Torah, similarly, assume a more physical character and be clad in the form of narratives, as is explained there in the Zohar.[78]

It is also known that by means of his Torah-study and his prayers and all the *mitzvot* that he performs, a *tzaddik* (holy man) creates an angel. And when God sends an angel to the *tzaddik* to assist him, it is impossible for the angel, who is indeed spiritual in nature, to come to this lower world without acquiring a physical character and garment that is itself less spiritual in nature. This is because the angel was created through

---

77. *Ma'or va-shemesh*, I, 23b.
78. Zohar, III, 152a.

combinations of letters that are in the *mitzvot* which the *tzaddik* fulfilled, letters which clad the hidden light of the *mitzvah*, while the garment that the angel clads when he comes to the lower world to be of service to the holy man consists of other letters.

And now we can comprehend the words of the verse immediately preceding, "Jacob went on his way and angels of God encountered him. When he saw them, Jacob said, 'This is God's camp'" (Gen 32:2–3). The expression, "when he saw them" can be understood in the light of the above suggestion, for when he saw them, he recognized that they came into being and are clad in the clothing of his Torah-study and *mitzvot* and of the combinations of his acts of unification. Then his heart directed him to utilize them, for he recognized that they came to be of assistance to him, as they were created through his own combinations and unifications.

But when he wished to send them to Esau, he understood that they are still too spiritual to send to him and must now assume an even more physical nature than was the case when they came to Jacob. For this reason it is written, "Jacob sent messengers ahead" (Gen 32:4)—meaning that as he sent them, he removed from them their spiritual garments. He understood *vayishlaḥ* ("And he sent") as derived from the word, *hafshatah* (removing a garment), like the expression, *m'shalḥei gelima de'anshei*,[79] understanding that he removed from them the angelic garments in which they were clad when they were in his presence so that they might appear to Esau as humans. [In that talmudic source, a root resembling that of *shalaḥ*, "send," is used to indicate "removing the garments" of creditors who lost money in a legal judgment.]

And the wording of the verse ("to his brother Esau") supports this understanding: it was necessary that they have a more physical character so that they might be able to exist in the presence of his brother, Esau.

Comment: The above passage is constructed upon the dual-meaning of the Hebrew word *mal'akhim*, which, in biblical use, can indicate either angels or messengers, and which lends itself to an equivalency in their meanings insofar as, in the biblical mindset, angels are messengers. But within this rather complex passage, the preacher tapped upon an important strain in Hasidic thought that, in its more complete sense, views everything in this world as having a higher root which transcends this world and its physical character.

79. *b. Ketub.* 85a.

The passage makes reference to the Torah in its higher core existence as being wholly spiritual, with the implication that it could be grasped on our level of being only through its acquiring a garment of narratives. Those narratives in themselves are not to be equated with the Torah (in its more sublime manifestation), though the Torah can be communicated to humans only through such narratives. Various other analogies exemplify this basic perspective: a person is not the body as such but something deeper and more intrinsically holy which, however, can exist in this realm of being only through such a physical, bodily form. Everything, even the food we eat, is a garment containing within it that which transcends the more apparent nature of the world which we inhabit.

In addition, this passage conveys something significant concerning the nature of a *mitzvah*, a holy deed. The passage understands a *mitzvah* as containing letters, sublime letters, just as does the Torah itself. That very thought challenges one to think of the *mitzvah* in a startlingly different way, transcending a more commonplace view of deeds.

The *Tzaddik*: Solitude and Community[80]

> "That same night Jacob arose ... he crossed the ford of the Jabbok. ... Jacob was left alone. And a man wrestled with him. When he saw that he had not prevailed against him, he wrenched Jacob's hip at its socket ...." (Gen 32:23–26)

It appears that one must comprehend this passage through an allusion, "The *Sh'khinah* (divine Presence) is present with every gathering of ten,"[81] and "a numerous people is the glory of a king" (Prov. 14:28). Concerning everything relating to holiness it is preferable that it take place within a group rather than by a single person alone. Even though in a state of prayerful solitude while praying alone, a holy man would be able to reach a higher level than when he prays together with others, nevertheless, in the process, he can acquire an accuser [based in a rather round-about way from the saying of Rabbi Halafta ben-Dosa, "Wherever ten sit together and engage in Torah, the divine Presence is found among them"[82]] and— God forbid—descend to a lower place. In doing the holy deed together

---

80. *Ma'or va-shemesh*, I, 25a.
81. *b. Sanh.* 39a.
82. *m. 'Abot* 3:7.

with a group, he will have no such accuser.[83] And this is the proof: even though the holy man might pray alone and his act ascends in the higher realms, he still cannot recite the *K'dushah* ["Holiness," a liturgical composition recited or chanted during the oral repetition of the silent prayer, *'amidah*] except with a quorum of ten.

Comment: The mention of Jacob being alone at the ford of the river brings the Kraków master to the question of the respective spiritual advantages of *hitbod'dut*, being alone in a way allowing for greater spiritual depth and intensity, and of fellowship and participation within a community. More precisely, Jacob's aloneness evokes the Kraków master's rejection of *hitbod'dut*, of being alone, when it involves the detriment of fellowship.

Hasidism, with its emphasis upon the community of followers, placed significant emphasis upon community. At the same time, however, a Hasidic community revolves around a mystic, one having a deep inner life attuned to the sublime. Having to decide between the two poles, the preacher clinched his case by resorting to a simple legal principle that basic parts of the prayer including the *K'dushah* require a prayer quorum (*minyan*), a group of ten worshippers. An individual, alone, even when his prayer reaches a higher level, is nevertheless ineligible to recite the *K'dushah*. It will be evident that the preacher frequently returned to engage that polarity, locating significant value in both, even while they continue to exist in a state of tension within his own mind.

Having to choose between the two poles, Kalonymus Kalman would place primary emphasis upon the importance of being part of a community setting, although it also becomes apparent that he is not completely satisfied with that kind of response. In the above homily, he notes that when a person is alone while engaged in prayer, his devotion might well attain much greater spiritual heights. The two poles of solitude and community suggest also a broader question of the basic primacy of the individual or of the group.

In other homilies in this collection, it will become evident that the tension between the two remained essentially unresolved in his mind as he continued to engage that issue in some highly interesting ways.

---

83. Zohar, I, 134a.

Vayeishev
The Two Poles Which One Must Avoid[84]

"When Joseph was taken down to Egypt (The Lord was with Joseph) and he was a successful man.... After a time, his master's wife cast her eyes upon Joseph.... But he refused,... 'How then could I do this most wicked thing, and sin before God?'... One such day, he came into the house to do his work. None of the household being there inside, she caught hold of him by his coat and said, 'Lie with me!' But he left his coat in her hand and got away and fled outside" (Gen 39:1–12).

It is known that the holy *Sh'khinah* went down to *Mitzrayim* (Egypt) with Joseph the Righteous [Jewish tradition often refers to Joseph as *Yosef ha-tzaddik*] and it says, "And the Lord was with Joseph" (Gen 39:2). *Vayehi* ("and he *was*"), an expression associated with sorrow, occurs in the verse, insofar as the divine Presence also went down into exile.[85] And being that the *Sh'khinah* was with him, certainly he guarded himself from all sin and iniquity and even from any very minute transgression and specifically from pride (*gei'ut*). For the Sages said, "One who feels pride and self-importance pushes away the feet of the *Sh'khinah*,"[86] and as the Sh'khinah was present with Joseph he certainly would not have felt even a minute speck of pride or arrogance.

But the explanation is as follows: "Now Joseph was well built and handsome" (Gen 39:6), indicating that he carefully guarded his body and its limbs in purity and holiness and was free of all iniquity and transgression. His was an illuminating soul, free of any blemish or any slight motion of sin as he engaged in acts of unification....

84. *Ma'or va-shemesh*, I, 28ab.
85. *Midr. Gen* 86:2; Zohar, I, 189a.
86. *b. Ber.* 43b.

But people with eyes of flesh did not know or understand the intention of the righteous person in his mannerisms (his decorative clothing and his curling his hair)[87] and his unifications, and they saw them as signs of pride. The blessed Holy One sought to reveal to them that Joseph was totally lacking in pride, and for this reason the test occurred with Potiphar's wife, also called the Evil Inclination (*yetzer ha-ra*),[88] who told him, "lie with me."

The saying of our Sages is known: all who are of haughty spirit are considered as though they committed immoral acts.[89] Arrogance is equivalent to immorality.... And if Joseph had even an ounce of physical pride, then he would have failed and succumbed to the advances of Potiphar's wife, for the consequence of transgression is further transgression.[90] If a person who committed a transgression should later have an occasion to commit another transgression similar to what he had done, he would proceed to commit that second transgression. But Joseph stood firm and did not succumb to transgression. Consequently, all would acknowledge and know that he truly lacked any sense of self-importance and haughtiness. His level of holiness and righteousness became evident in his deed.

When the Evil Inclination fails to bring the great *tzaddikim* to sin, it then pursues a different strategy and the *tzaddik* turns to a state of exaggerated solitude in which he scrutinizes his deeds and concludes in his own mind that he is the worst of the worst, full of transgressions and worthless, lacking all merit, for that is the way of the *tzaddikim* who spend much time alone, engaging in acts of repentance. And it is the strategy of the Evil Inclination to bring those *tzaddikim* to such a degree of sadness and depression—may God spare us from that—in which he would convey to himself that he is full of transgressions, and then the Evil Inclination would be able to grab hold of him and cause him to fail in something. But it is necessary for the *tzaddik* to realize that this is a tactic of the Evil Inclination, and he must immediately go forth from that mood to a sense of joy so that he might be saved from that strategy of the Evil Inclination.

This was the case with Joseph the Righteous: the Evil Inclination saw that it failed to force him to transgress, and so it brings him to engage in

---

87. Zohar, I, 190b.
88. Op. cit.
89. Zohar, I, 190b.
90. *m. 'Abot* 4:2.

a state of solitude in which he thinks of himself as worthless. The words, "none of the household being there inside" (Gen 39:11), indicate that he secluded himself, believing that he is guilty of transgressions, as the Evil Inclination sought to grab him and bring him to a state of sadness and depression so that in that way it might triumph over him. And the words, "she caught hold of him by his coat" (Gen 39:12), indicate that she grabbed him with transgressions in order to bring him to sadness, for through sadness, the Evil Inclination could bring him to failure.

The words, "But he left his coat in her hand and got away and fled outside" (Gen 39:12), however, indicate that he left his state of seclusion and his thoughts of self-incrimination which *tzaddikim* can sometimes have. And he "got away and fled outside" (Gen 39:13)—he affirmed himself and his true character, fortifying himself with joy. And this is the image of his father that he saw.[91] For the quality of Jacob is *Tiferet* (Glory). In this way he was spared from the snares of the Evil Inclination and all could know that Joseph was the Righteous, the Foundation of the World. [Kabbalah identifies Joseph with the *s'firah*, *Yesod*, foundation and sexual purity, and identifies Jacob with the *s'firah*, *Tiferet*.]

And this is the meaning of the verse, "See if I have vexatious ways, and guide me in ways everlasting" (Ps 139:24): ceasing to cooperate with the tactics of the Evil Inclination to bring him to moral failure, he seeks instead to relate once again to human society and its joys, as it is said, "And he fled and went outside." [The word ʻolam in the verse from Psalms indicates "everlasting," but the same word can also mean "world."] The Zohar[92] explains that the Sh'khinah dwells only in a place of joy.

Comment: As is evident in previous passages, Kalonymus Kalman, along with many others, tended to read a biblical passage in way that might seem quite extraneous to the text itself but which bears significance in terms of the complex of themes and values with which the expounder identifies. Drawing upon earlier readings, including those found in the Zohar, the biblical episode is here read as a warning against the two poles that stand out in this homily: one's sense of self-importance and haughtiness, on one hand, and on the other, an exaggerated introspection induced by a mindset of sadness and guilt as a person incriminates himself in his own mind and feels himself worthless. The latter could be understood as a perversion of

---

91. *b. Sotah* 36b; *Midr. Gen* 87:7 and 98:20 and Zohar, I, 222a.
92. Zohar, I, 180b.

the mystic conception of *'ayin* ("Nothingness").[93] Hasidic teaching warns of the pitfalls of self-castigation with its excessive focus on one's moral and spiritual failings in favor of a joyous pursuit of a life of piety.

Weaving together a number of statements and concepts from rabbinic sources and also from the Zohar, Kalonymus Kalman makes the case that Joseph is innocent not only of any immoral behavior but also of any sense of self-importance due to his position and success.

While the Kraków master sometimes tended to point to positive aspects of *hitbod'dut* (seclusion), he also exposed a fallible dimension in such solitary existence with its tendency to plant in a person a sense of guilt unrelated to any objective self-understanding. In that sense, this homily is not unrelated to an ongoing tension between seclusion and community which pervades *Ma'or va-shemesh*.

---

93. See Matt, "*Ayin*: The Concept of Nothingness."

Miketz

The *Tzaddik* Is Oblivious to Fame[94]

> "And it happened at the end of two years" (Gen 41:1) that the cupbearer remembered Joseph and mentioned his gift of dream-interpretation to Pharaoh.

. . . Joseph came to fear lest the cupbearer, now restored to his position, would publicize Joseph who accomplished wonders through his prayer, bringing people to act in a way favorable to him. For Joseph avoided anything that would bring his own role to public attention, except when it would be necessary to do so in order that God's Divinity might be revealed to the entire world. With these considerations, Joseph told the butler, *ki 'im* (except), which is a kind of condition that the cupbearer would not mention him to anyone, but should simply remember him in his own thoughts and heart, without relating anything to anyone else, except to Pharaoh. And he was to mention him to Pharaoh only when it would be necessary to disclose God's Divinity to the entire world so that faith everywhere would be strengthened. "You shall then recall me" as a recollection of something that had been forgotten by all concerned. And until that time, the cupbearer should have completely forgotten Joseph, not remembering him at all.

Comment: The homilist understood Joseph, along with other biblical figures, as a *tzaddik*, a holy man, and an example of human perfection, to whom fame, like pride, would be utterly alien.

Joseph is known in Jewish tradition as "Joseph the righteous" (*Yosef ha-tzaddik*), with the implication that he is thoroughly altruistic. While the biblical account itself might allow for a broader and more rounded view of

---

94. *Ma'or va-shemesh*, I, 30ab.

his personality and motives, the Kraków master analyzed the text in a way that Joseph specifically forbids the cupbearer's even remembering him until the crucial moment when Pharaoh is disturbed by his own dreams. In other words, not only did the cupbearer forget him until that point in time some two years later, but Joseph explicitly ordered the cupbearer to forget him during the interim.

Behind this interpretative exercise is the preacher's insistence on understanding the *tzaddik*-figure as beyond any concern for fame or any sense of self-importance. But beyond that, he was addressing a group of adherents to whom he imparted his message that concern for fame is illegitimate. In his speaking of *Yosef ha-tzaddik*, the righteous Joseph, his hope was that each person present might make the moral and spiritual effort to rise above all negative pride and above any concern for fame.

Vayigash
Submission[95]

We can likely understand this episode (of Judah's appeal to Joseph, whom he does not recognize, Gen 44:18–34) on the basis of the interpretation of the verse, "A gentle response allays wrath" (Prov 15:1). For it is impossible to come to that quality of gentleness except through submission (*hakhna'ah*) and humility (*'anavah*). Particularly if someone in greater authority wishes to act wrathfully toward someone of lesser rank, the latter must humble himself all the more. According to the measure of the other's stature, so will be his humility and submission.

But it is difficult to come to the quality of submission due to the force of the Evil Inclination which tempts one to think of himself in his own mind as a person of rank and position. Consequently, extraordinary actions are required of a person in order to cleanse his heart of the Evil Inclination and its way of thinking. And when one comes to submission, he naturally removes from himself, to an extent, his material character, for pride and lordship are bound up with materiality and worldly desires. But in coming to the quality of submission and seeing oneself as nothing, he severs himself somewhat from that very materiality, and every one, according to the extent of his submission, becomes freer of materiality as his spiritual self alone remains. He then cleaves to the higher worlds and becomes an instrument of submission, which draws him. . . .

Comment: While speaking of submission, Kalonymus Kalman is employing that term largely in the sense of humility. The Kraków master presented here an analysis of humility and of the impediments within oneself that do not easily allow for humility. Even facing the grim truth of their

---

95. *Ma'or va-shemesh*, I, 34a.

being trapped in a plot arranged by the powerful Egyptian official whom they do not recognize as their brother, it was a difficult feat for the brothers to overcome those impediments within themselves and to speak to Joseph in such a submissive manner.

The homily continues with the theme of uncladding one's materiality to read this phase of the Joseph story in terms of both Joseph's and his brothers' uncladding their materiality. The preacher, in this excerpt, was not offering any comprehensive literary analysis of the Joseph story; rather, he focused on a single theme, treating it quite independently of the larger narrative, but he delineated that one theme as one that can constantly repeat itself in life in a never-ending struggle between pride and humility.

The reader might well question whether such submission is a positive quality and a proper approach in speaking to power. And one might ask further whether this excerpt reflects either the situation of Kalonymus Kalman who had to make his peace with rabbinic authorities in Kraków who had little sympathy or tolerance for his own religious orientation or, going beyond that, might it reflect the psychological response of the Jew to the hostility of the larger population and its officialdom?

Vay'ḥi

Jacob's Final Testament and Failure[96]

> "And Jacob called his sons and said, come together and I will tell you what is to befall you in days to come. Assembly and hearken, O sons of Jacob, hearken to Israel your father." (Gen 49:1–2)

Rashi refers to a rabbinic midrash[97] in which Jacob wished to reveal the End (Redemption) but the *Sh'khinah* departed from him. . . . One cannot understand why first it is written "Come together and I will tell . . . ," while afterward, it is written, "Assemble," whereas normally both would be expressed by the same wording. And furthermore, why is it written, "Hearken to Israel, your father"?—What did he command them? Is there any sort of important testament mandating what they must do? Is it not rather the case that he didn't command them anything at all at that time? He only blessed them, and to some small degree he rebuked them, but did not command them at all concerning what they should do.

And concerning the saying of the Sages that Jacob sought to reveal to them the End (the ultimate Redemption) but the *Sh'khinah* (source of his inspiration) departed from him, we can ask: if it was proper to reveal the End, why did the Sh'khinah depart from him? And if it was not proper, why did he nevertheless seek to reveal it to them?

According to the Gemara,[98] Rabbi Yehoshua ben Levi asked the Messiah, "When will you come?" [According to tradition, Elijah is to announce the imminent coming of the Messiah.] And he answered him, "Today." Rabbi Yehoshua ben Levi then said to Elijah, may he be remembered for good, "But you did not come today," to which Elijah explained,

---

96. *Ma'or va-shemesh*, I, 37a.
97. b. Pesaḥ. 56a.
98. b. Sanh. 98a.

"Today if you hearken to my voice" (Ps 95:7).... It is written "I, the Lord, will speed it," followed by "in its time" (Isa 60:22). And the Gemara explains, "If they are worthy, 'I will hasten it'; and if not, then, 'in its time.'" And this is what the Messiah said: I would come today, but the matter depends upon Israel: If they repent, then I will hasten it and come today.

Jacob wished the repair of the world to begin in his own days, resulting from a proper repentance on the part of all the tribes (his sons). ... The concern of our father Jacob was their failure to repent properly. ... The *Sh'khinah* departed from Jacob, for the time had not yet come. And because the *Sh'khinah* had departed from him, Jacob was unable to bring them to a higher level of repentance. And so he told them that since it was not possible at that time to come to true repentance as he had wished, therefore "Assembly and hearken."

I heard from the holy mouth of the man of God, the late Holy Lantern, chief judge of the court of the holy community, Nashkhiz [Mordecai of Neshkhiz, in Volhynia, 1752–1800, known as a miracle-worker; author of *Rishpe 'eish*, Warsaw, 1869], that this has to do with the intent of persons in their journeying to the *tzaddikim*. Their core intent and motivation should be neither for prayer, nor for Torah, nor to witness the *tzaddik*'s high level; rather the journey must be for the sake of God—to know God and to cultivate reverence of God's sublime nature, knowing that He is the Root of all the worlds. And through joining together with the *tzaddikim*, it is possible to attain this realization.

And I've already said, "Turn to the Lord and to His might, seek His presence constantly" (Ps 105:4). "Seek the Lord" indicates prayer; and "His might" indicates the Torah which is called *'oz* (strength); but still higher is the counsel, "Seek His presence constantly"—to live in awe of God's presence, knowing that He is the Core and Root of all the worlds, and there is no place where God is not.[99]

... And this would illuminate what our father Jacob said, "Assemble and hearken, O sons of Jacob." When you *assemble* at the place of the *tzaddik*, *hearken* to your Father. Read the word *'el* (to) as *'El* (God). "Hearken" (not simply to hear, but) to understand that the God of Israel is your Father. Know whom you serve, and revere God, for that must be the principal purpose of your journey and gathering.

---

99. *Tikkunei ha-Zohar*, ch. 57.

Comment: Drawing upon older sources and, as was his talent, weaving them together to decipher a narrative within the text he was interpreting, Kalonymus Kalman provided for his following a portrait of Jacob as a failed *rebbe* who had failed to bring his followers (in this case, his sons) to a satisfactory state of repentance. The real thrust of this homily, however, takes off on biblical expressions indicating a gathering, as he defines what should be the true purpose of followers' making the journey to gather together at the place of their holy man, an actual practice that had become common in various Hasidic communities. Similar to what is found regarding several of these homilies, the preacher "discovers" within the toraitic account of Jacob and his sons an aspect of the stream's actual practice in his own time.

The master's reading of the episode of Jacob speaking to his sons before his death comprises what, to the preacher's mind, is a definition of what should ideally occur within a true Hasidic gathering of followers. That purpose, the master explains, goes beyond the means, expressions, and benefits of such a gathering to its more ultimate purpose, which is nothing other than reverence before God.

Jacob failed to bring his sons to a true sense of reverence, and hence to a wholeness of repentance. Relying upon some earlier interpretations, this homily presents Jacob as one who attempted but failed to make messianic redemption a reality. His intent might parallel that of Moses as found in a homily relating to the portion, *Va'ethanan* ("A Context for the Death of Moses"). But Jacob, in this homily, sought to bring his sons—his followers and disciples—to a state of truer and higher repentance not via any kind of cultic action, but only through trying to cultivate true reverence in the consciousness of his followers.

2

On the Second Book of the Torah (*Sh'mot* / Exodus)

Sh'mot
Torah and Time[1]

... It is known that our holy Torah transcends time, insofar as it pertains to all times and to all of time, for *ruaḥ ha-kodesh* (divine inspiration; revelation) does not cease. And even though when *ruaḥ ha-kodesh* spoke these words, they referred to happenings of that particular point-in-time, nevertheless clad in that same utterance is an eternal and infinite meaning. That understanding is expressed in the list of the names of the tribes (Exod 1:1–3) that opens the account: even though the tribes are given names relating to happenings described in the verses, nevertheless, since those names comprise part of a holy utterance, within the very recital of their names is clad a meaning that is not time-bound but is rather true of all time.

Comment: History is a record of the past or the quest of knowledge concerning the past, whereas Torah by its very nature, from the perspective of the classical Hasidic masters, necessarily addresses the present. In terms of its meaning, the text is ultimately heard and read not in the past tense, but rather in the present or, perhaps, in an "ever-present" tense which relates to all of time. Historical details concern specific occurrences that occurred at specific times, whereas the mindset of the Hasidic homilists read the exodus from Egypt to a large extent as alluding to a deeper, inner, more personal servitude and deliverance, the meaning of which goes far beyond any one-time happening and also beyond the societal context of

1. *Ma'or va-shemesh*, II, 1a.

the account as found in the Torah. The exodus, so grasped, is potentially occurring constantly in the inner life of every person.[2]

True Worship Requires Joy[3]

> The very nature of the worship of God is such that it must occur in a state of joy, as it says, "... because you would not serve the Lord your God in joy and gladness over the abundance of everything...." (Deut 28:47).

[The statement goes on to explain that prayer should take place in a mood of the joy of a *mitzvah* (*simḥah shel mitzvah*), a position voiced very clearly in the Zohar.[4]] God experiences delight when Israelites joyously raise their voices in Torah-study or in prayer, whereas worship that takes place in sadness brings about serious blemish in the higher realms. For this reason our Sages warned that a person should not pray in a mood of sadness or laziness,[5] and it is said in the Gemara [quoting a tradition of the sage, Rabba] that before study, one should even say something in jest,[6] as it is written, "Worship the Lord in gladness; (come into His presence with shouts of joy," Ps 100:2). Obviously a mortal with eyes of flesh would be unable to ascertain whether another person is serving God properly and joyously, and it is possible that even in one's joy a certain measure of sadness might be present, but the One who tests the hearts (*boḥen ha-l'vavot*) knows the truth and can ascertain whether or not worship takes place as is proper in joy.

And this is the meaning of the words, "And the Lord continued, 'I have marked well the plight of My people . . .'" (Exod 3:7), meaning that I see that affliction which precludes the possibility of their joyously worshiping His blessed Name and which brings them to serve Me in sadness due to the distress of their bondage. And I have no pleasure in that. But I heed their cry at the hand of their oppressors, for previously when they lifted their voices with praise and sang out joyously, their voice was sweet to me. And now, "I am mindful of their sufferings" (Exod 3:7). And

---

2. Note Wineman, "The Exodus in the Prism of the Hasidic Homily."
3. *Ma'or va-shemesh*, II, 1b.
4. Zohar, I, 180b, 197ab, 216b, and 229b.
5. *b. Ber.* 31a.
6. *b. Šabb.* 30b.

don't judge according to the seeing of your eyes, for even when they appear to worship joyously, as one who tests the hearts I am aware of their pain. And it is not even possible for them truly to worship joyously due to the distress of their subjugation. And so you shall inform them that I will bring them "to a good and spacious land, a land flowing with milk and honey" (Exod 3:8) where they will rejoice and sing energetically and serve Me with joy. For in that I will find delight.

Comment: The above homily appears to make the claim that it was not the physical subjugation in itself that was disturbing to God, but more precisely its effect upon the character of the prayer-life of the Israelites—a statement that might well raise serious questions in our minds. More likely, the homilist's intent was to focus upon the importance of worship in joy, a value assigned high priority in Hasidic life and worship, even if he may have raised that concept here to a seemingly absurd degree.

Certainly one aspect of his own activity in Kraków would have been to introduce and pioneer there a mode of joyous worship. That very model of prayer and joyous worship was obviously a very real factor in the spread of Hasidism in much of Eastern Europe.

Beyond that, the above passage testifies to the degree that Hasidic teaching directed the spotlight upon the inner aspect of everything, directing its focus upon the interior life of a person or of a community, rather than upon their external conditions.

The Descent of the Divine[7]

> "... have come down to rescue them." (Exod 3:8)

Why does the expression, "coming down," appear, something seemingly out-of-place in reference to God? Would it not be more appropriate to state simply, "I will bring them out (from Egypt/*Mitzrayim*)"?

... One can note in the writings of the *Ari z"l*, in an interpretation of the phrase "I, and not an angel,"[8] that there was great impurity in *Mitzrayim*, so intense that even the angels feared to go there lest they become materialized in its impure atmosphere. And if Israel were to remain there

---

7. *Ma'or va-shemesh*, II, 1b.
8. The *Haggadah shel Pesaḥ* on Deut 26:8.

even one moment longer, they would have drowned in the fifty Gates of Impurity. For this reason, God Himself—if it could be said—went down and disclosed Himself in Egypt and redeemed Israel, bringing out "one nation from the midst of another" (Deut 4:34) . . . [The homily-text adds: "as an embryo which a man removes from the stomach of a cow," an expression drawn from a rabbinic source.⁹]

Comment: As in other Hasidic homily-texts as well as in some earlier kabbalistic sources, *Mitzrayim* is understood not simply as a geographical area or regime, but rather as an extreme radicalization of material reality to the point that does not allow any space for soulfulness or spirituality. As presumed also in the preacher's comments on the creation-account, God's knowledge extends even to the precise degree of physicality and impurity that, if exceeded, would make any spiritual awareness impossible. [See above, "The Function of Shabbat" on *parashat B'rei'shit*.] *Mitzrayim*, on that symbolic plane, is the very antithesis of Shabbat and, in one form or another, always serves to threaten one's spiritual awareness and humanity.

Moses' Fear of Losing His Humility[10]

Moses, our Teacher—may he rest in peace—feared that were he to engage in some kind of significant action through which Israel would be redeemed, he would then occupy a level of greatness beyond that of all his people, and greater even than that of his brother, Aaron, who was known as a prophet of God. And furthermore, it would bring Moses himself to feel important and exulted in his own eyes, in a way in which he would be entrapped in arrogance. And it was for this reason that he resisted taking on this crown (position of public life and leadership).

But the blessed God taught him how he could be spared from that effect and could avoid looming large and important in his own eyes even with his role and mission. For God created all His creatures small and large, all according to His will, each with its own character and appearance and height. Some are greater and some smaller, and each one differs in nature from the others. And those differences did not account for any particular creature's having or not having a beautiful appearance. Rather

---

9. *Mek., Vayehi beshallaḥ*, ch. 6, 33a.
10. *Ma'or va-shemesh*, II, 1b-2a.

it arose in God's simple will to create each one with its own appearance designated for it without any basis to conclude that the deeds of one creature caused it to be more attractive than another. Similarly when God turns to a person, singling him out and lifting him up, it is due to His will that that person become the head and it is not his level or height or deeds that determine this.

In this vein, the blessed Holy One showed to Moses an example from the bush (Exod 3:1–3). That bush is obviously lower than the trees in its appearance and its height, and certainly it will not become so haughty as to claim that God chose it due to its important features. And Moses, our teacher, would be able to grasp that, like that bush, he would not consider it a mark of his own superiority over others, just as the bush does not think that God chose it due to its own laudable qualities.

Comment: In this homiletical fragment in which the homilist retold one element in the toraitic narrative, he remolded the meaning of that element in a way to situate within the account a theme not found or not recognizable on the surface-level of the Torah-text itself, but one that occupies a place of prime significance in Hasidic moral teaching and in Jewish moral teaching in general, namely the antithetical qualities of pride and humility.

True spiritual fire within the self leaves no space for pride or arrogance.

The Bush Aflame[11]

> "And Moses was a shepherd . . . And he led the sheep after the wilderness and came to the Mount. . . . And an angel of the Eternal One appeared to him in a flame of fire from within the bush." (Exod 3:1–2)

This scene alludes to what we have observed above on the portion, *Vayeḥi*, on the verse, "and listen to Israel" (Gen 49:2), namely that the essence of all worship is to grasp and become aware that God rules and supervises individuals and directs all the worlds and there is no place empty of His Presence. However, great efforts are required in order to truly grasp this realization, and it is necessary to seclude oneself and to be aware of its demands in all one actions and to be attentive to one's every movement.

---

11. *Ma'or va-shemesh*, II, 2a.

And one's heart must also be aflame like a burning fire with enthusiasm and longing for the blessed Creator. Then one will be able to come to truly know Divinity. And this is the essence of everything, as King David said, "Know the God of your father (and serve Him with a single mind and fervent heart, for the Lord searches all minds and discerns the design of every thought; if you seek Him, He will be available to you . . . ," 1 Chr 28:9). And acquiring that knowledge is the real purpose of the journey to take refuge in the shadow of the righteous of the generation . . . .

"In a blazing fire" (Exod 3:2)—for Moses' heart was always burning like a flaming fire to serve the Creator. "Out of a bush"—for even though the body is thick and is physical in nature just like a bush, nevertheless if one's heart is constantly burning with longing for the Creator, one will be able to acquire spiritual understanding.

Comment: The accent in such a comment by the Kraków master relates not to a people's deliverance from physical bondage and from their slave-status, but rather to one's acquiring spiritual awareness. When a Hasidic homily-text speaks of deliverance, the term most often applies to one's being brought out from a state-of-mind lacking such depth-awareness. Deliverance is the ability to grasp God's presence and to perceive a realm of meaning transcending the physical nature of our existence and its immediate needs.

The reader notes that elements in the text comprising the setting of the burning bush episode (Exod 3), such as the flame of fire and the bush itself, are read metaphorically in a way that they relate not to the physical setting in which the episode is situated, but rather to the self. The subject of fire has to do not with the bush in the desert but with Moses' inner life. And even more directly, it relates to the potential depth of passion within each person there in a Kraków prayer-room listening to Kalonymus Kalman's words which might kindle such a flame that continues to burn within their hearts.

The Infinite Names of God[12]

"Moses said to God, 'When I come to the Israelites and say to them "The God of your fathers has sent me to you," and they ask

---

12. *Ma'or va-shemesh*, II, 2ab.

> me, "What is His name?" what shall I say to them?' And God said to Moses, 'I Am That I Am.' He continued, 'Thus shall you say to the Israelites, "I Am sent me to you."' And God further said to Moses, 'Thus shall you speak to the Israelites: "The Lord, the God of your fathers, the God of Abraham, the God of Isaac, and the God of Jacob, has sent me to you: This shall be My name forever; this is My appellation for all eternity."'" (Exod 3:13–15)

And this was the holy way of our father, Abraham, may he rest in peace. Abraham was not content to worship in a way resembling *mitzvah melumdat 'anashim* (something that one simply learns from other people, Isa 29:13), such as learning from his father, Terah, to worship idols and the like. Rather, he wished to arrive at an understanding of what is true through his own efforts and intelligence.

At first he thought that the sun is the leader, but then when he saw that the sun set and then rose the following day in the East, he understood that the sun also must have a ruler and leader, and the same with the moon and the stars and the heavenly spheres, until from the source of his own wisdom he arrived at a sense of God who is the leader and Creator of all.[13]

And our father Isaac, seeing his father Abraham's example, did not want to worship in a mode and belief learned from others, but rather, like his father, he explored the truth of Divinity and of the holy in his own way until he, too, came to an understanding of the existence of the Divine. And similarly Jacob did not want to learn from his fathers and to duplicate their deeds without his arriving at a sense of spiritual truth drawn from his own intelligence.

And for this reason there are several Names for God. Through a person's own spiritual efforts and attainment, each one will arrive at a name for God. Our father, Abraham, whose worship was through love and kindness and who recognized God's greatness called Him *ha-gadol* (the Great One), and Isaac whose way of worship was through awe and fear, called Him *ha-gibbor* (the Valiant and Strong One), while Jacob, in line with the nature of his own worship, called Him *ha-nora* (the Awesome One). And for this reason, God is referred to as *ha-gadol he-gibbor v'-ha-nora* (Deut 10:17), suggesting that each one of the fathers called God by a name reflecting that person's own particular inner understanding and experience.

---

13. *Midr. Gen* 38:13; Ginzberg, *Legends*, 1:189; 5: 210, n. 16.

And in this way, we can grasp Moses' concern as to how to respond when the Israelites will ask him "What is His name?" (Exod 3:13). Moses was asking how to refer to God in line with the Israelites' own aspect and ability to serve Him. "Thus shall you say to the Israelites, AHYH ("I shall be") has sent me to you" (Exod 3:14), meaning that I will be (AHYH) called by each person according to the particular aspect of that person's service, so that they will not worship in the manner of "a commandment learned from people," but rather that each one might learn from you to serve Me with a name befitting that person's own quality.

For this reason He went on to say, "The Lord, the God of your fathers, the God of Abraham, the God of Isaac, and the God of Jacob, has sent me to you" (Exod 3:15). He specifically mentioned each one of the fathers individually, that from them you will learn that each person worships according to his own aspect as each one arrives at his own sense of God rather than accepting a name or concept "as something learned from others." And accordingly each one called God a name according to that person's own inner understanding.

And He continued, "This shall be My name forever" (Exod 3:15); the holy Name AHYH that I told you is hidden and is a marvelous and concealed mystery. "This is My appellation for all eternity" (literally, "from generation to generation") to be taught to all the generations to come. I will be called by each generation precisely in accordance with that generation's aspect and inner understanding. And comprehend!

Comment: The explanation of Abraham's search for truth and his arriving at his faith in a logical and rational way, a retelling of a much older aggadic tradition, might appear somewhat inconsistent with what is found in some other homilies in *Ma'or va-shemesh*. There the preacher emphasized that one's faith and grasp of life and its meaning comes from a place of depth within the self, a place deeper than words and formulations and deeper even than what can even be shared with others. Logic and reason are of the nature of what can be shared, whereas one's conception and faith in God, he maintained, is rooted not in reason, but in that deeper aspect of the self, in the very depth of a person's soul and ultimate uniqueness. A more contemporary discussion of the contrast between those two modes can be found in Heschel, *Man is Not Alone*, 170–71, "Faith and Reason."

The uniqueness of each person is noted and accentuated in several of the homilies in *Ma'or va-shemesh*. Note especially "The basis of Moses' hesitation" on *parashat Va'era* and "The Paradox of Religious Expression" on *parashat Nitzavim*. And in the above homily the preacher artfully read that same thrust into the biblical account of the dialogue between God and Moses at the scene of the Burning Bush.

His homily, moreover, is constructed upon an older tradition relating to those three appellations of God having been removed one-by-one by different biblical personages and later restored by the Men of the Great Assembly.[14] But Hasidic sources reshaped that tradition in a way to convey a very different type of meaning and to suggest that neither Isaac nor Jacob blindly followed in the path of Abraham as each added his own personal understanding to the faith of the first patriarch. In that spirit, an earlier Hasidic text conveyed the point, attributed to the Baal Shem Tov, that among the three patriarchs, "Isaac and Jacob depended not upon what they received from Abraham, but rather upon their own investigation of Divinity."[15]

This homily applies not only to individuals, but also to generations: the preacher considered not only individuals but also generations as being unique at a very deep and significant level. That note recalls a very interesting comment by a grandson of the *Besht*, Efrayim of Sydelikov. He noted the relationship of the word ḥodesh (month) in Exod 12:5 to the word ḥadash (new), a connection which he interpreted in terms of the intrinsic uniqueness of every generation which is expressed in that generation's particular interpretation of the Torah. Like each individual, also every generation has its own unique interpretation of the Torah, one related to the essence of that particular generation. It follows that one generation does not understand the Torah in the same way as does another generation and, furthermore, one generation's understanding of the Torah fails to satisfy and to speak to a later generation.[16] Efrayim of Sydelikov obviously felt that the Hasidic mode of interpretation exemplified in his own teachings was integrally connected with the soul and the essence of his generation.

---

14. *b. Yoma* 69b.

15. *Keter shem tov*, 15b.

16. *Degel Maḥaneh 'Efrayim* (Bo). See Wineman, "A Wrestling with Interpretation."

Va'era

The Basis of Moses' Hesitation[17]

> "And the Lord said to Moses, 'I am the Lord; speak to Pharaoh, king of Egypt all that I will tell you.' Moses appealed to the Lord, saying, 'See, I am of impeded speech; how then should Pharaoh heed me!'" (Exod 6:29–30)

On the basis of the text's simple meaning, it seems to me akin to what is written, "The counsel [or: secret] of the Lord is for those who fear Him" (Ps 25:14). One cannot equate the "secrets of the Torah" with the wisdom of Kabbalah and the writings of the 'Ari z"l and the Zohar, for those can be disclosed to others and explained clearly, and if so, since they are revealed, they are not in the category of secrets.

But what is the secret concerning which it is not even possible to disclose to any other person? It is the secret of God—Divinity itself that is past, present, and future and is "the essence and the Root of all the worlds"[18]—that is the secret that by its very nature cannot be communicated to anyone. Rather, every person contemplates for himself a sense of Divinity according to his intelligence and the inclinations of his heart.[19] And the greater the effort of self-purification that a person undergoes, the more one can attain, and in his pure mind he will attain more and more. It is not possible to disclose to any other person the way one's mind grasps Divinity from the depths of his own heart and intelligence; similarly it is impossible to speak of it to others in a way that the sense of the reality and awe of God can enter into their hearts.

Anyone who enters the way of true worship realizes that it is impossible to disclose to others all the secrets of one's heart. For that reason it

---

17. Ma'or va-shemesh, II, 4a.
18. Zohar, I, 11b (Int.).
19 See Zohar, I, 103b.

is termed *sod* (secret), for it truly is a secret; it is impossible for one to reveal to any one else what is located at the core of one's own heart and thought. Rather, every person understands according to his own effort and his own purification. And the more one grasps concerning Divinity in general or in detail and attains higher levels of an understanding of Divinity through further purification, it is all the more difficult to explain and to disclose to others the secrets of that person's heart, for he has more in his heart and thought which, by its very nature, defies disclosure or communication.

. . . And furthermore, it is impossible for such a person to communicate the extent of his grasp of Divinity to those who remain on a lower level. One who is less advanced in his understanding concerning the reality of Divinity can more easily explain to others what is in his heart, for such a person lacks the same depth in his heart that a greater one might have, and simple people can more easily understand him. It follows that one wishing to disclose the secrets of his heart in a way that others might comprehend has need of a translator [*m'turg'man*; in the ancient synagogues, during the public Torah-reading, the *m'turg'man* would provide for the congregation a verse-by-verse translation of the Hebrew text of the Torah into Aramaic which, over time, had become the vernacular], a man of lesser spiritual grasp from whom others are able to receive and comprehend . . . .

Comment: Also this passage exemplifies Kalonymus Kalman's more-than-occasional practice of locating within some aspect or detail of a biblical narrative a theme that would appear quite distant from the Torah-text itself but which is fundamental to his conception of the nature of faith.

This homily understands Moses' hesitation in going to Pharaoh, as commanded by God, as due neither to any kind of speech defect or difficulty in speaking nor to the difficulty in mustering the courage to speak to a person of immense power, but rather to the existential impossibility of one person's expressing to another one's deepest beliefs. Those beliefs are necessarily grounded in that person's own uniqueness and psyche and consequently another person would intrinsically be unable to grasp them. In this respect, the homilist continues to develop a theme that had preoccupied him in his comments on the previous Torah-portion and one with which he would continue to engage. (Note "The infinite names of God" on *parashat Sh'mot*, and also "The paradox of religious expression" on *parashat Nitzavim*.)

In the toraitic narrative, God tells Moses to take Aaron as his prophet. And in the preacher's analysis, Aaron fulfills the later role of the translator, one whom the master viewed as representing a more limited level of understanding, but who precisely for that reason can bring things down to a lower level allowing the people—and perhaps also Pharaoh—to understand, as Moses' own higher grasp is beyond the range of their comprehension. The translator who, in this analysis, represents a contraction (*tzimtzum*) of Moses' level of understanding, is better able to speak from a lower place, enabling others to comprehend on their own lower level. The role of such a translator or middleman echoes the Lurianic theme of contraction in the *'Ein-sof* that allows for the coming of the worlds into being. And, one might add, it echoes as well the contraction of the Innerness of the Torah as it assumes the form of a revealed text composed of words and narratives, another theme significant in *Ma'or va-shemesh*.

One might speculate that as a preacher, regularly communicating with those attending the prayer-services in his prayer-room in Kraków, Kalonymus Kalman identified his own role more specifically with that of Aaron who was able to convey his more limited understanding, even though the Kraków sage's own wisdom, like that of Moses, transcended that of his role as spokesman. Like the Torah itself as he grasped it, the master's words might allude to what reaches beyond his own discourse.

This passage and the suggestion it offers are rooted in that sense of the uniqueness of each person voiced in various Hasidic texts and teachings. Kalonymus Kalman's role as a communicator is itself paradoxical insofar as the implications of his understanding of the uniqueness of each person situate true communication on a spiritual level beyond the range of possibility. As suggested in "Why did Yitro journey to Moses" on *parashat Yitro*, however, communication can occur on an inter-personal rather than on a conceptual level.

Bo

Humility Renewed[20]

> "The Lord said to Moses and Aaron in the land of Egypt: This month shall mark for you the beginning of the months; it shall be the first of the months of the year for you . . . ." (Exod 12:1–2)

. . . Moses and Aaron were the humblest of all the persons who ever lived, as evidenced in their saying (in the face of rebellion and hostility) *v'naḥnu ma*, "For who [—or what—] are we?" (Exod 16:7). [In Jewish mystic texts, the word *mah* came to be used as an expression for *'Ayin*/Nothingness.]

In this respect, they are likened to the moon, which made itself small,[21] and this explains why the two of them (Moses and Aaron) merited the pronouncement concerning the new moon. That is the meaning of the verse, "this month shall mark *for you*" indicating that this renewal of humility belongs to you in that you, actually and personally, renewed that quality.

Comment: The above homily exemplifies one way in which culture ascribes human meaning to astronomical entities. While the light of the sun is powerful and majestic, that of the moon lacks precisely those qualities and connotations. The parallel of the moon—which, according to the agada, reduced itself to a smaller size—with the two leaders of the Israelites, suffers from the detail that, in the agada, the moon first complained concerned the equal status of the two lights, evidently desiring for itself the more powerful role. Both the Hebrew Bible and its rabbinic embellishment view Egypt generally—and Pharaoh in particular—as exemplars of arrogance, whereas, in contrast, Moses was said to be "a very humble man,

---

20. *Ma'or va-shemesh*, II, 8a.
21. b. Ḥul. 60b; Midr. Gen. 6:3.

more so than any other man on earth" (Num 12:3). It would easily appear that on a deeper level the struggle between Israel and Egypt is grasped as one between humility and arrogance.

In addition to the comparative brightness of the two lights, when the new moon first appears it is seen as only a tender, thin line of light in the sky, sometimes barely visible. Not only the moon itself, but its very tiny initial appearance contributes to its serving, metaphorically, as a mark of humility as well as of renewal and promise.

The comparison of the sun and moon reverberates in other passages from rabbinic agada, which note that while, during the day, the moon is barely visible due to the sun's much more powerful light, it becomes clearly visible when the sun goes down. The agada associates Esau (Edom which, in turn, came to symbolize Rome) with the sun, while Israel is said to be symbolized by the moon, which, though barely evident while the sun is shining, comes into clear view at night. The powerful empires have their day after which they fade from history, while the more humble entity, likened to the moon, endures the rule of the powerful forces and survives them following their decline and fall.[22] And just preceding this passage in *Ma'or va-shemesh* is mention that like the moon which made itself small, the *tzaddikim* do likewise "as they are broken-hearted and saddened and even despised in their own eyes."

The Meaning of *Matza*[23]

Our Rabbis differed among themselves[24] concerning the verse, "Of every tree of the garden you are free to eat, but as for the tree of knowledge of good and bad, you must not eat of it . . ." (Gen 2:16–17). They asked: From what tree did the First Person eat? And how would that First Person even know which tree is the tree of knowledge of good and evil, without any indication that God showed him?—and there is no such indication in the verse.

But one can maintain that the essential point in the command is that a person not be drawn after his desire to eat certain foods for the reason that they have a sweet taste and are lovely in appearance, while detesting all other food. It is the realization that a person should eat solely

22. *Midr. Gen* 6.3. also *Pesiq Rab Kah.* 54a (*Parshat ha-ḥodesh*).
23. *Ma'or va-shemesh*, II, 9a.
24. *Midr. Gen* 15:7.

for the purpose of maintaining the body in life and hence to be able to serve one's Creator, irrespective of the food's taste or appearance. . . .

And this is the meaning of the verse, "Of every tree of the garden you are free to eat" but not to distinguish in your eyes between food that is sweet to the pallet while rejecting all other food that does not taste sweet. That distinction is not permitted to you . . . . The tree of knowledge was not a particular tree; rather, humankind was commanded to regard all trees equally, without any distinction based upon their taste. And it was due to the need to purify themselves from their materiality and to shatter their desire by means of the yoke of servitude, hence repairing the sin of the First Man, that our fathers went down to Egypt.

It is for this reason that we were commanded on *Pesaḥ* (Passover) to eat the bread of poverty (*leḥem 'oni*, Deut 16:3), which is tasteless, lacking salt or any similar ingredient, as a way of teaching that a person not be drawn after imaginary human pleasures. And *matza* is called "the bread of poverty," as the poor person lacks the very possibility of choosing a food in which he takes delight but must eat whatever he finds, even if it is not sweet to his pallet. And so we eat *matza* made from dough without any amelioration in its taste, so that what is sweet and what is not sweet will all be the same in our eyes.

And the seven days (of the festival, Exod 12:15), when we hallow ourselves through eating *matza*, eating simply to preserve our lives so that we might serve God while refraining from seeking such worldly pleasures, represent the seventy years of our life-span (Ps 90:10).

Comment: The eating of unleavened bread (*matza*) is explained in the book of Exodus in that the Israelites had to leave Egypt (*Mitzrayim*) in haste, taking with them dough that had not yet leavened (Exod 12:34). The above homily bypassed that more familiar explanation of eating unleavened bread during the days of the *Pesaḥ* festival, an explanation with which those the preacher was addressing would certainly be familiar.

Following in the manner of earlier midrashic tradition which tended to interpret any word or detail in a biblical verse as bearing meaning independent of the very subject and context of the sentence,[25] Kalonymus Kalman skipped over that context of the practice of eating *matza* as clearly explained in the Torah. In his homily, there is only a secondary and rather weak connection of *matza* with the exodus, and in place of the context of the hurried

---

25. Heineman, *Darkhe ha-'agada*, 96–102.

departure from Egypt, the practice is given a very different context, one having to do with the tree whose fruit was forbidden to the human couple in the Garden of Eden (Gen 1:16–17). While a rabbinic text maintained that the identity of the tree was never revealed,[26] the homilist explained that the episode does not refer to any particular kind of tree, but rather to an approach to food and eating in general. That substitution of one context for another is quite central to the anatomy of the Hasidic homily in general and is, perhaps, a primary key to the art of the Hasidic homilist.

In much simpler and more prosaic terms, the Kraków preacher was conveying to those assembled in his prayer-room that food and eating constitute a means and not a supreme value or goal in life, and that consequently—in very simple terms—they should "eat in order to live, and not live in order to eat!"

---

26. *Midr. Gen* 15:7.

B'shallaḥ

The Miracle at the Sea[27]

> "And at daybreak [after the waters had parted and the Israelites crossed the Sea on dry land], the Sea returned to its normal state, and the Egyptians fled at its approach." (Exod 14:27)

Our Sages interpreted *l'eitano* (to its normal strength) as related to *tena'o ha-rishon* (to its initial terms to which the Sea had agreed when it was created). For at the time of creation, the Holy One, blessed be He, stipulated with the Sea that it would split for the Israelites at the time that they would go forth from Egypt.[28]

... The blessed Holy One created all the worlds so that they might praise Him and know that their very existence is due to the Creator, may He be blessed, and that even in this physical realm of being (*'olam ha-'Asiyah*) all created things would know of God's existence. For in this *'olam ha-'asiyah* in which existence assumed material form, all that was created could come to a state of forgetfulness, forgetting God's very existence as, over time, the world would assume greater and greater materiality.

Even the human being can more easily bear the yoke of Torah in his youth, for at that stage of life he hasn't yet lived so long in this material world and has not become so materialized to the point of completely forgetting the Creator. But as one moves on in years, a person becomes more and more accustomed to the order of nature and comes to view the world in a way in which everything occurs naturally, as the world behaves according to its own pattern and habit, just as we see that the sun rises in the East and sets in the West, and similarly that the moon behaves, each month, according to its own recurring cycle....

---

27. *Ma'or va-shemesh*, III, 12b-13a (*R'mazim l'Shvi'i shel Pesah*).
28. *Midr. Gen* 5:4.

Humans think in those terms, and not only humans, but also all material things—whether inert or vegetative or animals and beasts lacking intelligence—become more materialized as they continue their days in this world. For this reason, after having completed the making of the heavens and earth on the Sixth Day, the sublime holiness of the *Shabbat* descended so that all created things might know God's Oneness and realize that He created them. Unfortunately, however, with the continuing course of time, they all come to a state of forgetting. And in forgetting the clarity (which descended upon the world on the Seventh Day) they could easily transgress the Creator's will, for it seems to them that no one rules over them and that the world simply continues to function quite independently in its own manner and pattern.

For this reason, immediately after creation, concerned that all created things without exception would, in time, succumb to forgetfulness, the blessed Holy One decreed that the higher holiness descend occasionally so that created things could then remind themselves of that higher clarity (*b'hirut*) and light which they had experienced at twilight with the advent of the Seventh Day. In this way, even with the passage of time they would experience the clarity just as they did immediately following creation. . . .

In the Midrash we find that the Sea did not consent to divide.[29] This was the case precisely because it reached a state of forgetting and believed that it can do just as it wishes, forgetting that God is the Master of the world. . . . But the blessed Holy One reminded the Sea of the condition decreed upon it during the six days of creation. (God brought the Sea to recall) that high degree of clarity which descended with twilight just before that very first *Shabbat*. And so the sea remembered . . . and longed for that brightness and proceeded to perform the Will of the Creator, and it split (enabling the Israelites to pass through safely).

Even afterward, toward morning, there remained at the sea a trace of that light. The Israelites were prepared and had the strength to bear their experience of that light. But the Egyptians, unable to bear even the very trace of that light that lingered at the scene, "fled at its approach" (Exod 14:27); they lacked the inner strength to bear it, and so they ceased to exist and their souls departed. . . .

"And at daybreak, the sea returned to its normal state" (Exod 14:27). But even at daybreak when the sea regained its normal strength, it

---

29. *Midr. Exod.* 21:6. Note Schwartz, *Tree of Souls*, 105–7, and Fishbane, *Biblical Myth*, 37–52, 112–24.

nevertheless retained a trace of that clarity of light.... And "the Lord... threw the Egyptian army into panic" (Exod 14:24)—their very existence was annulled and they died, for they were unable to bear the light that the blessed Holy One brought down upon the sea....

The holy Torah applies to all time; its truth concerns every point-in-time and every era and every person. And we must understand what this verse alludes to us now in our generations.... We might understand with the help of a parable: Lacking understanding, a young infant does not obey his father out of love. He doesn't yet comprehend that idea. But as the infant continues to grow, he acquires understanding and grasps that his father is helpful to him and, knowing that his father is good to him, he follows his father's will out of love. But even though he no longer fears being struck by a rod, fear nevertheless continues to color his consciousness until he attains, even to a degree, an enlargement of intelligence (*gadlut ha-seikhel*) and understands and knows his father's wisdom and goodness. Then he obeys his father not out of fear, but out of love.

So it is with the service (*'avodah*, worship and worshipful living) of God. When beginning to enter into the gates of Torah and *'avodah*, a person needs a fear of punishment, lest he transgress God's will. That is external fear and not the essential form of awe. This is but a first stage of a lower level of understanding as one has a sense of God's greatness but is still immersed in the impure Shells (*k'lipot*) and turns to material desires. And at this stage, his obedience to God is still on the level of a fear of punishment.

A person must make the effort to pursue Torah and *'avodah* unceasingly until one goes beyond this fear and shatters his evil desires and comes to an enlargement of understanding. At this level he knows and understands that the blessed Holy One gives him his very existence, that goodness and kindness are from Him, and he now serves God out of love. At this point, both his spirit and his bodily matter have been purified—but not entirely. For at times he can still come upon some evil thought or lust, and he still holds onto the demonic Shells to some degree for the reason that his obedience still rests upon a consideration of receiving a reward. This can be called "a second stage of smallness," and he must serve and purify himself further until his evil or selfish desires and impulses vanish and the Shells are totally annulled within him. Only at this point has he attained an enlargement of understanding and becomes truly attached to God. And this can be called "the second stage of enlargement."

Only a few exceptional persons succeed in attaining this stage. But when the righteous Messiah will come, then God will make His divine Light evident, and evil will be thoroughly annulled. The earth will then be full of the awareness of God (*daʿat ʾElohim*), and we will all attain that level of understanding the Divine.

Earlier, before one takes the very beginning-steps on the path of *ʿavodah*, the blessed Holy One shows him, for a single moment, "a second enlargement of understanding" after which he proceeds with great longing and his soul thirsts for God. For this reason, one experiences no *ḥasidut* (piety) like its very beginning-point. But he doesn't know what that is, for his understanding is still on a lower level which immediately robs him of that attainment and experience. And so he returns to his prior stage of smallness which he must repair in order to go forward to a state of enlargement of understanding. . . .

In like manner, the Israelites in exile were subjugated by the Egyptians, and Pharaoh and his people ruled over them. The Israelites were immersed in the impurity of *Mitzrayim* (Egypt) and possessed a state of small understanding due to the Shells of *Mitzrayim* which served as masks and partitions (separating them from any deeper awareness). On the first night of *Pesaḥ* ("Passover"), the blessed Holy One made the light of divine clarity to appear over the world and the evil forces were annulled. The Israelites had attained an understanding of Divinity which was, however, immediately taken from them as they resumed their earlier state of lesser understanding and they came to the *Sʾfirah* [the counting of the days, Lev 23:15, during a seven-week period beginning with *Pesaḥ*, the feast of liberation, and leading up to the festival of *Shavuʿot*].

The intent of the *Sʾfirah* (Counting of Days) was that they might purify themselves and repair that "first state of smallness" and make their way to the "first state of enlarged understanding." And afterward, they could further purify themselves and repair their "second state of smallness." And with the Giving of the Torah (commemorated on *Shavuʿot*) they acquired that second stage of an enlarged understanding. . . .

So it was in the past, in *Mitzrayim*, and so it continues afterward, until the end of all the generations. And understand! [This homily has been somewhat abbreviated, due to the length and repetitive nature of the original text.]

Comment: This scenario is remarkable in that it provides an account very much at odds with that found in the biblical book of Exodus and in Jewish tradition in general. Whereas in the Song of the Sea (Exod 15) and in traditional Jewish liturgy, the God of Israel is praised for His display of power in defeating the Egyptian pursuers and, consequently, enabling the Israelites to safely advance in the wilderness, the account in *Ma'or va-shemesh*, it would appear, went far out of its way to provide an alternative understanding of the same episode, one in which God does not directly bring about the drowning of the Egyptians in the Sea.

The presence of that light appearing over the sea in the homily stands as a marked contrast to the midrashic reading in which the sea divided out of fear in seeing God's right hand placed upon Moses as the latter stretched out his hand over the sea.[30] The rendition of the death of the Egyptians in this homily from *Ma'or va-shemesh* contrasts both with that found in rabbinic lore[31] and also in the Zohar's treatment of that same episode,[32] in both of which God Himself engaged in a war to the end against the Egyptians in a battle-scene where both earthly and celestial armies fought and utilized magical strategies.

In the above homily, neither force nor might nor retribution, but the mere effect of a manifestation of divine Presence on those spiritually unprepared to bear that experience, resulted in the elimination of the Egyptian charioteers from the scene. Their drowning—the passage brings us to understand—was evidently due to an inherent flaw and darkness in Egyptian life, culture, and belief which could not tolerate the experience of the divine Light.

While the homily makes mention of the midrashic tradition of a condition which the sea accepted when it was created, the homily connects the Splitting of the Sea with another theme—that of the light which periodically recurs to remind the world of created things of their ultimate dependence upon and relationship to God. And whereas in the biblical account, the death of the Egyptian pursuers, bent on returning the Hebrews to bondage in Egypt, is associated with God's use of physical power, the homily in *Ma'or va'shemesh* significantly attributes the defeat of the Egyptian pursuers not to power, but rather to light. The reader cannot but detect an echo of the Lurianic concept of *sh'virah* in which the Shells (*k'lipot*) could

---

30. *Midr. Exod.* 21:6.
31. Ginzberg, *Legends*, 3:25–31.
32. Zohar, II, 48b–53b.

not bear the greater power of divine Light, in the incapability of the Egyptians to bear that more sublime light.

The reader notes that the preacher's scenario brings him to the theme of spiritual maturation, advancing from fear to a more mature motivation for religious commitment. It would seem that the tenor of the toraitic account did not mirror the preacher's own view of spiritual maturity. The conception of God's functioning as a punishing agent and the fear of His power, very much present in the toraitic narrative, exemplify what the master would identify as an essentially immature and childish motivation for man's service and obedience to God.

In re-wiring this episode of the splitting of the Sea and the destruction of the Egyptian pursuers, the preacher addressed a higher level of spiritual motivation than what is implied in the biblical account, and the reader might sense Kalonymus Kalman's groping toward a different conception of the Divine than what is found in the surface-level of the toraitic text. As becomes clear in the latter part of this homily, the very idea and fear of punishment mark a lower, immature level of spiritual awareness from which one must advance to a more profound relationship with the Divine.

The reader finds also other examples within *Ma'or va-shemesh* in which the master retold the biblical account in a way to negate the use of divine power for the purpose of punishment. Note, for example, "Sadness and the craving for food" on *parashat B'ha'alotkha*.

Miriam and the Dance at the Sea[33]

> "Then Miriam the prophetess, Aaron's sister, took a timbrel in her hand, and all the women went out after her in dance with timbrels. And Miriam chanted for them, 'Sing to the Lord, for He has triumphed gloriously; horse and driver He has hurdled into the sea.'" (Exod 15:20-21)

There is need to define precisely what Miriam the prophetess added in her words, for certainly the women had recited the Song together with Moses and all Israel, as we find in the Gemara that even embryos in their mothers' wombs joined in the Song at the Sea.[34] If so, then certainly their

---

33. *Ma'or va-shemesh*, II, 13b–14a.
34. *b. Ber.* 50a. also *Mek.* 35a (*Shirah* #1), and *Midr. Pss.* 77 (on Ps 8).

mothers had already sung those particular verses from the Song, and why would they repeat what they had already recited?

. . . More on those verses: Why was it important to make a point that Miriam brought out all the women? And where did she bring them? Also the word, *um'holot* (here: "in dance") is difficult as it seems to be superfluous, and in our holy Torah not even a single letter is superfluous. And why did Moses say *'ashirah* ("I will sing to the Lord" Exod. 15:1) in the imperfect (future) tense, while Miriam said the same in the present [actually the imperative], "Sing to the Lord"?

There would appear to be a solution to these questions in the talmudic statement that the blessed Holy One will arrange a dance [in the "Garden of Eden," referring to the Afterlife] for the righteous in which He will sit in the center as each one points with his finger, ". . . This is the Lord, in whom we trusted (Let us rejoice and exult in His deliverance!", Isa 25:9).[35] And Rashi explained *mahol* to indicate circular, "around," like a dance in the vineyard.[36] [The dance in Eden, mentioned nearing the conclusion of the talmudic tractate dealing with fasts, is occasioned by the tradition of unmarried women dancing each year on the fifteenth day of Av as men then choose their wives (*m. Ta'anit* 4:8).]

By way of explanation, when the thought to create the world arose in God's simple Will, the *'Ein-sof* first contracted the infinite Divinity to assume the form of a circle, in a way that it would extend equally to all the worlds. And only afterward, when the worlds assumed a material character, God went on to create the worlds with a straight line as a Contraction occurred with a sifting of the worlds. God's Divinity was contracted to a lesser degree in the higher world, and was further contracted in the next lower world, and that pattern continued through the very lowest of all the worlds.

Consequently we presently have no alternative except to grasp Divinity from below to above, as we need to separate the holy sparks (*nitzotzot*) and to advance by degree from one level to another, higher level. As a consequence, all the worlds and all created things have an aspect of male and female, in that one factor influences while another receives, for the higher world always impacts the next lower world, and the lesser requires the greater in order to receive and learn from it. Everything has an end-point, and the distance from the beginning to the end-point is

---

35. *b. Ta'an.* 31a.
36. Based on *m. Kil.* 4:1.

considerable. And everything that is above the end is closer to the beginning, as all that is higher than the next lower world is closer to the blessed Infinite One, and the smaller and lesser is in need of the greater in order to learn from it the way to serve and worship God, for that higher one has greater understanding and impacts the one having a more reduced level of understanding.

In the future, however, each person will directly repair his soul-portion to connect with its root and will raise up the holy sparks, and the external, destructive forces will be completely annulled. And then a brilliant light of God's Divinity will appear in all the worlds, assuming the form of a circle, and the worlds will be equal without any aspect of male and female (influencing and receiving), for all will acquire equally the light of God's Divinity just as in a circle there is neither beginning nor end. And none will have need of another in order to learn from him, just as in the vineyard dance . . . as is written, "No longer will they need to teach one another . . . for all of them, from the least of them to the greatest, shall heed Me—declares the Lord" (Jer 31:34).

And this is the meaning of the Gemara's statement: in the future, the Blessed Holy One will arrange a circle for *tzaddikim* and He will sit in the middle; the *tzaddikim* will attain a high level of comprehension of the sublime Light lacking any aspect of male or female, with no one of them having to learn from his fellow. For then the light of the clarity of God's Divinity will be revealed in all the worlds and will assume the form of a circle marked by equidistance, as in the vineyard dance, and all will be equally distant from the central point.

And this is the meaning of the *hakafot* (circular processions) which we form on *Hosha'nah rabbah* and *Sh'mini ha-'atzeret* (the seventh day of *Sukkot* and the additional holy day celebrated as *Simḥat-torah*): we perform *hakafot* based on the secret of the female surrounding the male ("a woman courts a man," Jer 31:22, indicating something new in the world), so that through those same circular processions we will extend the light of the Sublime One to a point where there will no longer be any male (influencing) or female (receiving) roles. [Note that this expression is found in the same chapter as the previous quotation from Jeremiah.]

And this was the intent of Miriam the Prophetess for which she brought out all the women to follow her and with them formed circular dances illustrating the secret of "the female will go around the male," all in order to extend the light of the Most High in a way lacking any distinction based on distance.

And for this reason Moses said, "I will sing to the Lord," for he represented the sense that the light of the clarity of the sublime has not yet appeared, and so he said, "I will sing," for they had not yet fully grasped His Divinity, and so he used the future tense, indicating that "when I will reach that level, then I will sing." Miriam, in contrast, drew the sublime Light within her circular dance and they then attained the fullness of understanding; therefore she said, "Sing" now, as their understanding was such that it could never be exceeded....

Comment: In his analysis, Kalonymus Kalman read gender-distinctions in kabbalistic terms as representative of levels of authority and subservience, specifically of greater or lesser proximity to the *'Ein-sof*, the infinite state of Divinity. In the light of that reading, Miriam's dance with the women, precisely in the form of a circular dance, serves metaphorically as the antithesis of a cosmos in which one world (or *s'firah*) is either subservient or superior to another, nearer or more distant from the Source of all that is.

In her dance with the women—the master explained—Miriam envisioned a view of the cosmos that is not based on differing levels of authority or spiritual quality. Hers was a grasp of Divinity that is fully accessible to all without any pattern of authority and subservience such as is represented by the kabbalistic *s'firot*. Her vision of a worldview, as the homilist conceived it, might suggest potential ramifications extending far beyond the scene of the Song and the dance at the shore of the sea.

Nehemiah Polen has examined this passage with great detail and insight in his article, "Miriam's Dance: Radical Egalitarianism in Hasidic Thought." For a somewhat similar theme, note also "As the stars of the heavens" on *parashat D'varim*, in which the stars, according to the homilist, similarly exemplify an alternative to hierarchical structure as such.

The Meaning of Manna[37]

> "And the Lord said to Moses, I will rain down bread for you from the sky, and the people will go out and gather that day's portion—that I may thus test them, to see whether they will follow My instructions or not." (Exod 16:4)

---

37. *Ma'or va-shemesh*, II, 14ab.

The manna was spiritual food ... which descended from a high world ... and as it descended to the earth it assumed a physical form, for even the angels were clad in human form when they came to our father Abraham.[38] And thus, the essence of the *mitzvah* concerning the manna was that the people were to eat with the intention of engaging in the worship of God, rather than eating for the sake of their own pleasure. They were to gather and sift out for themselves the holiness, leaving aside the materialistic aspect of the manna. But while the righteous did precisely that, the wicked would gather for themselves the physicality of the food, ignoring the holiness in that same food, and so they ground it up (Num 11:8) ...

"But on the sixth day, when they prepare what they have brought, it shall prove to be double the amount they gather each day" (Exod 16:5), for on the sixth day, when sufficient manna came down also for the holy Shabbat, it descended with even greater holiness than was the case during the other days. This is because the holiness of *Shabbat* is from *Keter* [the very highest of the *s'firot*, the emanations of the infinite Divine reality], and for this reason on *Shabbat* we recite the *K'dushat Keter*. [The Sefardic version of the *Musaf*, the Additional Prayer on Shabbat, is called *K'dushat Keter* for the reason that it begins with the word *keter* (crown); that form of the *K'dushah* is one of several features of the Sefardic liturgy that Hasidism adopted.]

Comment: Elsewhere, in his homiletical comments on the portion *'Eikev*, Kalonymus Kalman explained that manna was a purified state of food devoid of any dross or impurity which could be attributed to the *Sitra 'ahra* (the Evil Force). And for this reason it was easier to attain a sense of the innerness of that food, to go beyond its physical character and function and find, even in what we eat, its core spiritual dimension. That conception flows from the view that everything has an inner dimension, even the food we eat. And, furthermore, everything is a potential means for our connecting with the innerness of all that is, providing we view physical needs and delights in terms of their serving a spiritual function.

As in his comments concerning the eating of *matza* on the *Pesaḥ* festival, also the episode of manna in the wilderness directs the preacher to focus on different and contrasting relationships to food itself. Is food to be eaten as a strategy of life, directed and motivated by a higher meaning, or do we descend to a level at which one is driven by cravings for certain foods, even to the point of cultivating food-addictions, and view food and

---

38. b. B. meṣi'a, 86b, referring to Gen 18.

eating as ends in themselves? The gift of manna during the wilderness period became, to his mind, not a particular kind of food, but the kind of attitude with which one should relate to all food.

This passage conveys that, like the manna, all food is a material form assumed by what is more intrinsically spiritual in character and offers a delight that is deeper in nature than its sensual pleasure. As is found in the very same section containing this passage, "And so the *tzaddikim* ate it in the purity of holiness and tasted in it something akin to the World-to-Come (*'olam haba*)."

Kalonymus Kalman viewed in the manna not simply a divine act of compassion for the Israelites amidst the difficult conditions of desert life or even a way of proving to the people their dependence upon God. He grasped manna as a way of preparation for a more spiritual orientation to life. In that sense, the significance of the manna is not limited to one particular stretch of time but rather bears relevance to all time, to every day or every occasion on which a person eats.

Similarly, the thrust of his interpretation lies not in any emphasis upon manna as a miraculous, supernatural happening and phenomenon, some kind of divine "meals on wheels," but rather as a relationship to eating and to food. One might paraphrase the Kraków sage's remarks in that, depending upon one's attitude toward food and toward the very act of eating, all food is potentially manna. It is eating for the sake of bodily life and health, gifts which themselves are then to be utilized for a higher purpose.

As the observance of *Tu b'Shvat* (the fifteenth day of the month of *Shvat*, marking the New Year for Trees) falls during or close to the week of the portion, *B'shalah*, Kalonymus Kalman related that occasion to the same thematics emphasized in his treatment of manna. He suggested that appetite is weaker in times of excessive heat and excessive cold, while early spring, when the warming of the atmosphere is still in an early stage, is a time of increased appetite.

Accordingly, he related the New Year of Trees to a critique of eating for the sake of satisfying a physical desire. Both eating less and eating only to sustain the body and not for the sake of one's sensuous delight in food—he maintained—are healthful in themselves and have a beneficial effect on the mind. Overcoming physical cravings in favor of focusing upon spiritual desire, even in connection with the act of eating—the preacher suggested—can be likened to a pail that draws up water from a well. In this case, however, it draws down beneficial blessing from higher realms, blessing which has a positive impact on the inert world as well as on the realms of plant, animal, and human life.

Yitro

Why Did Yitro Journey to Moses?[39]

> [Kalonymus Kalman probes the question, Why did Yitro, the father of Moses' wife, Tzipora, come to Moses with his daughter and her two sons? After considering a number of possible answers and discounting some of them, he offered his own response to the question.]

In order *leval yidaḥ mimenu nidaḥ* ("that no one can be kept banished," based on 2 Sam 14:14), in every generation, the blessed Holy One sends to this world great *tzaddikim* graced with exceedingly holy, elevated souls and great and holy understanding. The fire of the altar always burns within them with inner enthusiasm and awe and love, fiery sparks of a divine flame. And as Jews, we are commanded in the Torah to cleave to those learned in Torah. It is in this spirit that in explaining the words, "holding fast to Him" (Deut 11:22), Rashi asked, "Is it really possible to hold fast to God?" [—who, in Deut 4:24, is likened to a consuming fire![40]] and answered, "But one is able to cleave to the wise ones who teach the Torah." So when the Israelite journeys to the *tzaddikim* in his generation, drawing near to a holy man with great desire and love, then, as a face is reflected in water (*k'mayim ha-panim 'el-panim*) [on the basis of Prov 27:19], the *tzaddik*, through his holiness, influences him to be like a faithful, sturdy peg that will never leave or fall out.

Yitro realized that the service/worship of the Lord is exceedingly great and precious, and that one does not enter into that path and commitment immediately, but only after great efforts and bonding with the *tzaddikim*. . . .

---

39. *Ma'or va-shemesh*, II, 16a–17a.
40. *Sipre* on Deut 11:22.

Understanding that no person is able to rely simply upon his own intelligence, Yitro grasped that he must connect with Moses, from whom one might learn the awe of God. There is no other possible route. And with that understanding, he left his own land and came to Moses. . . .

And Moses then came forth to greet him and kissed him, for a kiss is a cleaving of one spirit to another. Through Moses' kissing Yitro, Moses' very spirit cleaved to him. Yitro's heart was then drawn to Moses, and through this Yitro was drawn even further to a state of repentance. Though Moses was able to speak to him of all the wonders of the blessed Creator, if not for his kissing him first, his telling him would have had no effect, for Yitro would never have believed him.

Comment: Moses' kiss engendered a soul-level attachment between the two, enabling Yitro to be open to a different understanding of the Divine. The window to deepening one's understanding is not a matter of conventional communication, but rather an interpersonal act of love and a deep respect for the other person.

We have noted previously that, to the mind of the Kraków preacher, an inherent difficulty lies in the way of one person communicating his deepest thoughts and beliefs to another person, as those thoughts are necessarily rooted in a person's own unique individuality and emerge from a depth within the person that others cannot share or comprehend. But the *tzaddik*'s love, felt by the person coming to him, serves as a bridge over that existential gulf.

In his re-casting the scene of the meeting between Moses and Yitro, the master has emphasized that a person's true influence upon another takes place not on the level of words or ideas or logical argument, but rather through the relationship that a person feels in the presence of another. This point, which has been emphasized by G. Dynner and Z. Gries, is in accord with Martin Buber's interpretation of Hasidism as a life of true encounter in which a person ("I") truly recognizes the reality of the other ("Thou") as one's love of God encompasses the world.[41] Note also "Blessing requires love" on *parashat Naso*.

(At the same time, the homily goes on to mention that had Yitro kissed Moses, the kiss would have been damaging to Moses, a reflection of the

---

41. Note Dynner, *Men of Silk*, 198; Gries, *Sefer, Sofer v'sippur*, 65; Buber, *The Origin and Meaning of Hasidism*, 198.

highly suspicious view of the outsider as one who can have a dangerous impact. That fear of the outsider was also part of Kalonymus Kalman's world.)

A Portrait of Moses as a Judge[42]

> "When Moses' father-in-law saw how much Moses had to do for the people, he said, 'What is this thing that you are doing to the people? Why do you act alone while all the people stand about you from morning until evening?'" (Exod 18:14)

Yitro noted also that through the entire day Moses would maintain a state of attachment (*d'vekut*) to God even while all the people were standing around him.... And Moses explained to his father-in-law, "When the people come to me to seek God, seeking to learn from me the service and worship of God, were I to descend completely from my state of attachment, they would not benefit at all." You might ask, "Since you are separated from them in your state of attachment, how will you decide and clarify the judgment having to do with one person and his fellow or between a husband and wife?" But the text explains, "When they will have a dispute, it comes before me" (Exod 18:16), meaning: if they erred in any matter causing a blemish, they "*come to Me*" ('to God'), an intimation of *t'shuvah*.

Moses explained, "In their coming near, I awaken in each person repentance and regret, with the natural consequence that one reconciles himself to his fellow and does not cause him any further injustice or wrongdoing." And that is conveyed in the words, "And I decide between a man and his neighbor" (Exod 18:16)—I awaken him to repentance and regret, and he stands near me, and when he comes home, even though I had not spoken with him about that matter, due to my awakening him to repentance, he immediately becomes reconciled with his fellow. And hence, "And I decide" (in the Hebrew, *v'shafat'ti*: I have judged"—"I have already judged him," and hence the verb is written in the past tense.

Comment: The account in the Torah, to which this comment refers, presents Moses in a way that, in retrospect, recalls the role of the *rav*, the rabbi in the traditional community who attends to any conflicts or disputes among the Jews of the place and who is able to render judgment based

42. *Ma'or ha-shemesh*, II, 17b–18a.

upon his superior knowledge of Jewish legal texts. In the description that emerges from Moses' explanation in *Ma'or va-shemesh* however, Moses' role goes beyond rendering a judgment as he speaks to the hearts of the litigants.

In his retelling this scene of the Israelites standing in a long line to bring their disputes before Moses, Kalonymus Kalman explained that Moses' activity was so time-consuming for the reason that Moses' intent was not simply to weigh the claims of persons in a dispute; he endeavored to change the heart of each person with whom he dealt. He strove to bring that person to an inner change (*t'shuvah*) so that he would no longer be envious of others or have any desire to transgress another's boundaries. This he could accomplish only by patiently and seriously relating to each individual seeking his help. Not content with resolving disputes, Moses healed the blemish in the person's character and with that kind of inner change in a person, reconciliation naturally followed.

Moses' aspiration was to alter the basic feelings of the litigants in a way to avert future disputes on account of actions that would naturally follow from any continued ill-feeling. As presented in this passage from *Ma'or va-shemesh*, Moses is more a *rebbe* than a *rav*. More than a judge functioning within a system of law, he strove to be a healer of the heart. In this insightful excerpt the master re-wired a passage and scene from the biblical narrative. Moreover, in effect Kalonymus Kalman situated within his reading of the toraitic narrative itself his vision of the ethos of Hasidic community and leadership and the depth-connection between the *tzaddik* and his followers.

The homily, however, goes beyond that implied parallel as it involves a transformation of the very setting of Moses' judgment; the partners to a conflict ultimately stand not only before Moses, but before God, the true Judge and Healer. Through Moses' patient and careful endeavor, his explanation and his very role and activity represent, symbolically, the true divine Healer who brings about a turning of the heart.

Going still further, Moses, in this homily, explains to Yitro that the Israelites come to him to inquire how to serve and worship God. They come to him, not in connection with grievances or conflicts with their fellows, but in his role as a spiritual mentor.

The Status of the Sinaitic Event in Context[43]

> "Moses came and summoned the elders of the people and put before them all the words that the Lord had commanded him. All the people answered as one saying, 'All that the Lord has spoken we will do.'..." (Exod 19:7–8)

Upon hearing from Moses our Teacher that the blessed Holy One wants to give them the Torah, the Israelites responded enthusiastically as they longed to grasp the Oneness of God *from within* themselves as did the holy fathers. And, similarly *from within themselves*, they willed to do all the necessary actions that bring delight to their Creator. Afterward they heard from the mouth of God, "They did well to speak thus" (Deut 5:25), for when their deeds would be of that level and character they would naturally walk in the ways of the Torah even without ever having heard it in advance. And this is what they exclaimed before the Giving of the Torah, "All that the Lord has spoken we will faithfully do" [literally: "we will do and we will obey"] (Exod 24:7), indicating that first we will do in a way flowing from our own selves, and only afterward we will hear from the mouth of God.

"And Moses brought back the people's words to the Lord" (Exod 19:8). From the start, Moses simply relayed their answer concerning his mission, conveying that Israel agreed to accept His Divinity. Then, the blessed Holy One said to Moses, "I will come to you in a thick cloud, in order that the people may hear when I speak with you" (Exod 19:9), and the people will overhear My conveying to you the Torah and the *mitzvot* so that they might know how to fulfill God's Will. "Then Moses reported the people's words to the Lord" (Exod 19:9), telling Him of their will to do and fulfill the Torah even without first having heard it, since theirs was a fierce desire to make the effort with all their strength and minds to attain a sense of the greatness and majesty and oneness of God, just as the holy fathers did.

But as nothing is hidden from Him, God knew that their strong desire would last only the length of a passing hour, and that, though freedom of choice is in man's hands, he will nevertheless surrender to his desires (on the basis of Prov 21:1). The Holy One said to Moses, "Go to the people and warn them to stay pure today and tomorrow..." (Exod 19:10); they are to prepare themselves over three days, for perhaps through just

---

43. *Ma'or va-shemesh*, II, 19ab.

that kind of preparation they might truly attain the necessary level. But afterward when they fell from their higher level, they requested of Moses, "You speak to us . . . and we will obey" (Exod 19:16).

It is not written "and we will do" but "we will obey" (*nishma*, also meaning "hear"), indicating that first we will hear in order to know how we should conduct ourselves. And on that level, every person will be able to serve the Lord, first hearing—so that a person will not transgress the words of the Sages, but will rather fulfill all the Torah in its entirety—and through this he will be able truly to grasp the majesty of God.

It is concerning this that the blessed Holy One said, "They did well to speak thus. May they always be of such mind, to revere Me and follow all My commandments, that it may go well with them and with their children forever. Would that their hearts would so revere Me all the days" (Deut 5:25–26), that they will first hear and then do and fulfill what they will hear from the mouth of the Sages and their students and not transgress My will. And this too will be pleasing before Me.

Comment: Does one begin with a commitment to fulfill the divine Will or need one first hear a statement of that Will? That question is grasped traditionally as the contrast between an *a priori* commitment and one requiring a prior knowledge of what is expected of him, a polarity which, in traditional exegesis, rests here upon the order of words in a biblical verse. Placing a priority upon hearing is understood as less than a wholeness of commitment, whereas the Israelites—as spelled out in Jewish traditional interpretation—did not condition their covenantal commitment upon a prior statement as to what it actually entails. They did not ask to read the small print before signing their agreement!

Kalonymus Kalman, however, inserted within that polarity another kind of polarity. The response of the Israelites at Sinai is contrasted with the example of the three fathers, the patriarchs of Israel who, it was claimed, did not require any revelation prior to their actually living the Torah. A rabbinic statement has it that Abraham, for example, fulfilled the entire Torah including even rather minute details of rabbinic law.[44] The fathers preceded the revelation at Sinai and, in addition, did not learn the Torah and its requirements from rabbinic scholars. The fathers, Kalonymus Kalman maintained here, knew the Torah instinctively from within themselves and conducted their lives in accordance with it. And the comparison that

---

44. *b. Yoma* 28b.

emerges places them on a higher level than that of the Israelites at Sinai; in that sense, the example of the fathers and their higher level of spiritual intuition overshadow and even dwarf the scene of the revelation at Sinai.

The latter, in the perspective of the Kraków master, is contingent upon the need of a person to hear, from beyond oneself, a statement of how one is to live in this world. That other might be God or Moses or Torah-students of any generation. The source is something other and beyond themselves. It is no longer something intrinsic, flowing from one's own innate sense of things, but allows—or requires—an external authority on some level. In contrast, it is maintained that the fathers were capable of grasping the way of Torah without hearing it from any such authority beyond the self; theirs was an intrinsic sense of the divine Will.

At the same time, the reader notes that the passage moves from that kind of comparison and contrast to a note of acceptance, expressed in God's own voice as deciphered in the text of the Torah. The higher, more ideal level is not always within the realm of possibility, and so God—and the preacher—must be content with a lower, more indirect source of knowledge. The passage concludes on a note of accepting that state of things, even while realizing that it fails to represent the very highest level. The comparison, though, remains. And although the homilist comes to terms with a more indirect and imperfect relationship, that more ideal relationship in which such knowledge is understood within oneself, remains in the background, much like a tall mountain hovering over a scene of a lower terrain.

For a broader background of this theme, the reader is directed to Arthur Green's *Devotion and Commandment—The Faith of Abraham in the Hasidic Imagination*, to which one might add statements of that theme in Isaac of Radvil's *'Or Yitshak*, discussed in A. Wineman, "Hewn from the Divine Quarry."

The Gate of Humility and Its Recurrence[45]

It is known from the words of elevated holy ones that on all festive days [the three festivals of the Jewish year, *Pesaḥ, Shavu'ot* and *Sukkot*] the theme of the festival can be experienced in all its initial power. And so on the festival of *Shavu'ot* (the Festival of Weeks) one who purifies himself is able to re-experience great holiness, similar to that of the Israelites

---

45. *Ma'or va-shemesh*, IV, 4b (*Rimzei Shavu'ot*).

when, on this holy day, the entire people stood at Mount Sinai. And just as the gateway of humility was then opened for the Israelites, so in every generation the gate of humility opens for everyone who purifies himself on this holy day.

Comment: For the contemporary reader, this excerpt, found within a much larger and rather complicated discussion on the *Shavu'ot* festival, might bring to mind Mircea Eliade's conception of sacred time as an earlier, primordial, time that is accessible and periodically restored. One who participates in a festival can experience the very beginning of the world just as though that person were living in that kind of time which preceded the de-sacralization of time itself. For that person the world can be experienced as new, as in the time of its origins.[46] It might, furthermore, suggest the understanding of a mythic event as a happening that can be re-experienced and re-lived in the consciousness of a tradition's adherents.[47]

What recurs, however, is explained in this excerpt not as the revelation at Sinai itself but, more specifically, the Israelites' acquiring the quality of humility after what was a clear failure on their part to acquire that quality. The homilist wove together a number of motifs found in the Talmud, some having to do with Yosef Ketanta, a rabbinic sage mentioned only in those few connections in the entire talmudic literature. It was his practice to obtain a special calf to be prepared for him in celebration of *Shavu'ot* (*'atzeret*) for the reason that if not for the giving of the Torah, celebrated on *Shavu'ot*, he would be simply one of many others working in the marketplace.[48] And elsewhere, he is mentioned, somewhat strangely, as one who pointed to himself as proof that humility has not disappeared in Israel.[49]

The preacher, however, wove these together with another motif, namely the desire of the Israelites at Sinai to "see their King." That motif is found in the *M'khilta*, the ta'anitic midrash on *Sh'mot* which, filling in a gap within the biblical narrative in Exodus, ch. 19, has the Israelites' telling Moses that "our desire is to hear from the King Himself, as hearing it through a veil (*pargod*) is not like hearing it (directly) from the King," and God responded with a willingness to grant their request. Another version

---

46. Eliade, *The Sacred and the Profane*, ch. 1; *Myth and Reality*, chs. 2–3. Also, Wineman, "Mircea Eliade and the Jewish Holy Day."
47. Armstrong, *The Bible—The Biography*, 238.
48. *b. Pesaḥ.* 68b.
49. *b. Sotah* 49b.

of that motif then appears in the same text, "We want to see our King, as hearing is not similar to actually seeing," and God similarly responded by granting their request.[50] And, as a consequence, Adonai descended upon the mountain to the sight of all the people, all of whom saw what (later) even Ezekiel and Isaiah were not granted to see.[51] Those comments from the *M'khilta* do not include any note of criticism of the Israelites' request. In his comment on Exod 19:9 Rashi refers to that request, explaining it in that "Hearing something from a messenger is not similar as hearing it from the King," and adds, "Our wish is to see our King." In his comment on Exod 19:21, however, Rashi speaks of this request to see their King as *ta'avah*, a word connoting lustful desire and associated with the tree of knowledge of good and evil (Gen 3:6).

Kalonymus Kalman built his *Shavu'ot* homily upon that note, and in doing so he went against the grain of the much more general glorification of the Israelites at Sinai to read into the account a contest between the Israelites' utter lack of humility in wishing to "see their King" and their repentance which followed with their acquiring the quality of humility. The preacher read their very request and intention as an expression of arrogance on their part as they viewed themselves as prepared and worthy of such a visual experience of God. They saw themselves as occupying a rank far exceeding their inner preparation for the event of divine revelation, and their standing *at the foot of the mountain* (Exod 19:17) represents their failure to measure up to the mountain and its own humility. Not only the Israelites, but even Moses, who elsewhere is held up by God as the prime human exemplar of humility (Num 12:4), had to retreat and descend (Exod 19:25) from his own wish to see God. And only upon the Israelites'—and Moses'—overcoming their own pride and exaggerated self-esteem, did God then begin to speak His Words; in the text, Moses' *descent* (Exod 19:25) is immediately followed by God's commencing to *speak* the Ten Utterances (Exod 20:1). Revelation could occur only in the wake of humility.

A conglomeration of strains and themes together served as raw material in the construction of this homily. What stands out most prominently is the master's brilliant re-conception of the account of the Israelites at Sinai as precisely their acquiring humility after their prior betrayal of that very quality. And what could easily be grasped paradoxically from the talmudic source as the sage Yosef's pride in his humility—even his boasting of his

---

50. Mek. 63b, *Yitro, Baḥodesh ha-sh'lishi*, end of *parashah* 2, on Exod 19:9.
51. Mek. 64a, *Yitro, Baḥodesh ha-sh'lishi, parashah* 3, on Exod 19:11.

own humility—emerges in this homily instead as an expression of gratitude for humility itself, and in that spirit Yosef celebrated the festival of *Shavu'ot* in his special way, because only through the merit and impact of that day could he himself, much later—on the same date in the calendar—acquire that very quality of humility.

Mishpatim

Justice and Worship[52]

"These are the rules that you shall set before them." (Exod. 21:1)

Rashi explained that this portion (*Mishpatim*), containing civil laws, is located adjacent to verses pertaining to the altar (Exod 20:19–23) to indicate that you shall situate the law-court (Sanhedrin) next to the altar (in the Tabernable or Temple)....

"And if you make for Me an altar of stones, do not build it of hewn stones, for by wielding your tool upon them you have profaned them" (Exod 20:22). The altar, Rashi explained, was created to lengthen man's days (through the opportunity for atonement which it allows), whereas iron (employed as a weapon of killing), was created to shorten man's days, and therefore it is only reasonable that iron which is employed to shorten one's lifespan not be wielded over what can lengthen a person's life.[53]

Furthermore, this collection of civil laws appears adjacent to laws pertaining to the altar, making it clear that you are to situate the court (Sanhedrin) adjacent to the altar . . . for the altar alludes to (sacrificial) worship. And now prayer (*t'filah*) comes in place of sacrifice, as it says in the Gemara, "Prayers were instituted corresponding to the daily offerings."[54] . . . And it is known that a person is more easily able to pray with inner enthusiasm and with awe and trembling than to study with the same passion and emotional intensity. For this reason Rashi concluded that the court is to be situated near (the altar). He intended that the study of Torah and, in particular, of the civil, legal judgments associated with the Sanhedrin shall be held on a par with the altar, which is associated with

---

52. *Ma'or va-shemesh*, II, 22ab.
53. *m. Mid.* 3:4; also *Mek.*, 74a, *Baḥodesh*, ch. 11.
54. *b. Ber.* 26b.

worship, as you will engage in Torah-study with the same qualities of deep inner spiritual enthusiasm, awe and trembling associated with worship.

We learn that when a person brings sacrificial offerings at the altar, he certainly has first engaged in repentance so that he might find atonement for his deeds. For without repentance, "the sacrificial gift of the wicked is an abomination" (Prov 21:27). For atonement is possible only through a person's having engaged in repentance prior to his making the offering, and it is by virtue of his repentance and atonement that his life is prolonged....

The eyes of all Israel are directed toward one who, through God's beneficence, serves as a rabbi and leader of the community. Such a person must always convey a pronounced ambiance of submission and remorse, living with the sense of a broken heart and constantly examining his ways virtually every moment. And he must be perpetually engaged in repentance, for it is impossible for him to be completely free of sin.

In connection with the words, "In case it is a chieftain (*nasi*) who incurs guilt by doing unwittingly any of the things which by the commandment of the Lord his God ought not to be done, and finds himself culpable..." (Lev 4:22) [referring to a tribal leader, but later interpreted as referring to judges], it is noted in the holy Zohar that concerning all others it is written "*if* he will sin," while concerning the *nasi* it is written, "*when* a *nasi* will sin," indicating that it is certain that he will sin.[55] Being that at times he feels a sense of pride vis-a-vis the community and acts as though he were on a higher level than others, he could easily arrive, even unintentionally, at a wrong judgment, and so it is impossible for him to avoid any possibility of sin. And if he fails to engage in repentance, it is clear that he will not prolong his days, as our Sages said (in reference to the kings of Judah), "Woe to the position of authority which buries those who occupy that position."[56] It is therefore incumbent upon a judge to examine his deeds carefully and constantly and to engage in penitence for his deeds. And if so, God will then certainly forgive him and lengthen his days and years with goodness and pleasantness.

That is the meaning of the adjacent locations, within the text of the Torah, of the civil law with laws pertaining to the altar, telling you to situate the law-court near the altar. One who sits on the court must always be in a state of submissiveness and repentance so that his judgeship might

---

55. Zohar, III, 23a.
56. b. Pesaḥ. 87b.

bring him length of days. . . . Hence the rabbi (judge) must always engage in repentance, and if he does so he will lengthen his days and years. And understand!

Comment: A judge must not only pursue justice but must be forever conscious of the very real possibility of his erring and betraying his commission of justice. His role and his duties hence require that he never trust himself and his own inclinations, but rather must ever be on guard against committing an injustice through his judicial verdicts. The judge must therefore engage his own judgments with trepidation and weigh them, guarding against any lack of objectivity in his thinking. He must, in other words, engage in a never-ending spiritual process akin to what is devotional in nature. In the adjacent positions of laws relating to the altar and to civil law, Rashi explained that the Torah views the two as, indeed, very closely related.

In addition to communicating the gravity of the role and position of a judge, a theme given unquestionable emphasis in rabbinic sources and clearly enunciated in the quotation from Rashi's commentary cited above, this passage and its overtones might also be read with an eye to its cultural and polemical context. While Hasidism tended to place an emphasis upon prayer and the depth of spiritual struggle and intent and energy, the more official and conventional mode of Jewish religious life at the time looked upon *study* as the apex of Jewish living and held aloft the role of the rabbinic scholar, whose role in the community revolved around his serving as a judge on the basis of his erudition in Jewish legal literature. It is not difficult to overhear in this passage the spiritual pitfalls precisely in the very position that was most esteemed by those who had been the opponents of the Hasidic camp.

In a broader sense, prayer is more easily experienced as inspirational than is a law book or a record of court proceedings. A significant theme in Hasidic teaching emphasizes that spiritual experience is not to be restricted to a particular corner of life but should permeate all of life, a theme that, in its way, is voiced in that more earlier interpretation of the proximity between the scene of legal proceedings and the altar in the Tabernacle.

T'rumah

Moses as the Model of the Tabernacle[57]

> "Exactly as I show you—the pattern of the Tabernacle, and the pattern of all its furnishings—so shall you make it." (Exod 25:9)

This verse, addressed to Moses, is not readily understandable. It reads, "exactly as I show you," not "to you," which would be *l'kha*, but rather *'otkha* (the object of the verb), indicating that He is showing "you" to someone else.

And also the words, "the pattern of the Tabernacle . . ." is problematic. Was not the higher Tabernacle which God showed to Moses the actual (or original) Tabernacle itself, while the Tabernacle that Israel constructed was built in the pattern of that celestial Tabernacle, but located within the camp in this lower world?[58] [The concept of a celestial Tabernacle as the model for the earthly Tabernacle is thought to reflect an old Semitic worldview in which everything on earth mirrors what exists on a higher sphere.]

And how is it fitting to speak of *showing you* the pattern of the Tabernacle? A further difficulty arises in that He said "so shall you make it," employing the plural form both of the pronoun and the verb. Did all the Israelites make the Tabernacle? Also how would they understand how to construct it simply from what they saw? And is it at all possible to convey to human intelligence how to construct according to a spatial pattern something that is spiritual in nature?

But the verse can be understood in light of the ways that Moses our Teacher, may he rest in peace, purified himself from all kinds of physicality to the point at which he became totally spiritual and hence served

---

57. *Ma'or va-shemesh*, II, 27b.

58. *Midr. Exod.* 33:4, *Tanḥ* (Naso) #19, *Pesiq.Rab Kah.*, 4b; also b. Pesaḥ. 54a and *b. Ned.* 39b.

as a chariot of the *Sh'khinah* [a bearer of the divine Presence, echoing the image in Ezek 1]. Moses himself served as the pattern of the higher Tabernacle, and from him his contemporaries were able to learn how to serve God in a way that they too might be able to reach his own attainments. And that is the meaning of the words, "Make for Me a holy place and I will dwell among *them*" (Exod 25:8)—namely, that every Israelite is to purify himself thoroughly in order to be such a chariot (vehicle) of the *Sh'khinah*.

Certainly not every person knows in what way he will come to merit that level of attainment. And so the Torah says, "Exactly as I show *you*—the pattern of the Tabernacle and the pattern of all its furnishings—so shall you make it," voicing the intention that you can find a direction and guideline in what you see in Moses. It is him that I show to the people of your generation. This means that *you*, Moses, are the pattern of the higher Tabernacle, and the Israelites are to learn to be like you, so that each of them can serve as a chariot of the *Sh'khinah*. For every person is able to reach what Moses our Teacher has himself attained.

From those words we can understand that the purpose of our worship is to purify the self in order to serve as such a chariot of the *Sh'khinah*. For in this way, God's presence will dwell in this lower realm, fulfilling the very intention of creation. And may His Kingship be revealed soon.

Comment: It should be clear to the reader by now that Kalonymus Kalman viewed the Tabernacle not simply as a physical structure drawn to certain specifications, but rather as something that is essentially spiritual rather than physical in nature. Echoing the thinking of the sixteenth-century commentator Moshe Alshekh, who himself was likely influenced directly or indirectly by the tenor of Sufi spirituality, the Hasidic masters viewed the Tabernacle essentially as a symbol of the human being who is to make of his life and of his very being a dwelling-place for the Divine.[59]

In this homily, the preacher referred to Moses as the model of the Tabernacle—neither the physical person, nor some disembodied spiritual entity, but the concrete Moses who has purified his physical nature. He is ultimately the model of the meaning of the Tabernacle, a model from whom the Israelites can learn the way of self-purification allowing for God's Presence in the world. And he is ultimately the model of what each Israelite, in his own way, is to become in order to realize that broader

---

59. See Wineman, "Sufis in the Hasidic *Mishkan*."

conception of God's dwelling in this world. The homily makes it clear that Moses is not held up as the one single, absolute manifestation of that ideal; rather, each person is to seek to purify himself as Moses has done and is able to reach the level of what Moses attained.

In the context of an accent upon the uniqueness of each individual voiced in these homilies, one must understand that while Moses is held up as the model, the ultimate blueprint, the particular details of the blueprint differ from one person to another. Each person is to produce a particular version of the same model, namely a purification of one's whole self to serve as a "bearer of the chariot."

From Each Only according to His Ability[60]

> "They shall make an ark of acacia wood, two and a half cubits long, a cubit and half wide, and a cubit and a half high. Overlay it with pure gold—overlay it inside and out—and make upon it a gold molding round about. . . . Make two cherubim (winged figures above the Ark in the 'Holy of Holies' within the Tabernacle) of gold—make them of hammered work—at the two ends of the cover." (Exod 25:10–18)

The Midrash noted that in regard to all the other artifacts of the Tabernacle it is written, "And you (singular) shall make," but concerning the Ark it says, "And they (plural) shall make" (Exod 25:10). According to Rabbi Yehuda bar Shalom, the blessed Holy One said, "Let them all come and participate in building the Ark so that they might all merit from Torah-learning."[61] The point is that every Israelite has a portion in some letter from among the letters of the Torah, and the principle of a person's involvement with Torah-study is that one study for the sake of the unification of the blessed Holy One and His *Sh'khinah* [making for a unification of the spiritual reality that underlies all existence].

Even though he is not able to learn the entire Torah, each person is able to engage in the Torah according to his own strength and capabilities, provided he does what he is able with the intent of providing delight to His Maker and Creator.

. . . God demands of each person only according to that person's own capability. You find that when the blessed Holy One gave the Torah

---

60 *Ma'or va-shemesh*, II, 27b.
61. *Midr. Exod.* 34:2.

to Israel, had He come with all His force, the Israelites would not have been able to endure. . . . But He came to them in terms of *their* own strength, as it says, "The Voice of the Lord in strength" (Ps 29:4), not "with His strength," but rather simply "in strength"—according to the strength and capability of each one of them.[62] And for this reason the Midrash explains in regard to the verse, "And *they* shall make an Ark," that each person should engage in Torah according to his own ability, provided he have the desired intent (*kavanah*).

Comment: This passage, too, can be understood in terms of the divide in Eastern European Jewry between this Hasidic camp and its opponents (*Mitnagdim*). The latter, more normative sector revered the exemplars of intense learning and erudition. They held aloft the image of the exceptionally learned Jew, steeped in talmudic learning. Hasidism, despite the charges leveled against it, likewise emphasized Torah-study, but did not associate the study of Torah solely with those having outstanding accomplishments in knowledge. Its conception of Torah-study tended to place the emphasis more on the place of study in the life of all Jews and, especially in its earlier period, was very critical concerning the moral traps of pride and haughtiness and impure, egotistical motivation to which, they believed, the class of elite scholars often succumbed. Their Opponents, on the other hand, accused the *Ḥasidim* of belittling Torah-study and its diligent scholars. In the above homily, the reader can overhear something of that divide and of the criticism evoked in the two camps.

The midrashic passage bearing the name of Rabbi Yehuda bar Shalom to which the larger homily refers focuses upon the use of the plural in the command to make the Ark which the Midrash viewed as symbolizing Torah-study. Referring to the saying of Simeon bar Yohai concerning the three crowns,[63] the table in the Tabernacle is thought to represent the crown of royalty, and the altar, the crown of the priesthood. The recipients of those crowns are determined by one's parentage and hence unavailable to others. In contrast, the crown of learning (*keter torah*), represented by the Ark, is potentially open to all who find a place in their lives for such study.

Furthermore, in a note bearing a distinctly democratic ring, the midrashic passage maintains that the crown of Torah, which is available to all, occupies a higher position than the other two crowns which are limited in

62. *Midr. Exod.* 34:1.
63. *m. 'Abot* 4:17.

each case to a particular family or class or lineage. That midrashic excerpt also focused upon the word *zer* (in this case, a golden border set around the top of the Ark), a word that, however, could be vocalized to signify what is foreign and alien (*zar*). Learning could serve either as such a gold border, similar to a crown, or could lead to one's alienation from true devotion and learning. Learning can have pitfalls as well as achievements.

That space for criticism is clearly implied in the following passage which emphasizes the need to repent precisely in connection with study, a theme that brings to the surface the moral pitfalls which the Hasidic teachers sometimes associated with the learned class and its preoccupations.

Repentance Before and After Study[64]

> "They shall make an ark of acadia wood . . . ." (Exod 25:10)

This verse must be understood in terms of what the particular artifact represents: the Ark ('*Aron*, which is said to contain the Tablets of the Law and which, in a much later time, came to house the Torah-scroll) alludes to Torah (study). And it is known from all the holy books that when a person wants to study Torah for its own sake (not for any extraneous, personal or egotistical motivation), he must engage in repentance before he begins his study, "for there is not one good man on earth who does what is best and doesn't err" (Eccl 7:20). "And to the wicked, God said, 'Who are you to recite My laws, and mouth the terms of My covenant, seeing that you spurn My discipline, and brush My words aside?'" (Ps 50:16).

For this reason, before beginning to study, one must carefully examine his deeds and locate the blemishes in his behavior, and he must desire from now on to be a true servant of God, learning and fulfilling God's will. And, similarly, following his study, after he has studied his lessons, he must similarly examine carefully whether his study was free of any extraneous motivation or, God forbid, of any intent other than for the sake of Torah itself. And the person must ponder, in repentance, his failure to study properly and sincerely, God forbid. It follows that all his days must be devoted to repentance. And similarly in his fulfilling the *mitzvot* (holy deeds), one must likewise engage in *t'shuvah* (in the sense of soul-searching and self-examination) both before and after fulfilling any such commanded deed.

64. *Ma'or va-shemesh*, II, 28a.

... The Ark symbolizes Torah-study, and the curtain alludes to repentance. And the veil (*kapporet,* which hangs from the top of the Ark) is related to the verb *l'khaper* (to atone).[65] It follows that one must engage in *t'shuvah* prior to his studying Torah. And this is the meaning of the command to make "two golden cherubim" (Exod 25:18) which, Rashi explained, have the appearance of infants. A person must engage in *t'shuvah* and must be humble in his own eyes, as though he were a day-old infant who has not yet fulfilled any *mitzvot* or good deeds.

And hence twice it is necessary to engage in *t'shuvah* in order to remake oneself to be like such an infant (devoid of any merit)—both before and after his study—and the *two* cherubim allude to both what precedes and follows one's study. For both before and after study, one must feel that he is but an infant [without having yet performed any meritorious or praiseworthy deeds and without having achieved any feats of learning].

Comment: Torah-study is a holy activity, but like other holy acts and activities, it can flow from various motivations, not all of them grounded in sincerity and holiness. The call for repentance both before and after one's study rests upon the very real possibility that one's learning can be motivated by negative as well as positive motivations.

The two golden cherubim have themselves a curious problematic presence as they fall in the category of molten images, normally forbidden, and these are to be situated precisely above the Ark in what was regarded as the most holy area within the Tabernacle. Suggesting seemingly quasi-mythological images, they would appear quite out-of-place in a cultic site specifically lacking all such images. In this homily, building on Rashi's identification of the cherubim as infants, Kalonymus Kalman offered his interpretation of those two graven figures as a sign that Torah-study, represented by the Ark, must take place with a consciousness lacking all sense of self-importance and accomplishment, as though the student or scholar, of whatever age, were but a young infant, innocent of any sense of personal pride and accomplishment.

---

65. *Midr. Exod.* 50:4.

T'tzavveh

Fellowship and Mutuality[66]

> "You shall further instruct (*t'tzavveh*) the Israelites to bring you clear oil of beaten olives for lighting, for kindling lamps regularly." (Exod 27:20)

These words are addressed to the High *Tzaddik* in his generation who commands the Israelites how to serve the Lord according to the holy Torah. But the word, *t'tzavveh* (you shall command), can be understood also as an expression for joining together as one fellowship [from the Aramaic word *tzavta*, "together"]. In other words, the *tzaddik* is to join himself to the Israelites to be together with them in one fellowship. Great benefit comes to the *tzaddik*, in that they will "bring you clear oil of beaten olives for lighting," for through their joining with you, the blessed Holy One will bring to the *tzaddik* oil, an allusion to Higher Wisdom. "And they shall bring you," must be understood as their role, through their awakening, in your own attaining Wisdom, symbolized by pure olive oil.

Comment: The teaching, referring to the role of fellowship as followers join together with the *tzaddik*, emerges in the discourse of the Kraków master relating to a distinctly cultic practice, the kindling the oil-lights in the Tabernacle. Life is not divided into clearly distinct realms, and from the realm of ritual, one might derive understanding pertaining to a realm transcending ritual itself.

    The comment on this verse is grounded in a not uncommon practice in Hasidic homily literature, namely providing for a word in the text an etymology quite foreign to the word itself. That particular strategy, though

---

66. *Ma'or va-shemesh*, II, 28b.

highly questionable as a linguistic explanation, has occasioned many highly creative and fruitful readings of the biblical text.

This kind of creative etymology enabled the master to transform the command to kindle the oil-lights into a relationship of togetherness and mutuality between the *tzaddik*, as leader and center of a community, and his followers. In his thinking, each stands in need of the other. Rather then viewing their relationship as a one-way street in which the holy man gives and the followers receive, a different model is suggested: without the indispensable role of the followers (*Ḥasidim*), the *tzaddik* is unable to reach his own potential spiritual heights.

In a somewhat earlier Hasidic source, the same reading of that root, *tziva*, as having the meaning of *b'tzavta* (together), has elicited an understanding of the word, *mitzvah* (commandment, holy deed), as an act in which God and the human partner are both present together.[67] The same thought echoes in the writings of the late Abraham Joshua Heschel, who spoke of the *mitzvah* as a place of meeting between man and God.[68]

Note that Aaron, the first high priest, is referred to as the "high *tzaddik*," an unusual expression which would view him as a mirror of the Hasidic holy man. This is but one example in which Kalonymus Kalman, like many others before and after him, viewed the past in terms of his own present and conceived of the Hasidic *tzaddik* as a contemporary parallel of the biblical priest.

---

67. *Likkutim yekarim* #136, 44b.
68. Heschel, *God in Search of Man*, 289, 312.

Ki tissa

The Seventh Day as a Day of Renewed Existential Connection[69]

> "The Israelite people shall keep the Sabbath, observing the Sabbath throughout the ages as a covenant for all time: it shall be a sign for all time between Me and the people of Israel. For in six days the Lord made heaven and earth, and on the seventh day He ceased from work and was refreshed." (Exod 31:16–17)

It follows that in every generation it is incumbent upon the *tzaddikim* of the generation to extend the holiness of Shabbat even to simple people, those who, during all their weekdays, must occupy themselves with worldly matters and are burdened in their work, so that they too might experience the holiness of *Shabbat*. It is written, "On the seventh day God finished the work which He had been doing . . ." (Gen 2:2). This is one of the things that the scribes altered for King Ptolemy[70] [who is said to have gathered together seventy-two scribes, each of whom was then commissioned to translate, independently, the Torah into Greek] to read "And God completed on the sixth day and rested on the Seventh." But in truth, as our Sages said, God finished on the Seventh Day, for what did the world still lack? It lacked rest (*m'nuḥah*). The Shabbat came and with it came rest.[71]

The real point is that during all the first six days the created things were distanced from their Root. For with the creation of the worlds God contracted His Divinity, and the worlds evolved from the higher to the lower with numerous contractions extending to this lower world which, in the process, acquired physical form. And during the weekdays, it was very

---

69. *Ma'or va-shemesh*, II, 29b–30a.
70. *b. Meg.* 9a.
71. See Rashi on Gen 2:2.

difficult for anything to awaken to attach itself to its Root. But with the coming of the Shabbat, the blessed Holy One brought down the holiness of Shabbat to all the worlds and all the created things could then experience the holiness of Shabbat, something they were unable to experience during the preceding weekdays due to the world's physical character.

And on the holy Shabbat, they began to feel the holiness which was revealed to them and would begin to glisten and yearn to ascend to become attached to their Source. In such ascents, by means of effort and devotion, all the worlds, from the lower to the highest, ascend and cleave to the blessed Infinite One. And from where does that longing emerge?— From God's bringing down the holiness of Shabbat upon all the worlds. When that occurred, they all began to yearn to ascend and to connect with their Root. For *vai-khal* (finished, completed) comes from the expression conveying a longing of the soul (*kilyon-nefesh*, Ps 84:3). [The same root *k-l-h* could indicate either "becoming complete" or "longing," and the homilist is here following the suggestion of Hayyim ben-Atar.[72] The same interpretation is found in "A longing permeating all existence" on *parashat B'rei'shit*.]

Vayinafash ("and became refreshed, renewed") means that God brings down a higher holiness on Shabbat. God brings down an exceedingly small measure of the holiness of His Divinity, some small measure of God's own spirit—if one could speak in those terms—so that every person, according to his own aspect and preparation, might experience the holiness of Shabbat. And in that way every person will grasp that he can draw to himself that higher holiness to the extent that he becomes a chariot of the divine Presence.

And it goes without saying that he will also grasp that he has the possibility to draw the higher holiness down to material things. This can be done by means of acts of unification and combinations of names worthy of the Tabernacle and undertaken for the purpose of the presence of the *Sh'khinah* . . . .

Comment: Immediately following mention of the appointment of Bezalel and his assistant, Ohali'av, the master craftsmen to head the work on the Tabernacle (Exod 31:1–11), the Torah-text devotes several verses to the importance of the observance of the Seventh Day (Exod 31:12–17). The connection between those two passages is made clear in a single word,

---

72 *'Or ha-ḥayyim* on Gen 2:2–3.

Akh, understood here as "nevertheless" (Exod 31:13): even considering the importance of constructing the Tabernacle and all its artifacts, work involved in the making of the Tabernacle must not be done on the Seventh Day. The holiness of Shabbat takes precedence over that of the building and artistic embellishment of the Tabernacle.

The Kraków master, however, seeking a more intrinsic connection between those two passages, posited a distinct parallel between the Shabbat and the Tabernacle (*Mishkan*): the Tabernacle signifies the divine Presence in this lower world, and Shabbat, too, allows for an awareness and connection with God, even in this lower realm of being.

In the process, the preacher went on to present perhaps an even more striking connection between the Seventh Day which, according to the account in Genesis, culminated the week of creation, and every Shabbat. Creation—or more precisely, the evolution of the worlds from the all-encompassing Infinity of the *'Ein-sof*, based on conceptions spelled out in Lurianic Kabbalah—involves a distancing between the divine Root of all existence and between any and every existent being or object in the world. Shabbat, in contrast, allows for a renewed sense of connection with that Root. In that sense, every Shabbat is like the very first and serves the very same function.

Shabbat, the master explained, is nothing less than a miniscule example of the holiness of Divinity itself. The observance of the Shabbat allows a day each week on which we can reconnect with that from which we and the world necessarily became distanced as the condition of our very being. Ours is the experience both of absence and presence, and Shabbat is the key to a sense of presence.

In Kalonymus Kalman's comments upon the Creator's "becoming refreshed," that refreshment and renewal itself acquires a deeper meaning and resonance. It applies directly less to God than to ourselves as parts of a world that is necessarily distanced from our real Root. The real "refreshment" lies in expanding the dimensions of our awareness and consciousness beyond the limitations imposed by a necessary work-week and the pressing concerns with meeting the needs of life; these potentially create an existential distance from our true Root and Source and, hence, from our truer selves. In that sense, Kalonymus Kalman has likened Shabbat to a kind of homecoming following that unavoidable sense of alienation and distancing from our truer selves and our ultimate Root.

For Each Soul to Know Its Initial Location[73]

The First Man contained all the souls that were destined to come to the world.[74] Many of those were contained in the forehead of the First Man, and numerous souls were in his nose and in his lips and his eyes. And many souls were hanging from his beard. The purpose of divine worship is that each person might repair the root of his soul in terms of where (*'eifoh*) his soul was within the body of the First Man. This is what God asked Job, "Where (*'eifoh*) were you when I laid the earth's foundation?" (Job 38:4), meaning, where within the First Man was your soul? This is found in *Midrash rabbah* on this portion.[75]

The First Man was the place of all the souls, for had the First Man not sinned, he alone would have repaired everything according to the Will of God who created him precisely for that purpose, and there would have been no need to bring any other generations into existence. He would simply repair himself with all the souls that he encompassed. Only in the wake of his sin, the *Sh'virah* (cataclysm) transpired and with his sin, souls fell. It is only for this reason that there was need for other generations to come into being, so that every single soul might be repaired in terms of its original location within the First Man.

This is what King Solomon, may he rest in peace, said, "But, see, this I did find: God made men plain, but they have engaged in too much reasoning" (Eccl 7:29). The intent of the blessed Holy One was simply to form the First Man alone and he would then repair everything. As a consequence of his sin, however, it was necessary to bring forth many generations consisting of the souls that he himself had encompassed in order that each one might repair the particular root of his own soul. And that is the principal goal of the worship and service of God.

This is what the Holy One sought in Israel, namely the ability of each person to serve and discover himself in terms of his soul's location within the First Man and hence to repair his own soul-root. But if, God forbid, the divine Presence does not dwell among the Israelites, especially in this bitter exile, it will no longer be possible to locate one's original position and to repair it. And for this reason, (Moses) said: "How shall it be known *'eifo* (where) . . . ?" (Exod 33:16, as Moses pleads that God continue to

---

73. *Ma'or va-shemesh*, II, 31b.
74. *Tanḥ (P'kudei)* #3. Vital, *Sha'ar ha-gilgulim*, Int. 6.
75. *Midr. Exod.* 40:3.

accompany the Israelites on their way through the desert)—How will each of the Israelites locate his own soul in its precise location where it was situated within the First Man so that he might repair the root of his soul? Is it not in Your proceeding together with us, allowing Your Presence to dwell among us? Only then will each person be able to discover himself in order to repair his soul-root. And this is easy to comprehend.

Comment: The preacher here connected Moses' request that God continue to accompany Israel on its journey with a theme drawn from Lurianic Kabbalah and its worldview, a significant part of the lens through which Kolonymus Kalman viewed the text of the Torah. The midrashic passage to which the homily referred spoke of Adam as originally a lifeless mass (*golem*) which, however, contained all the souls which later descended from Adam, including that of Bezalel who was, even in that state, already destined to construct the Tabernacle.

The master himself constructed his reading of the primordial selection of Bezalel in the light of the Lurianic idea that each person whose soul was included within the soul of the First Man has, in terms of its location within that primordial figure, a particular quality that he must himself repair or fulfill; each has a unique task that only that particular person can accomplish. Behind this rather abstruse conception, the reader can, nevertheless, recognize a theme of undeniable significance to Kalonymus Kalman, namely the individuality and uniqueness of each person rooted in a place of depth within the self.

This very idea was expressed in mythic Lurianic terms as the unique position of one's soul within the soul and body of the First Adam. The same accent is heard distinctly in the kabbalistic theme that there is a specific interpretation of the Torah corresponding to each individual Jew, based upon the tradition that the number of (male) Israelites at Sinai corresponds to the number of letters in the Torah.[76]

K. E. Gronzinger, in a chapter entitled, "No One Else Could Enter Here, for This Door was Meant for You Alone,"[77] interestingly pointed to that same basic concept in the writings of Franz Kafka.

---

76. Hayyim Vital, *Sha'ar ha-gilgulim*, ch. 17. Scholem, *The Kabbalah and its Symbolism*, 64–65.

77. Grozinger, *Kafka and Kabbalah*, 46–50.

The Veil over Moses' Radiant Face[78]

"(Moses came down from Mount Sinai. And as Moses came down from the mountain bearing the two tablets of the Pact,) Moses was not aware that the skin of his face was radiant, since he had spoken with God. Aaron and all the Israelites saw and they shrank from coming near him. But Moses called to them, (and Aaron and all the chieftains in the assembly returned to him, and Moses spoke to them. Afterwards all the Israelites came near, and he instructed them concerning all that the Lord had imparted to him on Mount Sinai.) And when Moses had finished speaking with them, he put a veil over his face. Whenever Moses went in before the Lord to speak with Him, he would leave the veil off until he came out . . ." (Exod 34:29–34).

In examining the text carefully, certain questions arise. Who informed Moses that the skin of his face was radiant, so that he then placed a veil over it? Does it not say, in fact, that Moses did not know? And there is no mention of any person who informed him of such. And furthermore, why did he place the veil over his face? When speaking with Israel, he did not cover his face, for it is written that when Moses would come before the Lord to speak with Him, he removed the covering until he would leave, and he then left and spoke to the Israelites concerning that which he was commanded to relay to them, and only afterward he placed the veil on his face. Why afterward did he place the veil over his face? Would it not be proper and appropriate that the Israelites revere him when he is not speaking with them? And also one must understand the matter of the covering itself: what was it, and did he always go with his face covered like a bride? . . .

But it appears that one can explain this episode on the basis of its plain meaning, for it is known that God made man in His Image (Gen 9:6). What is the Image of God? It is known that the divine Names are *AHY'H, HVY'H, ADN'Y,* variants of God's revealing His Name ("I am") to Moses (Exod 3:14). And when a person hallows himself in all his 248 limbs and 365 sinews and walks in the path of holiness at all times, then those holy Names are present in his face, and that is actually the Image of God: the divine Names. And this is what is said, "And all the peoples of the earth shall see that the Lord's Name is proclaimed over you, and they shall stand in fear of you" (Deut 28:10), meaning that they will see the

---

78. *Ma'or va-shemesh,* II, 32a.

Ineffable Name actually engraved upon his face and will fear him. And certainly now in this generation, I have seen that a number of people have achieved that state, and people have remarked that they have seen the Ineffable Name engraved on some person's face.

And certainly in relation to Moses our Teacher, may he rest in peace, who so thoroughly purified himself, the Names of the holy Blessed One were actually present on his face. In *g'matria*, the (numerical values of the) letters of the Names *AHY'H*, *HVY'H*, *ADN'Y* add up to the equivalent of the letters in the word *masveih* (veil or covering). The people feared to approach him because his face was actually radiant. Only when Moses came before God, to speak with Him, the lights present in his face were then annulled as is a candle in the presence of a torch, for this is found in the Gemara: "To what can the righteous be likened in the presence of the *Sh'khinah*?—to a candle in the presence of a torch."[79] And so the veil was annulled from upon his face. But when he came before the Israelites, immediately the holiness that he acquired from the *Sh'khinah*, those Names which are equivalent to the values of the letters of the word, *masveih* (covering), were actually radiant. Those letters comprised the covering over his face. . . .

When he would speak with the Israelites, transmitting to them the divine Will as he had been commanded, he descended a certain degree from his own level, for a teacher/rabbi must contract his mind when he studies with pupils [a theme emphasized in the teachings and parables ascribed to Dov Baer, the Maggid of Mezherich, in reference to God and Torah].[80] For this reason, in speaking with Israel a measure of his brightness was removed, and so it is written, "And when Moses had finished speaking with them, he put a veil over his face," for immediately when he ceased speaking with them, that great brightness was again present in him.

Comment: Probing difficulties in the wording of the episode of Moses' radiant face upon his second descent from Mount Sinai, the master provided a rather unusual understanding of that account. Whereas the Torah presents Moses' radiance as something that took place concerning Moses alone at a specific point-in-time, Kalonymus Kalman tends to grasp that

---

79. b. Pesaḥ. 8a.

80. *Maggid d'varav l'Ya'akov*, 229, #132; *K'dushat Levi ha-shalem*, 278 (*le-Rosh hashanah*); Wineman, *The Hasidic Parable*, 52–55.

occurrence as something that is hardly so rare as the text would indicate. This exemplifies a broader tendency of the Hasidic homily to view the narrative in the Torah as alluding to what occurs beyond a one-time happening to suggest what can be recurrent in human experience. And perhaps of greater significance, the veil is understood not as a way of concealing that radiance but, rather, as an expression of the radiance itself.

The talmudic image of the vastly diminished light of a candle when in the presence of a torch occurs in a passage discussing the use of a candle in the search for unleavened bread-products prior to the *Pesaḥ* festival.[81] The subject in that passage does not relate to Moses' radiant face, but rather to God, as it refers to a verse from the prophet Habakkuk, ". . . His majesty covers the skies, His splendor fills the earth: It is a brilliant light which gives off light on every side . . ." (Hab 3:3–4). And the talmudic passage which asks to what are the righteous (*tzaddikim*) comparable before the presence of the *Sh'khinah*, answers with that analogy of the light of a candle in the presence of the much vaster brightness of a torch. Perhaps the preacher noted that the subject in that analogy is not Moses with his radiant countenance, but rather the *tzaddikim*. Furthermore, the same discussion in the Talmud also made reference to the verse from Proverbs, "The lifebreath (soul) of man is the lamp of the Lord" (Prov 20:27), the analogy referring, even more broadly, to humankind in general.

Like Moses in that one passage, which stands alone in all the Torah, Kalonymus Kalman viewed the *tzaddik* as one who has succeeded in thoroughly purifying his very body in all its aspects. He has, in that sense, gone beyond his own material, physical nature and has become essentially spiritual in character.

And like Moses, the *tzaddik* (understood here as the leader and center of a Hasidic community) cannot become fully apparent and known to his followers, for an essential gulf separates them. He is able to reveal to them some aspect of his understanding and spiritual awareness, but in relating to human beings who are not on his own level he cannot reveal his entire self and consciousness. He is like the teacher who must retreat to a certain degree from his own actual level and understanding for the purpose of communicating with his pupils on a level on which they are capable of comprehending. The complete radiance of his mind and its vision is not easily communicated to his followers, as the range of his own mystic mindset is likely beyond their ability to grasp and share.

---

81. *b. Pesaḥ.* 8a.

While Moses is depicted as one who "speaks with God," he also had to speak with human beings, and that, in fact, was essential to his role. And like Moses, similarly the *tzaddik* as a teacher and educator must remove something of his own radiance, toning down the impact of his mystic experience and consciousness so as not to erect a barrier between himself and those with whom he must communicate. The *tzaddik*'s removing that radiance implies that he must make the effort to present himself and his thinking on a level closer to the frame-of-reference of those with whom he is engaging in discussion and only in rare moments can he communicate what transcends the level of their norms and understanding.

The reader might well ponder to what extent was Kolonymus Kalman alluding to his own role as a communicator? To what degree was he conscious of his sharing only part of his own deeper grasp and understanding? And, in line with a larger theme in *Ma'or va-shemesh*, to what degree does that circumstance reflect something broader and more universal insofar as the depth within any individual defies communication?

Vayakhel

Exploring the Parallel between Creation and Tabernacle[82]

Our Sages said that at the hour that the blessed Holy One created the world, it continued expanding until He rebuked it and halted its expansion, as it is written, "I am *El Shaddai*" (Gen 17:1; 35:11), meaning, I am the one who said to the world, "Enough" (*dai*).[83]

This can be understood in that God realized that were the world to expand any further, it would bring about a degree of materialization in which it simply would not be possible for man to turn and connect himself with his Root, the blessed Infinite One, and for this reason God said to His world, "Enough!" For God's chief delight is in man's purifying his very physicality and his choosing the good and connecting to his Root.

And so for this purpose, the blessed Holy One brought down the holiness of Shabbat, an unbounded legacy,[84] a spiritual expansion free of any materiality whatsoever. For had the material expansion continued even just a tiny degree more, it would never have been possible at any future time for the holiness of Shabbat, as a spiritual expansion, to be revealed. And for this reason God said to His world, "Enough" (*dai*), that it might expand only to the point at which it could still allow for the possibility of grasping the spirituality of Shabbat.

And this is as the Sages said, "Shabbat entered as a hair-breadth,"[85] meaning that on Shabbat God established a boundary allowing only a limited space for materialization beyond which it could not continue to expand. By means of the holiness of Shabbat, materiality, even on the

---

82. *Ma'or va-shemesh*, II, 35b–36a.
83. b. Ḥag. 12a.
84. b. Šabb. 118a.
85. *Midr. Gen* 10:9.

weekdays, would lack the power to further expand, for something of the holiness of Shabbat sparkles even during the work-days. And this explains why God created the world with the Name ʾ*El Shaddai*, saying to His world, "Enough" (*dai*), so that it would not expand further to acquire an even more physical character.

The principle intent in the creation of the world was that God's Presence be located in this lower world. Nevertheless, with the destructive nature of the deeds and evil actions of the generation of the flood and that of the dispersion (following the Tower of Babel), the divine Presence departed[86] and its disclosure was concealed. Still later, with the giving of the Torah the impurity ceased,[87] allowing for a resumption of the divine disclosure and Presence below, although degeneration again occurred to a serious degree with the making of the golden calf. And in that way, a wall of partition barring divine disclosure emerged.

And for that reason God commanded to build the Tabernacle (*Mishkan*) with all its artifacts in order that the divine Presence might dwell within it and manifest His Divinity among the Israelites, as it says, "... that I may dwell among them" (Exod 25:8). And with the Tabernacle, the divine intent to be present within the world would be truly fulfilled.

For this reason it is said that the Tabernacle was constructed according to the pattern of creation, for with the erection of the Tabernacle, the original intention expressed in creation would be realized. And for this same reason it was necessary to construct the Tabernacle with profound intent, to impact it with a deep spirituality so that no aspect of it would become materialized to the point at which its physical state would not allow for the Tabernacle's greater spirituality. In this sense the making of the Tabernacle precisely parallels the creation of the world. For if its physical character had expanded even an infinitesimal amount at the expense of its spiritual meaning, the very intent expressed in the Tabernacle would have been defeated.

As God gave Bezalel "skill, ability, and knowledge" (Exod 31:3), he knew exactly how to impact the necessary spirituality to the Tabernacle and to every single one of its implements without its material aspect reaching the point at which it could not support its spiritual purpose. And this is what our Sages indicated in their statement that Bezalel knew how to combine the letters with which heaven and earth were created, as

---

86. *Midr. Gen* 19:7.
87. *b. Šabb.* 146a.

well as the meaning of the midrash concerning his name, *b'tzeil Shaddai* ("in the shadow of the Divine"),[88] for he brought a halt to the materialization of the Tabernacle just as the Creator halted the materialization of the world. . . .

Comment: Building upon elements within the Torah-text and upon interpretations found principally in rabbinic sources, the preacher, in this passage, evoked a sense of Bezalel as much more than a skilled and knowledgeable builder and artist. The Tabernacle, to his mind, was not an ordinary building project, even as it remained, on one level, a physical object. Its physicality, however, could easily get out-of-bounds and override its spiritual character and meaning. Bezalel's determination that such not happen has to do not with architectural blueprints and the execution of building projects according to such plans, but rather with the realm of the craftman's intent.

Within the dialectic involved in this passage, Bezalel emerges as a sage fully aware of the tension, even the very sharp tension, between the spiritual and the material character of any edifice or similar project. Such an endeavor could pass the muster of design and execution and, nevertheless, fail as to its real purpose. This homily defined Bezalel's core concern as preventing the Tabernacle from becoming subject to the materialization potentially inherent in everything in the world.

The parallel that had been suggested between Bezalel, the master craftsman, and God in His role as Creator is here defined in terms of their shared concern for setting bounds in order to prevent a materialization of their respective works. The Kraków preacher raised the Tabernacle to a very high level where, unlike on our plane of things, everything rests upon the quality of the intent of its builder. In that sense, the core-Hasidic emphasis upon inner intent recast the biblical Tabernacle in its own image.

The Joy of Giving[89]

> "Thus the Israelites, all the men and women whose hearts moved them to bring anything for the work that the Lord, through

---

88. *b. Ber.* 55a.
89. *Ma'or va-shemesh*, II, 36b.

Moses, had commanded to be done, brought it as a freewill offering to the Lord." (Exod 35:29)

This verse would appear to be quite superfluous, for along with all the other verses detailing the contributions, the text already spelled out the response of the people, "And everyone who excelled in ability and everyone whose spirit moved him came, bringing to the Lord his offering for the work of the Tent of Meeting and for all its service and for the sacred vestments. Men and women, all whose hearts moved them, all who would make a wave-offering of gold to the Lord, came bringing brooches, earrings, rings, and pendants—gold objects of all kinds" (Exod 35:21–22). Why, then, is this verse (Exod 35:29) even necessary?

The import of this verse, however, might be understood by noting its very wording: "The Israelites . . . brought a freewill offering to the Lord." Our Sages said that one who explains the *mitzvah* to send off the mother-bird before taking her young (Deut 22:6–7) purely as a matter of mercy is to be silenced, for he fails to understand the passage simply as a divine decree. And we also find in the Gemara that one should not say "I have no desire to eat of the flesh of a pig," but rather "I have desire for such, but the Holy One has forbidden it."[90] For while there are several transgressions which are themselves acts that people naturally detest, a person's proper motivation for not transgressing should not be his viewing the act as detestable; rather, one must make a break with that natural tendency and obey the law purely because it is something which the King has forbidden of his servants.

Similarly, there are several prohibitions which would be obligated simply on the basis of intelligence alone, but one should desist from the act not on that basis but rather because it is a command of the blessed Creator who, as Lord over His servants, forbade the thing. . . .

This is true in regard to all the *mitzvot*. But the mitzvah of *tz'dakah* (charity and charitable deeds) follows a different pattern. It is human nature to love much money and to pursue money, and in that sense it is counter to human nature to do something resulting in a loss of money through *tz'dakah*. For this reason the Torah commands in connection with the *mitzvah* of *tz'dakah*, "Give to (your needy kinsman) readily and have no regrets when you do so . . ." (Deut 15:10), for human nature is such that a person resists giving money, thereby decreasing one's own

---

90. *b. Ber.* 33b on *m. Ber.* 5:3, *Sipra* on Lev 20:26, and Rashi's comment on the same verse.

funds. For this reason, it is necessary for a person to shatter that aspect of his nature so that not only will he not feel any regret in giving, but that he will give with love. And that, indeed, is something very difficult.

But there is a greater level of *tz'dakah* among exceptional people, those who, every moment, actually look forward to a poor person coming in need of financial help or of some other charitable deed. And when the blessed Holy One provides for them an opportunity to engage in *tz'dakah*, they experience an exceedingly great joy, as though God has given them a good gift.

And so we find in the Zohar [building upon the paradoxical language in Exod 35:5, "Take—*kaḥ*—from among you gifts to the Lord...," and connecting the verse with Isa 58:7] that the coming of a poor person is a gracious gift to the master of the house,[91] for the opportunity to give *tz'dakah* is a gift from God to one who is deserving of that *mitzvah* to feed the hungry and clothe the naked and to assist brides and orphans at their weddings. And so such a person praises and extols the Creator for choosing him to be able to fulfill such *mitzvot*.[92]

And this is the meaning of the verse quoted above, indicating that the Israelites gave their contributions for the Tabernacle with a joyous and beneficent heart. And in connection with their offering, they thanked the blessed Holy One for giving them the opportunity and merit of performing this *mitzvah*. "The Israelites ... brought it as a freewill offering to the Lord"—they viewed their act of bringing an offering as a divine gift given to them and were grateful that God chose them for this deed.

Comment: The Zohar already connected the wording of the command to make willing contributions toward the building of the Tabernacle with one's providing assistance to a poor, needy person. Maintaining the same connection, the Kraków preacher, in this passage, brought to light a moral gem within the Jewish ethical tradition, revealing the paradoxical character of *tz'dakah* as a person views the very need and opportunity to give as a divine gift. In that sense, one who gives is the real beneficiary as he receives a greater kind of gift. This example, along with others throughout the collection, reveals the master's fondness for such paradoxical relationships.

---

91. Zohar, II, 198a.

92. Also Zohar, I, 104a, *Sefer ha-yashar*, ch. 13, also *The Zohar*, tr. Matt, VI, 127, n. 57.

Bezalel and Humility[93]

Work on the Tabernacle required an especially high level of holiness and purification. These were required so that those involved could engage in the acts of unification in their work; only in that spirit could they prepare a dwelling place for God's very Presence, bringing to concrete fulfillment the very intent of creation itself.

And certainly a person whom God has mercifully designated as qualified for such work would be one who is as nothing in his own eyes, one feeling even that he is unworthy of that role. For God would not approve for that role a person having a high self-estimation or even one who considers himself capable of working on such a high level. As was said concerning Moses our Teacher, all that he merited was due to his deep humility in that he regarded himself as unworthy of God's revealing Himself to him. . . .

And when Bezalel and the others gifted with a heart of wisdom saw that they were selected by God in connection with this holy work, they added holiness upon holiness and worshipful deed upon worshipful deed, because they still did not feel themselves adequate, in terms of their skill and intelligence, to construct a Tabernacle for the very Presence of God. And, moreover, they succeeded in extending their own holiness and willingness of heart to all the people of Israel. While they were pounding with hammers and other implements of their labor, the fire of their love and of their willingness of heart entered into all the Israelites who were then drawn to bring still more and more.

Comment: As the Tablernacle was not an ordinary building-project, it required qualities beyond those of technical and artistic skill. Accordingly, Bezalel the designer and builder is here painted as a moral and spiritual model, one who paradoxically merited his role precisely because he believed himself unworthy of that very role. Once again, a striking element of paradox colors the homilist's reading of what might otherwise appear to be a highly prosaic account.

---

93. *Ma'or va-shemesh*, II, 37ab.

P'kudei

An Accountant of the Spirit[94]

Moses was the sole treasurer for the work on the Tabernacle, as no one else would be able to measure in his mind the extent of the holiness and the unifications (acts of deep devotion aimed at a unification of the spiritual reality underlying all existence) represented in the response and contributions of the Israelites. Moses alone would understand the extent and value of their thoughts and inner intentions. Nevertheless, Moses went to Bezalel to gain a clearer estimation and saw that more was contributed than was needed for the construction of the Tabernacle, though he could already see in his own mind that there was already an abundance of holiness beyond what was required.

And he said before the blessed Holy One, "Master of the world, we have constructed the Tabernacle and we have garnered together greater holiness in connection with the contributions offered than could be utilized. What shall we do with the surplus?" God confirmed that the excess holiness evoked by the Israelites' response exceeded the need at this time. He told Moses, "Place the vast holiness and love and awe and enthusiasm within the Torah, in those portions relating to the Making of the Tabernacle. For the Torah is called testimony [*'edut*, as in 'the Ark of Testimony' (Exod 25:22), and in *g'matria* the total numerical value of the letters comprising the word *'edut* is equivalent to those in the word *talmud* [study; the letters of each word add up to 480].... When Israel occupies itself with the Torah-portions relating to the Tabernacle, they will then have the strength to continue to garner holiness from the higher spheres that were actually awakened through the Making of the Tabernacle."

---

94. *Ma'or va-shemesh*, II, 38a.

And Moses did just that. In writing the Torah, he placed within our holy Torah itself the tremendous holiness represented by Israel's willingness to contribute, in order that when we engage in studying those portions centering on the Making of the Tabernacle, we might awaken our hearts to draw upon us the presence of the *Sh'khinah* and to evoke in us acts of unification that were achieved from that time on.

Comment: While the subject of the Torah-text in this portion is the excess materials contributed for the construction of the Tabernacle, spelled out concretely in terms of the kinds of material as well as their quantity, that fact, intrinsic to the passage, is radically altered in the above homily of Kalonymus Kalman. Almost in a kind of magician's act, the passage with its mathematical accounts, necessarily concerning what is *quantitative* and measurable, is transferred to a very different wavelength where it pertains to what is purely *qualitative* in nature.

The Kraków preacher would instinctively seek in the text what transcends any kind of material subject and measurements, transcending the world of numbers itself, and would hear—or overhear—in it a statement concerning the realm of human innerness, devotion and intent. Echoing the original call for "every person whose heart so moves him" (Exod 25:2) to bring gifts, in the Kraków master's explanation what is measured is not the amount of excess materials, but rather the depth of that willingness of heart. That kind of transformation is the achievement not of a magician, but of an artist who severs a passage from its own context and substitutes for it a much more sublime context.

One part of the homily makes a passing reference to a midrashic passage[95] which raised the question what to do with the surplus materials contributed toward the building of the Tabernacle. The answer suggested in that much earlier source was to utilize them to construct a second Tabernacle beyond the confines of the camp. We note that in the above homily, Kalonymus Kalman repeated the very same question while he refashioned the response in a very different and remarkable direction. The surplus of materials listed in the Torah-portion symbolizes, for the homilist, the spiritual power expressed in the people's "willingness of heart" which is then deposited in the corresponding chapters of the Torah; that same spiritual energy can then be experienced—in non-quantitative terms—by those studying those very chapters.

95. *Midr. Exod.* 51:2; *Tanḥ.* (*P'kudei*) #5; Ginzberg, *Legends*, 3:177, n. 369.

Presumably anyone, with or without a calculator, might be able to add up the quantity of the excess materials. But the homily would presume that only Moses could grasp and measure the "excess of inner motivation." This kind of transformation from the quantitative to the qualitative, from what is material in nature to what is inner in character, is symptomatic of the interpretative art in Kalonymus Kalman's readings of the toraitic text and in kindred Hasidic texts. A reference relating to the field of *things* becomes an insight into the field of inner intent and devotion. For the material context found in the toraitic passage, a much more sublime context is provided, and the inspiring effect of that substitution exemplifies the art of the homilist perhaps at it highest peak.

3

On the Third Book of the Torah
(*Vayikra* / Leviticus)

Vayikra
The Implications of Humankind's Uniqueness[1]

"(In God's mind) "Israel arose first" (before all other aspects of creation).[2] This was the case so that the Israelites might unify the Glory of God's kingdom, a kingdom encompassing all the worlds, raising them upward to the blessed Infinite One. Unification of this nature requires binding together all the worlds, all that was created in this lower world and all four worlds [*'Atzilut, B'ri'ah, Y'tzirah,* and *'Asiyah,* the four planes of existence in the Kabbalistic world-picture] and elevating them all to their Source. For they were all hewn from the simple Oneness that is their Source. And of all living things of a physical nature, man alone is able to realize that (likening the world to a palace) "there is no palace without one who owns the palace."[3]

Humankind is able to connect all the worlds and all forms of life to the Light of the blessed Infinite One, connecting with that Light all that his mind, together with his senses of sight and hearing and of taste and smell, can attain....

And underlying the sacrifices, offered when the Temple was standing, is this very idea of connecting the created animals to their Root, so that all that exists becomes connected with God, sweetening the Judgments at their root and allowing kindness and good influences to be drawn upon the people of Israel.... Through the offerings of cattle and sheep, it is possible to connect even animality itself to the Infinite One....

1. *Ma'or va-shemesh*, III, 2a.
2. *Midr. Gen* 1:5.
3. *Midr. Gen* 39:1.

Comment: The third book of the Torah opens with instructions concerning sacrificial offerings, chiefly offerings of cattle, sheep, and birds. The Kraków master read those biblical laws in a way that refracts a vision of the oneness of all existence, a oneness that, on one level, is less a fact than an aspiration. The animals (*b'heimot*) serving as sacrificial offerings connote, in his homilies, the quality of *b'hemi'ut* ("animality"), which is subhuman but which also serves a role in the penitential process through the bringing of sacrificial offerings. *B'hemi'ut* suggests that which, in character, is furthest from the nature of the divine Oneness and its Light but which also exists within the human being.

In this way, the sacrificial animal-offerings become a language for lifting up to the divine Oneness that very animality within a person, including his urges and responses and egotistical actions. Everything, including every aspect of our being, must be raised to connect with the Divine, and in this process of uplifting, those impulses become redeemed to find their rightful place in the economy of holy living. With the understanding that the animals that were to be offered upon the altar represent animality itself, the Kraków master explained the sacrificial ritual symbolically as a way to redeem such animality by raising it to its divine Source.

Kolonymus Kalman's comments go on to liken each person required to bring a penitential offering to the very First Man in that each such person has the capacity to repair the First Man's primordial sin.

Every Person Is as the First Man[4]

> "When any of you [*'adam*, a human] presents an offering . . . to the Lord . . . ." (Lev 1:2)

Rashi already pointedly asked, why does this verse speak of *'adam* (humankind) rather than simply *'ish* ("a man")? Perhaps it is because the one who brings an offering must first humble himself and engage in complete repentance, thinking that, God forbid, through his sinful act he has brought on a guilty verdict for the whole world. A rabbinic saying has it that a person should always regard himself as half worthy and half guilty . . . and in his doing a *mitzvah* he might alter the verdict to one of merit for the entire world.[5]

---

4. *Ma'or va-shemesh*, III, 2a.
5. *b. Qidd.* 40b; also Maimonides, *Mishne torah, Hilkhot t'shuvah*, 3:4.

The sin of the First Man, though unintentional, was nevertheless of the utmost gravity. As he was the first of all those to come to the world, through his sin he cast a judgment of guilt extending to the end of all the generations. For this reason, his is considered a severe sin, and the man who offers a sacrifice for his own sin should consider, in his mind, that his own sin similarly effects the lot of the entire world. And for this reason he should bring his offering in humility and complete repentance. In doing so, he will repair the nature of the sin of the First Man.

And that is why the verse speaks of 'adam: the person needing to bring the penitential offering should consider that his own sin has import and consequence for all the world (just like the sin of the First Man). Accordingly, he should first repent sincerely and wholly and with absolute humility. If so, then afterward, in his bringing his offering, he brings about a meritorious verdict for the entire world and repairs the sin of the First Man. . . .

Comment: Kabbalah, in which Hasidism is rooted, placed much greater emphasis upon the sin of the First Man than does rabbinic teaching. And the theme of that primordial sin appears in several of the homilies of Kalonymus Kalman, including the above passage.

One notes here both the recurrent repercussions of the sin of the First Man (Adam) along with the duty of every person to repair that primordial sin. In some sense, that initial sin is constantly repeated with its grave consequences, and with that understanding, it is no longer read as a past occurrence, but as an ever-present possibility. And of equal significance, that status as an ever-present possibility applies also to the repair of the primordial sin which lies within the reach of each and every person. Each and every person has the capacity and the opportunity to repair the primordial sin, and in that sense every person is the First Person (*'Adam ha-rishon*).

Tzav

The Fire to be Kept Burning upon the Altar[6]

> "The Lord spoke to Moses, saying: Command Aaron and his sons thus: This is the ritual of the burnt offering: The burnt offering itself shall remain where it is burned upon the altar all night until morning, while the fire on the altar is kept going on it." (Lev 6:1–2)

... From the fire that is kept burning on the altar, we can grasp that even though we are forbidden to kindle fire on Shabbat, ... it is, nevertheless, a *mitzvah* to keep the fire burning on the altar even on Shabbat, for that fire is from a high root and from a holy place.[7]

... The entire intention of Pharaoh was that the letters indicating mercy not give light and hence have impact within the letters of the divine Name. In that case, the force of judgment and punishment would not be challenged and the Israelites would remain in exile under his rule. But when God saw that the Israelites were drowning within the fiftieth gate (of impurity) from which they would never be able to rise, He brought down the light of the fifty gates of holiness, which are gates of repentance, equivalent to the World of Thought (a level deeper and higher than that of speech). In this way, the external, demonic forces would no longer be empowered, and Israel then went forth from Egypt. For this reason, they were commanded to take a *seh*, a lamb or a kid, the word consisting of the first letters of the two words, *sha'arei ha- t'shuvah*, "the gates of repentance." [Depending upon the specific word and its vocalization, the same letter can be pronounced either as *s* or *sh* (as *sin* or *shin*).]

---

6. *Ma'or va-shemesh*, III, 3a.
7. Note *b. Šabb.* 87b, and *Pirqe R. El.* ch. 53

Comment: The fire burning on the altar came to connote a depth of feeling and passion, a connection emphasized in *No'am 'Elimelekh*, in which the everlasting fire on the altar alludes to an inner enthusiasm kindled within the heart of the priest.[8] But not all passionate feelings are positive or desirable, and heated emotions and contention can have disastrous consequences. The sacred fire is differentiated from other kinds of intense emotions including those associated with Pharaoh's intent.

The Torah is spoken of as fire, *'eish dat lamo* (Deut 33:2) and even God is referred to as "a consuming fire" (Deut 4:24). A talmudic agada, however, depicts the Evil Inclination, source of impure passion, as a pillar of fire.[9] Not all fire is light!

The homily on this portion appears more as a random collection of topics rather than as a cohesive discourse. Beginning with the portion *Tzav*, which concerns various kinds of sacrificial offerings and the fire upon the altar, the preacher hastened to connect that reading with its position in the calendar as read (depending on the year) on the Shabbat prior to *Pesaḥ*, the festival commemorating the exodus from Egyptian bondage. This explains his turning to the *seh*, the young animal of the herd, which each Hebrew family was to prepare just days before the actual going-out from Egypt (Exod 12:3). The import resulting from that rather flimsy connection allows an understanding of the exodus as a form of repentance. In this vein, the homilist explained that the exodus itself could occur only through the possibility of repentance on a depth-level, and on a still deeper level, the liberation from bondage itself comes to be understood as a process of repentance (*t'shuvah*).

---

8. *No'am 'Elimelekh* on Lev 6:2 and also on *T'tzavveh*.
9. b. *Qidd.* 81a.

Sh'mini

The Inner Experience at the Core of a Cultic Act[10]

The eighth day of the consecration rite (initiating the priests, Aaron and his sons, into their cultic role) was intended as an atonement for the making of the golden calf and as a revelation of the divine Presence (within the Tabernacle).

It is known that the economic worth of a sacrifice is indicative of the severity of the sin for which it comes to atone: a severe sin would require a large sacrifice, while a slighter sin would require only a smaller sacrifice. This is made clear in an incident found in the Zohar concerning a person commanded to bring a cow as a burnt offering to atone for a thought and who grasped, in this way, the actual severity of his sinful thought, as he not only immediately vowed never to repeat his sinful reflection but, in addition, became a very devout person.[11]

And so, on the eighth day, when Aaron himself would actually participate in the rite of atonement, Moses called to him, instructing him concerning the procedure to be followed. He told him, "Take a calf of the herd for a sin offering (and a ram for a burnt offering, without blemish, and bring them before the Lord," Lev 9:2), for from the type of sacrifice imposed upon him as an atonement, Aaron would be able to grasp the real extent of his iniquity (in connection with the Making of the Golden Calf). Moses then commanded the Israelites, in contrast, to bring a relatively smaller offering, for after their witnessing the graver expression of repentance and the humble submission in Aaron's offering, they proceeded to bring their own offerings in the very same spirit. The requirement of Aaron's larger offering was to bring the people-at-large to

10. *Ma'or va-shemesh*, III, 3b-4b.
11. Zohar, III, 9a.

a sense of humble submission, as in witnessing Aaron's repentance and humility they grasped the severity of their own sin.

... During the first seven days (of the consecration-ritual), Moses himself served in a priestly role prior to Aaron's functioning as a priest. One can understand the change in their roles in terms of a parable of the beasts that disobeyed and angered their king, the lion. The animals feared for their very lives and could not bring themselves to approach their king. But the fox, the wisest of the beasts, deceitfully convinced the other animals to accompany him to speak to their king: he would speak on their behalf as he knew hundreds of parables (which would elicit a forgiving response from the lion). After proceeding for part of the journey to the lion-king, however, the fox turned around and told them that he now forgot one-hundred of his fables and would have to suffice with those he remembered. The same thing happened somewhat later as he forgot another hundred parables. And upon coming still nearer to the king's court, he told them that he has forgotten all of his fables, and so each animal would now have to speak for itself.[12]

Similarly Moses, bringing the people before God, explained to them that each person must himself bring an offering as atonement in order to be spared a punishment of death (and they cannot depend upon the leader's doing this on their behalf). [The same parable of the fox and the lion-king appears in "The limits of relying upon one's leader" on *parashat Vayeilekh* in connection with the imminent death of Moses.]

Moses never continued afterward to serve in a priestly capacity, something we may understand through a rabbinic comment that he served with a white tunic (*ḥalik*) without a border.[13] Moses himself was without any guilt whatsoever in the making of the golden calf, and consequently the atonement for that episode could not be brought about through him, the white *ḥalik* indicating that he was thoroughly innocent. Only one who acts with a sense of his own guilt and feels a personal need for atonement can bring others to a state of atonement; anyone else would lack the necessary sense of humble submission (*hakhna'ah*) which necessarily requires a sense of one's own personal need for atonement....

Aaron himself (in the episode of the making of the golden calf) sinned neither in the realm of his thinking nor in that of his action, as his intent was solely for the sake of God and was not based at all on personal

---

12. *Midr. Gen* 78:7.
13. *b. Taʿan.* 11b.

considerations. [This view reflects a justification of Aaron's motivations found in the Midrash.[14]] But atonement (and its ritual expression in the form of a sacrificial offering) was nevertheless required of him for his action for the reason that no other person could have known his motivation, and so in that sense his action involved a (potential) ḥillul ha-Shem, a Profanation of the Name of God, requiring atonement.

... His true atonement was achieved not in his offering a sacrifice, but rather in his utter amazement and shock concerning his own deed and in his determination, in his own heart, never to repeat such a foolish action and in his humbling himself before his Creator concerning what he had done. And the actual offering served merely to complete the process of atonement.

And we find in holy writings that when a person comes before the priests of God to seek atonement, prior to his offering his sacrifice the priests are to strive to humble the sinner so that he might repent with all his heart. They signal to the Levites who begin singing as a way of awakening his sense of a broken heart through their pleasant voices. And only then is the person's offering given and accepted.

... And in this manner, when the Temple and its altar were standing and functioning and the priest served there, bringing the people to atonement, both the Levites and the priests (kohanim) were able to know the actual thoughts of such people, knowing whether or not they had truly and sincerely undergone inner change. And if the priests and Levites realized that they had not succeeded in moving their hearts to the intense degree required for complete repentance, the priest would then find a way to signal to the Levites, who would proceed further to provide music to awaken the person to a true and complete repentance. This is brought out in *Sefer b'rit m'nuḥah* [a Spanish kabbalistic text of uncertain authorship, often ascribed to Avraham ben Isaac of Granada, fourteenth century] ...

Comment: In his reading the details of the eight-day consecration-ritual initiating Aaron and his sons into the priesthood, Kalonymus Kalman specifically read the priestly function and the role of the priests with an accent not on the details and forms of sacrificial worship themselves, but upon the inner intent and experience he believed to be central in that ritual-system. Hasidism's basic thrust upon innerness and inner intent radiates

---

14. *Midr. Exod.* 41.5; *Pirqe R. El.* ch. 45.

this rendition. The forms of any system of worship can easily become ends in themselves, as a preoccupation with detail can avert attention from the deeper meaning of the rite. The preacher, it would appear, was clearly aware of that danger involved in any type of ritual behavior, as he went to great lengths to emphasize what was to transpire precisely within the consciousness of the person bringing the sacrificial gift to the altar.

In this homiletical discourse, the Kraków master envisioned in the rite and in its various aspects a way to touch the heart of the person bringing the offering. The priest (*kohen*), he maintained, was capable of perceiving the person's inner thoughts and state-of-mind and hence could know whether or not the person bringing a sacrifice was truly penitent. In his descriptive portrayal of the rite, the priest utilizes the services of the Levites (*Levi'im*) who, through the music they provide, were able, when necessary, to deepen the contrition of the person bringing such a sacrificial offering. In the Torah, the *Levi'im* who served the priests (*kohanim*) engaged in manual tasks such as taking the Tabernacle apart and carrying the artifacts as the camp folds up and moves to a new location in the desert. Only considerably later, in the Second Temple period, did the *Levi'im* become associated with a musical role in the Temple-ritual. In this homily, or more accurately in the text from which Kalonymus Kalman drew, the *Levi'im* utilized their musical skills to awaken the person's contrition.

Elsewhere, too, in *Ma'or va-shemesh*, the preacher emphasized the role of music in impacting a person's consciousness, touching a person at a very deep place within the self. That emphasis likely reflects the role which the *niggun*, often a chant without words, occupies in Hasidic prayer-life. And more broadly, the Kraków master attributed to music and song the power both to touch a person's heart and to voice one's depth of consciousness more adequately than can words.

Tazriʿa

On Laws of Purity and Impurity[15]

(In reference to the animals that are permitted for food,) if you eat them, you should do so only in a spirit of holiness and purity, in which case even from the animals and their earthiness and physicality, holiness comes into being. For everything, including even the animals, becomes attached to what is above, to *ḥayot ha-kodesh* (the beasts bearing the divine Chariot in the angelic world, referring to the vision in Ezek 1) . . . . As the righteous, holy person connects all that is earthly and physical to that which is higher, so the very beasts and animals and fowl which are consumed as food here below become attached to what is of a higher level.

Furthermore, the very order of the regulations as found in the book of Leviticus corresponds to the four bearers of the Chariot (in Ezek 1) which bear the image of a lion, an ox, an eagle and a human. The image of the man is mentioned last, because precisely by means of the human *tzaddik*, everything below connects with what is on a higher plane. Similarly in the order of creation (Gen 1), those animals preceded the human, for all is "sweetened" (redeemed) by man who becomes a *tzaddik* and attaches all that is below to what is above and, in the process, draws down beneficial influence from higher realms to this lower world. And understand this.

In the *Tikkunim*[16] and the holy Zohar,[17] it is explained that if not for the sin of the First Man, we would have no need to distinguish between what is forbidden and permitted, between what is proper and what is improper, between purity and impurity and, instead, we would be able to learn the

---

15. *Maʾor va-shemesh*, III, 6a–7a.
16. *Tikkunei ha-zohar*, ed. Margoliot, 99a.
17. Zohar, I, 53a.

innerness of the Torah directly. But due to the sin of the First Man, good and evil became fused together causing confusion, and consequently we are required to separate ourselves from forbidden and impure foods in order to separate out the proper food from the waste and worthless element and to elevate the holy Sparks (imprisoned within the latter).

. . . In our world or plane of existence (*ʿAsiyah*), what is impure is much more abundant than is proper food. Moving upward from one realm of existence to another, each plane consists of progressively greater holiness and less waste and confusion or fusion of the holy with the impure. And in the highest of the four worlds, *ʾAtzilut*, only the holy exists and there is no waste-element whatsoever. Consequently, one whose soul is from that world of *ʾAtzilut* is not prone to sin, for the *Sitra ʾaḥra* (the evil force manifesting impurity, the antithesis of what is holy), has no power or presence there.

And corresponding to those four worlds are four dimensions of Torah. The simple, surface level of the Torah corresponds to our world, *ʿAsiyah*, while the dimension of *d'rush* [exemplified in Midrash which explicates the Torah-text in a way that reveals further meanings generally associated with rabbinic Judaism] corresponds to the next higher world, *Y'tzirah*. Proceeding further upward, the level of intimations in the Torah corresponds to the world of *B'riʾah*, while the secrets or mysteries of Torah (mystic wisdom) correspond to the highest world, *ʾAtzilut*.

And corresponding to those four dimensions of Torah are the layers of soulfulness in the human being: *nefesh, ruʾaḥ, n'shamah* and *y'ḥidah*. The lowest of those, *nefesh* (which humans share with animals and) which gravitates toward material desires, corresponds to this world of *ʿAsiyah* in which man must make the effort to purify his soul, separating himself from forbidden foods and other forms of impurity, including even those based only on rabbinic interpretation, and he must refrain from causing blemish with his limbs and eyes and mouth, for their proper use is crucial for the repair of his soul. A person can acquire the next higher level of *ruʾaḥ* only by guarding his behavior in all those areas, and in this way he is able to deepen his understanding of the Torah.

. . . But without first repairing the self on the level of the plain, surface meanings of Torah and their midrashic readings, one will not find his way to understand what is intimated in the Torah. Without guarding oneself from forbidden foods and taking heed in matters of purity and impurity, a person cannot progress in his pathway through Torah, for each person consists of aspects of all the worlds.

3—(Vayikra / Leviticus)

... The blessed Holy One, of course, would be able to draw down all the beneficial influences (alone, without need for our own effort in that process). However, in creating the world it was His will that all such beneficial influences be drawn down through an awakening from below (*hit'aruta d'letata*). In this way, man can awaken himself from below and purify himself from all materialistic seeking and connect the lower with the higher levels, longing to attain the divine blessings, and awakening the process of drawing down the higher lights through the efforts of the Assembly (people) of Israel [identified also with *Malkhut/Sh'khinah*, the lowest of the ten *s'firot* in the kabbalistic worldview] as a woman who longs for and arouses her husband [allusion to the Blessed Holy One].

Before the blessed holy One created the world, when the very thought of creating the world arose in His simple Will in order to bring blessing to His creatures, there was a sexual oneness (neither masculine nor feminine), requiring no one to awaken and arouse the other. After He created the world, however, all the good influences are drawn down through an awakening from below which succeeds in uniting the higher with the lower worlds.

Comment: The master felt the need to relate, or at least reconcile, the laws of levitical purity and impurity found in the third book of the Torah with the deeper and higher mystic wisdom that he associated with the Torah's inner character. Challenged by a sense of a gulf separating the two, one of which appears to relate to seemingly external matters, while the other more directly relates to what is sublime, he sought to overcome that polarity.

Following teachings found in the Zohar and in later Kabbalah, the preacher explained that the collection of laws found in this part of the Torah became necessary only due to a failure in the original plan of creation. And given the consequence of that failure, in our own complex reality, we are able to attain that higher wisdom, the innerness of the Torah, only by careful adherence to laws based on categories of purity and impurity. For the larger context of this theme in post-Zoharic kabbalah, Pinchas Giller points to the view that the sin of Adam, together with the generations of rabbinic casuistry, brought about a fusion of darkness with the purity of the higher *s'firot*, resulting in a complicated struggle between the holy and unholy.[18]

It becomes apparent, however, that the more difficult course, necessitated by the primordial sinful act on the part of the First Man (Adam),

---

18. Giller, *The Enlightened Shall Shine*, 40, 77.

is required for a more basic consideration. It is of the nature of the Kabbalistic cosmos that we can reach the higher strata of existence not directly, but only via the lower strata—hence the concept of *hit'aruta d'letata*. And, as brought out in the above passage, the phenomenon of sexual intercourse is thought to represent and symbolize that relationship between the higher and lower realms of being. That conception echoes in the understanding that we can connect with the sublime spiritual reality only via the way we relate to the Divine in our more complicated everyday world and its needs.

The Affliction of Pride and False Piety[19]

"When a person has on the skin of his body a swelling, a rash, or a discoloration, and it develops into a scaly affection on the skin of his body, it shall be reported to Aaron the priest or to one of his sons, the priests. (The priest shall examine the affection on the skin of his body: if hair in the affected patch has turned white and the affection appears to be deeper than the skin of his body, it is a leprous affection; when the priest sees it, he shall pronounce him unclean." Lev 13:1–3.)

It seems to me that when the awe of God begins to sparkle in a person's heart, the person experiences a powerful drive to serve God, igniting in his heart a fiery torch to engage in the Will of the Creator and he experiences a brightening within him. This, however, can activate his imagination to sin against the Maker (alliteration: *masi'o ha—yetzer*—inclination—*laḥ'to la-yotzer*—Maker) by his thinking of himself as a righteous and holy person of a high level. Having some small degree of enthusiastic attachment and brightness, he feels joy and thinks of himself as exceedingly righteous and holy. All this is, however, the temptation of the Evil Inclination to entertain such strange thoughts which, then, actually bring him to the very lowest possible level.

And this is the meaning of the words, "a person has on the skin of his body a swelling"—a rising "in his skin" (*b'or*) as burning (*bo'eir*), from the expression *mashi'in mashu'ot* (igniting a tall bonfire as a signal)[20] that he has some enthusiasm for the worship of the Creator. "Or *sapaḥat* (rash)"—expressing his cleaving to the service of God, "or *baheret* (discoloration)"—from the word for brightness that he experiences in the worship of God. And whenever the word *ve-hayah*—when it happens

19. *Ma'or va-shemesh*, III, 7a.
20. m. Roš. Haš. 2:3.

that—appears, it signifies the joy that he feels in considering himself a *tzaddik*. "And in the skin of his flesh a leprous affection (*nega'*),"—as people are wont to say, there is nothing that makes one feel better than delight (*'oneg*) and nothing that makes him feel worse than affection/affliction (*nega'*). [The two words, meaning affliction and delight, are comprised of the very same letters simply placed in a different order.]

And his healing will occur through his attaching himself to the righteous of the generation, learning from them submission and the shattering of one's self-image to allow for humility. And he will sit and be healed. And this involves his being brought "to Aaron the priest or to one of his sons, the priests"—to connect himself with the righteous of the generation, for in that way he will be healed.

Comment: While the biblical priest did not engage in treating those who became subject to such skin-afflictions, it was his responsibility to diagnose the afflictions and, when necessary, to quarantine those so affected who then had to remain beyond the borders of the camp. And later, if the affliction appeared to have passed, it was again the priest's task to examine them and, if it turned out that the affliction has indeed passed, to re-admit the person to the camp accompanied by a rite of purification and re-admission.

Much earlier midrashic readings of these chapters, approaching the text with various word-games, suggest a causal relationship between the physical skin-afflictions, subject of this Torah-portion and the following portion, and certain types of behavior such as arrogance and slander or other misuse of speech.[21] Kalonymus Kalman, like some other Hasidic homilists, often went further in reading those chapters as a code, the physical afflictions serving merely as code-names for the real diseases which are moral, rather than physical, in character. The actual disease is largely identified with a person's succumbing to the cardinal sin of egotism. And in this light, the homilies tend to center around those temptations and openings for egotism which can be clad in a cloak of religiosity and religious behavior.

With this understanding, the Hasidic readings of this subject represent a radical and creative transformation of the Torah-text itself and of the role of the priest. If the disease is one of pride and a person's false self-estimation, the healing consists of the person's acquiring a sense of humility. Only in that way could the homilist identify with the ancient priest

21. Note *b. 'Arak.* 15b–16ab; *Midr. Lev.* 15:2,5,9; 16:1–6;17:3.

and his role in these chapters of Leviticus. The *tzaddik* was not a medical examiner, but he was viewed as one potentially capable of bringing a person to overcome false pride and to find healing in humility.

The Danger Caused by Deception[22]

A person can easily distance himself from the wicked who openly throw off the yoke of God's kingship, as one can clearly see that their ways are not good. But definite effort is required to protect oneself and distance oneself from those who deceive, pretending that they are among those who attend the academy of learning and behave in ways of piety and abstinence, while in reality they simply act one way while pretending to act in a very different way. For such a person more than taints the worship of honest people when coming together with them for study or prayer. The deceiving person, in that case, brings the others who truly serve God and who possess a holy spark tending to reach upward to its Holy Source, to a state of sadness or to laziness, causing them to descend from their own fervor and spiritual longing.

 . . . [U]nderstanding the text on the level of intimation, it seems to me that God caused the worlds to develop and descend world by world, from ʾAtzilut to B'riʾah, and from B'riʾah to Y'tzirah, continuing consistently through ʿAsiyah (this lower world). And as those worlds developed through *tzimtzum* (a restriction or partial withdrawal or cladding of the divine Presence), each one more than in the case of its predecessors, the divine holiness came to assume a hidden state within everything that is in the lower worlds. The Divine is consequently present, but concealed, within garments and masks.

And this is in accordance with God's simple Will concerning the creation of the worlds in a way to allow a space for freedom of choice and will and for reward and punishment. For to the degree that one acts according to what is good and walks in the ways of God, those masks and garments fall away and the holiness of the Divine that is hidden within everything becomes evident and illuminates the person's consciousness. This, however, requires considerable effort in the way of self-purification, directing one's thought to be continually pure and clear in its devotion to serve God in all matters, through Torah-learning and prayer and good

---

22. *Maʾor va-shemesh*, III, 7b–8a.

deeds and through repairing their own qualities such as love and fear, pride, domination and the like . . . .

Comment: Here, again, the master and preacher warns that while piety can be inspiring when it is sincere, pious behavior can also, at times, serve as an exquisite but deceiving garment cladding and concealing a person's actual behavior and values.

Beyond that caution, the above teaching, like much of Hasidic wisdom, appropriated Lurianic teaching and themes even while refining those same ideas. God is hidden in our world, but God is hidden within everything and in all things we can experience the presence of the Divine. There is no aspect of life or reality apart from God's Presence, even when that Presence might be concealed and even smothered and imprisoned. Our task is, therefore, to liberate and redeem the divine Sparks present within all that is.

In *Ma'or va-shemesh* and kindred homily-texts, the biblical body of laws concerning details relating to skin-ailments has been transformed into a moral document revealing very poignant psychological insight.

M'tzora

The Sadness That Leads to Joy and Healing[23]

> "... the priest (*kohen*) shall go outside the camp. If the priest sees that behold (*ve-hineih*) the afflicted one has been healed of his scaly affection ..." (a rite of purification and re-admission is called for, Lev 14:3)

That word *ve-hineih* ("and behold") appears to be quite superfluous. The verse could be worded simply, "and the *kohen* saw that he has been healed." Earlier commentators, in particular Hayyim ben-Attar [author of 'Or ha-ḥayyim, an eighteenth-century commentary on the Torah] pointed out that the cure is not dependent upon some natural cause in the way a disease is cured through the use of certain drugs and the like. Rather the afflicted one's dwelling alone (beyond the camp) intensifies his sadness (and in that state of sadness he gives thought to repairing his deeds and his character). . . .

In the natural course of happenings, a person's sadness relating to his wrongdoings would only intensify the sickness. But when one is completely broken-hearted in contrition and humility before the Creator, that very sadness brings him to a wholeness of joy, [as the Zohar notes in relation to Ps 100:2, "Worship the Lord in gladness"].[24] The word *ve-hineih* in the above verse [Lev 14:3] is an expression for joy,[25] conveying, paradoxically, that the afflicted one in his repentance was so completely broken-hearted that he comes to experience joy. . . . "That the afflicted has been healed"—certainly God has forgiven him, for beyond all doubt he has repented and repaired (the qualities which contributed to his wrongdoing).

---

23. *Ma'or va-shemesh*, III, 8ab.
24. Zohar, I, 163a.
25. See *Midr. Exod* 3:17.

Comment: This passage testifies to the attraction of the Kraków preacher to paradox. While sadness and joy are normally thought of as antithetical moods, the master views the deep sadness evoked in the wake of isolation precisely as a path to joy. This occurs, of course, when one's sadness and isolation bring one to serious soul-searching and repentance.

Again, while rabbinic agada connected some of these afflictions with undesirable behavioral qualities and viewed the disease to be a consequence of such traits, Hasidic interpretation frequently went beyond that causal relationship to speak of the character-traits themselves as the true disease which requires healing. This relationship situates the priestly role on a very different plane on which the *kohen* deals, essentially, not with symptoms of skin-ailments but rather with character deficiencies. While the Hasidic homilists could hardly sense any identification with the biblical priests in regard to their task of recognizing, examining, and quarantining people with physical afflictions, they could much more easily identify with the role of the priest as it is recast in a text such as this, in which the *kohen*-figure is instrumental in correcting a person's moral and spiritual blemishes.

And a somewhat earlier classical Hasidic homily-text explains the word *ha-kohen* ("the priest") as actually referring to God who cleanses and forgives the person in the wake of the person's remorse and repentance.[26]

---

26. *Ma'or 'einayim*, (*M'tzora*).

ʾAḥarei mot

Concerning Those with Whom We Share a Higher Soul-Root[27]

All the people of Israel (of all generations) are joined together by a very strong connection as one single complete entity, and all are of a single root as it said in Job, "Where (ʾeifo) were you when I laid the earth's foundations...?" (Job 38:4).

Our Sages explained that all the souls of Israel were dependent upon one ʾeifah (very small measure) of the First Man, whether it be from the brain, or from the forehead or the eyes or the heart or the hands or feet or of the numerous hairs,[28] and every soul is a complete entity in itself. [The Midrash refers to the First Man, Adam, when he was still a formless mass (golem); God's asking Job where is his ʾefah is hence read as asking where was his soul within the all-encompassing soul of that very First Man.]

So it will be in the future when all is repaired, and so it was prior to the First Man's sin, before the souls fell with the cataclysm (Sh'virah) due to his sin. Holy Sparks fell from the holy souls into what is inert matter and into vegetative life or animal or human life (literally, "having the use of speech and language"). A person must repair the root of his soul, lifting up all the Sparks (nitzotzot) that belong to it. And to the extent that the person purifies his soul and his behavior in regard both to one's dwelling-place and one's utensils, doing so for the sake of God, that person raises up the Sparks that are imprisoned in inert matter. Afterward when he goes on to acquire ruaḥ (the next higher level of soul), he is able then to raise up the fallen Sparks found in plant life.

---

27. Maʾor va-shemesh, III, 13b.
28. Based on Midr. Exod. 40:3.

And afterward, when he acquires a *n'shamah* (the still next higher level of soul), he raises up the Sparks that are in living things (animals and the like), and all these require repentance on his part. When he goes on to acquire *yeḥidah* (a still higher level, beyond the normal and natural), he still has to repair some small inclination or disturbing or prideful thought which stands in the way of wholeness in his worship or in his learning or in some *mitzvah* (holy deed) of his. And when he repents and repairs that lack of total wholeness, then through his repentance he also awakens those people who belong to the root of his soul, so that they too will repent. Insofar as they are of the root of his soul, through his own high level of spiritual improvement, he also awakens them to repentance and repair of a similar nature.

... [A]nd to the degree that he draws them near to the proper level of worship of God, he raises those Sparks that are in the humans. But so long as he has not lifted up the Sparks belonging to the root of his soul, he is required, through metempsychosis, to return to life once again until he succeeds in repairing all the Sparks belonging to his own soul-root. And a person whose soul has no further Sparks to repair is unable to draw other persons to his own worship.

We find this instruction in the Talmud, "Do not appoint anyone to serve as a *parnas* (administrator) over the community unless he has a basket of impure reptiles on his back"[29] [as a person beyond all blemish could easily become arrogant], for in order to draw people who are of one's own soul-root to the true worship of God, it is necessary that the person first raise up holy Sparks of his own soul that fell with the *Sh'virah*, including perhaps even some disturbing thought of pride or self-glorification that occurs in his mind. And since a person lacking any further need to repair himself is unable to effect others ("cannot be appointed over the community"), his own life-span will not be extended.

Concerning the verse, "The Lord spoke to Moses after the death of the two sons of Aaron who died when they drew too close to the presence of the Lord" (Lev 16:1), the souls of Nadav and Avihu were of a high level. None of their Sparks fell with the *Sh'virah*, and so they were able to repair their Sparks very quickly. And for this reason they were not granted length of life. But the soul of Aaron himself had many such fallen Sparks, and so through his high level of worship and repentance, he was able to draw others close to the true worship of God. And furthermore,

---

29. *b. Yoma* 22b.

through repairing those others with whom he shared the same soul-root, he himself reached a still higher level of holiness.

It is important to note that it is possible to draw near only those who have at least some small measure of regret concerning their deeds and their ways, but not those who are thoroughly alien and closed to any sense of regret and repentance.

Comment: The first half of the portion *Aḥarei mot*, (Lev 16), consists of instructions for the ancient observance of Yom Kippur ("the Day of Atonement"). In this discussion of Yom Kippur, Kalonymus Kalman, like other Hasidic masters, focused not on the biblical ritual as detailed in the text, which centered around the purification of the Tabernacle from defilement, but rather on the nature of Yom Kippur as it developed later in rabbinic Judaism. That holy day became a day of repentance, when each person, believing himself to be standing in judgment before God, endeavors to judge himself and to become aware of his own wrongs and failings and of his own need to strive spiritually upward.

Reflecting themes that evolved within Lurianic Kabbalah and later found a home within Hasidism, the Kraków master conveyed in his discussion a sense of a depth-bond connecting persons on a level far beneath any surface-connection. That outlook maintains not only that each person shares a particular soul-root with many others, but that the very possibility of repentance is dependent upon such underlying and unknown bonds.

The passage builds also upon the concept that the *tzaddik* (a holy man serving as the center of a Hasidic community) can impact his followers only if he himself is imperfect and is aware of some imperfection on his part, even if that blemish came about through his connection with others. For only as he engages with his own need for repentance is he able to impact others in the same direction.

The chapter in the Torah devoted to Yom Kippur (Lev 16) opens with reference to the death of two of the four sons of Aaron, the first Israelite priest according to biblical tradition. The death of those two sons, Nadav and Avihu, is reported somewhat earlier, in that they brought "alien fire" upon the altar (Lev. 10:1). That unspecified accusation was later interpreted in various ways which viewed their death as a punishment for their less-than-perfect execution of the laws and practices of the priesthood while serving at the altar in the Tabernacle.

In line with his renditions of other narrative-passages found in the Torah and following the approach of Hayyim Ben-Attar in *'Or ha-Ḥayyim*, who, along with others, influenced early Hasidism, Kalonymus Kalman viewed the death of Aaron's two sons very differently. He saw the two sons not as erring in their task, but rather as wholly righteous and as having completely attained the repair of their soul-root. Having fulfilled that purpose, they had no further need to continue in life.

This homily, like other Hasidic homilies, does not identify the priest as associated primarily with his cultic role at the altar, but rather as one who brings others near to God and to the paths of repentance and true worship. While the biblical *kohen* officiated at the altar in connection with sacrificial offerings (*korbanot*), the Hasidic homily literature presented the *kohen* as one who *m'karev*, who brings others closer to God and to the Torah. (Both those words derive from a common root, *k-r-v*.) This emphasis and transformation in the meaning of the priesthood reflects how Hasidic teaching understood the role of its own leaders. In addition, that definition, without question, is impacted by Hillel's famous comment concerning Aaron, the very first priest himself, as one who "loves people and *brings them near (um'karvan)* to the Torah"[30]

We have noted the Kraków master's struggling with the sometimes conflicting claims of primacy on the part of the individual and of the community, a theme that is also discussed in our very next passage. Here, however, we meet the conception of another type of community, mystic in nature, consisting of those who share the same soul-root. That community need not have any connection with family bonds and relationships, and a person may never have met many with whom he or she shares a common "soul-root." At the same time, a traditional Hasidic community centered around a *tzaddik* (holy man) is thought of as being based, ultimately, upon that more mystic community whose members are naturally drawn to one another and to the *tzaddik* (holy man) due to their sharing a deeper soul-root.

---

30. *m. 'Abot* 1:12.

K'doshim

The Paradoxical Relationship between Solitude and Community[31]

> "And the Lord spoke to Moses saying, 'Speak to the whole Israelite community and say to them: You shall be holy, for I, the Lord your God, am holy.'" (Lev 19:1–2)

That introductory verse comes to teach us that it is not possible for a person to attain holiness alone without his being part of that larger assembly and population and acting in accord with them. This is made clear in that most of the core-elements of the Torah, such as prayer, depend upon a larger assemblage [for example, being part of a *minyan* or quorum of worshippers]. It is the community of Israel that, as a community, is commanded to be holy.

One might err in the belief that it is possible to attain holiness by secluding and separating oneself from the community. For this reason, Rashi wisely explained that this portion was declared in a gathering of all of Israel, all of whom are nevertheless commanded to guard themselves, even when alone, from all that obstructs their divine service. In this vein a midrashic source specifies that precisely this portion was pronounced at the scene of a gathering of all the people, lest one claim that a person should seclude himself and isolate himself, thinking that in this way he will attain a higher level of holiness. The Torah specifies, ("You shall be holy) for I am holy," signifying that "My holiness is higher and of a different nature than yours," for the blessed Creator is truly One by nature, whereas a person seeking to extend the holiness of God upon himself can serve God only together with a community[32] . . . .

---

31. *Ma'or va-shemesh*, III, 16a.
32. *Midr. Lev.* 24:9.

One can rightly ask, how is it at all possible for us to be holy as God is holy (insofar as God is by His very nature One and we are many)? And how would it be possible for all the people of Israel to be secluded in solitude? . . . There are those who think that the way of serving God, the way to attain a state of attachment to God, requires that a person seclude himself, studying in a closed room secluded from others, neither speaking to anyone nor even being seen by anyone else as one strives to arrive at the truth. But one might seclude himself over a period of many years and still never arrive at the truth. . . .

The core element in *'avodah* is to join with righteous members of the community of Israel and to learn from their good deeds. And what is really required is seclusion in thought in a way that at all times, even when situated within a large gathering, one will nevertheless direct his mind to God's exalted state. In the chapter of *p'rishut* (seclusion and ascetic behavior), the author of *Hovot ha-l'vavot* ["The Duties of the Heart" written by Bahya ibn Pakudah in eleventh-century Spain] wrote that the central element of isolation is that even in a house full of people, one can nevertheless imagine himself as alone, as though no one else is present, as he himself in his thinking, even in that setting, is attached to God and will hardly be aware that anyone else is present. And during prayer in particular it is important to feel as though no one else is present other than God. That is the real principal of seclusion: to be alone in the realm of one's thought which is directed solely to God.

"You shall be holy" (Lev 19:2) can be read as "You shall be set apart" (from all others) even when in a large assembly. And even within a crowd, you can be (in that sense) completely alone.

The words, "You shall be (*tihyu*, plural) holy," convey that even when you are together as part of a large holy community, individually you shall be *parush* (separated from the large group) as each one individually attaches and connects his thought to God, just as though each person is alone, with no others present, similar to that analogy of being alone even in a house full of people. God is saying, "Just as I am separate (*parush*)"—even as God fills and surrounds all the worlds and there is no place empty of His presence—nevertheless at the very same time, God is separate from all that is material in nature. Correspondingly, even as you are situated within a larger assembly, you shall be separate from them in the sense that (in your thinking and consciousness) you are attached only to God. . . .

K'doshim

Comment: The Kraków preacher opened his homily by contrasting the emphasis upon *hitbod'dut* (seclusion, solitude) as the path of attaining holiness with his own accent upon being part of the larger community of Israel.

The eleventh-century work *Ḥovot ha-l'vavot* ("The Duties of the Heart") was impacted by Sufi thinking and practice and, possibly, also by Christian ascetics. While Baḥya expressed qualified admiration for ascetics who went to live in caves or out in the desert, at the same time he questioned the value of such retreat from human society.[33] Two centuries later, also in Spain, Baḥya ben Asher, in his commentary on the Torah, viewed Moses' work as a shepherd in the desert in a solitary environment as preparation for his role as a Prophet.[34] And Kalonymus Kalman's mentor, Elimelekh of Lyzhansk, similarly associated the Torah's reference to *midbar-Sinai* (Exod 19:1) with *hitbod'dut* and suggested the impact of solitude in enabling the Israelite population to be spiritually prepared to receive the Torah at Sinai.[35]

Seemingly in contrast, Kalonymus Kalman Epstein, following earlier teachings made the point that the prescriptions in the portion, *K'doshim*, are explicitly addressed to the entire assemblage of Israelites, accentuating the importance of being part of that large assembly and negating *hitbod'dut* as the path to holiness. However, as the Kraków master proceeded to analyze the contrast between those two emphases, he actually struck a mediating position between solitude and community.

While making it clear that holiness is an ideal designated for the entire Israelite population, he highlighted, at the same time, the importance of each person's thinking of himself as alone, even when he is part of that larger communal situation. One then participates in the larger community specifically as an individual who, in the province of his own consciousness, is solely attached to God. The Kraków master's mediating position on this issue might remind the reader of Ralph Waldo Emerson's insistence that even as a member of society, the individual, in his own inner life, must remain in some important sense a single, even solitary individual. (Note especially Emerson's essays, "Self-Reliance" and "Society and Solitude").

As Kalonymus Kalman declared elsewhere, a thousand people can pray together in a large hall; yet the prayer of each person is different.[36]

---

33. Baḥya Ibn Pekudah., *Ḥovot hal'vavot*, Gate 9, 429–40.
34. *Baḥya ben Asher* on Exod 3:1; also on Exod 13:20.
35. *No'am 'Elimelekh*, 154, on Exod 19:1 (*Yitro*); also 143 on Exod 13:20 (*B'shalaḥ*).
36. *Ma'or va-shemesh*, V, 7b. (*Va'etḥanan*).

Throughout his collection of homilies, the role of community is accompanied by the clear importance of the inner life of each person as a unique individual. It is in the province of one's inner life that one connects with his deeper self and his higher, divine Root, and it is that connection that enables a person to become a member of a community in a meaningful and beneficial sense. While traditionally, Jewish prayer occurs in a group-setting, the Kraków master was well aware that by its very nature, prayer itself derives from something that takes place within the depth-consciousness of the individual participant.

The key both to the complexity of this issue and to the preacher's mediating position can perhaps be traced to the comment of Rashi on the second verse of this Torah-portion in which the eleventh-century exegete, while emphasizing the collective context of Lev 19, also explained the word *k'doshim* ("holy") as *p'rushim*, those who separate themselves from immoral behavior for the purposes of holiness. And the word *parush* came later to signify one who lived an essentially solitary life out to devotion to an ideal of holiness.

In this fusion of community with the depth of each person's rich inner life, the modern reader might grasp a vision of an ideal community as carved in the mind of the preacher as one whose members are spared the force of conformist tendencies within the group, and one in which a community does not become a "crowd." While the Kraków master was, undoubtedly, thinking of the ideal Hasidic community of his own time, the same vision might apply to any kind of group or community.

ʾEmor

The Inner Meaning of the Calendar[37]

During the days of the *S'firah* [the "counting" of forty-nine days beginning on the second evening of *Pesaḥ* to the day prior to *Shavuʿot*, "the Festival of Weeks"], a person must repair the lack of unity and oneness, as it is written, "And they journeyed from *R'fidim* and came to the wilderness of Sinai" (Exod 19:2, to the scene of revelation).

[In light of a shift from plural to singular verbs, midrashic comments read the geographical movement from the one location to another as conveying a moving away from contention to a state in which mutual respect and consideration prevailed in the Israelites' thinking and behavior.[38]] Rashi explained that they then all became "as one person with one heart." And for this reason they were able to receive and understand the Torah when it was given.

The Midrash went on to explain the words, "seven whole weeks" (Lev 23:15) in that those weeks are whole only when the Israelites fulfill the divine Will.[39] For it is God's desire that all the people of Israel become "as one person with one heart," acting out of love and brotherly feeling. And then the Midrash went on also to explain the words which follow, "And you shall bring an *omer*" (a singular noun, referring to the offering of new grain, Lev 23:16) in that precisely by means of that sense of oneness, you will be able to receive and comprehend the Torah, given on the Festival of Weeks.

---

37. *Maʾor va-shemesh*, III, 18a.
38. *Mek.* (*Yitro, Baḥodesh hashlishi, parashah* #1) on Exod 19:2.
39. *Midr. Lev.* 28:3.

Comment: All references to the festival of *Shavu'ot* in the Torah present that occasion purely as an agricultural festival. It marks a high point in the harvest which then continues until its culmination with *Sukkot*, "the festival of ingathering," when all that remains of the harvest's yield is brought in from the fields before the onset of the winter rains.

Later, perhaps at some point in the rabbinic period, however, *Shavu'ot* acquired a significance transcending its agricultural importance. Building on the reference to the third month of the year in Exod 19:1 (the biblical year begins in the spring, as *Pesaḥ* begins on the full moon on that first month), *Shavu'ot*, which falls during the third month, became associated with the giving of the Decalogue and of the Torah as a whole. The biblical episode of the revelation of the Decalogue (Exod 19–20) itself grew into a much broader and richer conception of *matan-torah*, the giving of the Torah, understood as including both the entire text of the Written Torah (the Pentateuch) along with the body of traditional oral interpretation, all of which came traditionally to be attributed to the revelation at Sinai.

That connection between a point in the agricultural year and the commemoration of revelation became further enriched over time. The midrashic sources referred to in the above homily read geographical details mentioned in the Torah to convey a psychological transformation of the Israelite population: the Israelites' coming to the Sinai wilderness experienced an inner change as self-centeredness and contention gave way to a sense of oneness encompassing an entire community. And in a stroke of both moral and artistic brilliance, that very sense of oneness and identification with the other was understood as a prerequisite-condition for receiving and understanding the Torah at Sinai. Building upon earlier kabbalistic interpretation, Hasidic homilists seized upon that connection to regard the seven weeks prior to the revelation at Sinai as a period of inner, spiritual growth repeated each year as the practice of the counting of the days of the Omer (Lev. 23:15) became a time of renewed introspection and repair of personal attitudes and traits.[40]

The Zohar refers to a profusion of dew from the divine heights which descended during the weeks before the revelation at Sinai and purified the Israelites from the legacy of filth originating with the primordial sin of the First Man, hence allowing for the giving of the Torah at Sinai.[41] The theme of purification is heard much later in *Ḥemdat yamim* where it occurs not as

---

40. Agnon, *Atem re'item*, 46–50 on Exod 19:2.
41. Zohar, III, 97a.

a one-time occurrence as a result of descending heavenly dew, but rather as an annual period of spiritual preparation for the festival on which the giving of the Torah is celebrated.[42]

The above homily by the Kraków preacher brings into focus a detail of the agricultural ritual which it then views through the lens of a sense of true oneness within a community, a theme of true moral import. The homilist has remarkably brought these very different strands together in a way that mirrors and is built upon the fruits of a fusion, over time, of a harvest-celebration and a tradition of revelation.

---

42. Ḥemdat yamim, III, 41d.

B'har
Satiety[43]

A person should make his Torah-study ongoing and central in his life and regard his work through which he earns a livelihood as secondary in importance. For "How does one benefit from all his labor beneath the sun?" (Eccl 1:3). Sometimes even though one pursues vexing matters during all his days and even his nights, he nevertheless fails to benefit beyond a small measure of bread; but if the same person were to trust in God and devote his efforts and energy to Torah and worship, he might more easily earn a livelihood. . . .

From the jar of manna which Aaron placed before the Lord to be preserved through the generations (Exod 16:33), one learns not to engage in the passing vanities of the world. And accordingly, one should not devote effort in commerce beyond the point at which he obtains what he needs for his livelihood. And should God grant him considerable wealth, he should not go on to further pursue endeavors in order to acquire still greater wealth. And certainly he should not lend to others for interest or add additional trading ventures to his own regular earnings, seeking more and more, while closing his eyes to his poor Jewish brethren and failing to make them more secure through compassionate deeds lest they become destitute. For that is not the way. Rather, one should engage in trade only according to the measure of his needs, and beyond that point he should engage, instead, in merciful and charitable deeds. And then it will be well with him in that he will be able to engage in Torah-study and in worship and also assist his brethren, lending to them without interest so that his brothers, too, will be able to get along in life.

---

43. *Ma'or va-shemesh*, III, 19a.

And we can grasp the very essence of the Land of Israel in that it is given to Israel only so that each person might sit beneath his vine and his fig-tree and be able to earn a livelihood without difficulty, without his increasing his efforts in trade beyond what he needs. And the balance of his time he should devote to charitable and merciful deeds. Had they followed in this way, the Israelites would not have been exiled from the Land. For it is due to their engaging in trade beyond their actual needs and to their journeying beyond the Land in quest of further business and becoming like the peoples of those lands and learning their ways that the Land spews them out.

... "And you shall eat your fill" (Lev 25:19). This means that a person must value his serving God above all else and ignore his material desires. And in that case, whatever he eats, even if it be but a small measure, will satisfy him, for he does not eat for the purpose of filling his stomach. And this is the meaning of the words, "and you shall eat your fill"—whatever you eat will satisfy you. And in this way you will know even greater security.

Comment: This excerpt is from a homily relating to the law of the Seventh Year, the *Sh'mitah*, during which the owner of land is neither to plant nor reap his field (Lev 25:1–7). During that Seventh Year, according to the law, the owner of the field may reap his field if he and his household are in need of food; otherwise it must be left for the poor and landless as well as for animals in quest of food.

While the Torah, including the law of the Seventh Year, reflects a society in which virtually everyone, save for the landless tribe of Levi, worked in agriculture and each family owned a parcel of land, the homily in *Ma'or va-shemesh* reflects a very different kind of society, one with which the Kraków preacher would have been familiar. That society would consist largely of traders, ranging from petty traders often having a very insecure livelihood, to a few more affluent merchants who engaged even in foreign commercial trade. It also reflects a stage of Jewish religious life in which study, in particular study of rabbinic texts, occupied an important place. In his envisioning the past through his present, the preacher went on to interpret the law of the Seventh Year as conveying the primary place of Torah-study in one's life, and the antithesis of such study would not be agriculture but rather a pursuit of trade and commerce.

Echoing the biblical promise that if the Israelites refrain from planting on the Seventh Year the land will, on its own, continue to produce food and "you shall eat your fill," Kalonymus Kalman went on to interpret the law of the Seventh Year in terms of a more comprehensive concept of satiety, one that is not necessarily limited to the Seventh Year. He advocated that, at any time, a person should not strive for more than what one needs. It is important to be satisfied with what one has and not strive to go beyond that.

The same ideal of satiety, in turn, is translated into devoting one's efforts to Torah-study and worship rather than succumbing to the impulse always to seek more material benefit than one actually needs. In his analysis, a lack of satiety goes hand in hand with a neglect of Torah-study.

In the Kraków preacher's interpretation of the law of the Seventh Year, the words "And you shall know your fill" are read not as a reward or consequence of obeying the law prohibiting planting and reaping during the seventh year, but as the very essence of the law itself. That ethic of satiety is further bound up with the sense that one's primary concern in life be in the area of Torah-study and merciful actions, viewing the earning of a livelihood as but secondary in importance. This viewpoint is hardly original with *Ma'or va-shemesh*. Earlier writings, too, understood work and commerce not as one's primary activity in life, but as necessary only for the purposes of sustaining a person and his family in life and hence as enabling one to devote time and energy to Torah-study and acts of compassion.[44]

---

44. *m. 'Abot* 1:15; *b. Ber.* 35b; Maimonides, *Mishnah torah, Talmud-torah*, 3:7.

b'Ḥukotai
The World's Benefits from Torah-Learning[45]

> "If you follow My laws and faithfully observe My commandments, (I will grant your rains in their season, so that the earth shall yield its produce and the trees of the field their fruit. Your threshing shall overtake the vintage, and your vintage shall overtake the sowing; you shall eat your fill of bread and dwell securely in your land. I will grant peace in the land, and you shall lie down untroubled by anyone . . . ." Lev 26:3–6)

For God created all the worlds and their fullness by means of the holy Torah and through combinations of the Names intimated in every single letter among the letters of the Torah. And when occupying themselves with the holy Torah, the Israelites add strength and life to all the worlds and to all that was created. Indeed, in giving the Torah to His people Israel, it was God's basic will that in the course of their study, whenever they focus on the Torah's mention of anything in the world, they give life to that thing. This occurs when they occupy themselves with the subject of the creation of heaven and earth as found in the Torah, or with any component of the world. For this reason we must engage in Torah with awe and trembling, in order that we might give strength and life to every thing, as one relates to its mention in the holy Torah.

Comment: This homily makes the claim that studying Torah gives life to the world and, in particular, to whatever aspect of the world we touch upon through the study of Torah. That thought is an expression of the conception of the Torah and its letters as comprising the very blueprint of the world, of existence itself. That relationship, which would appear to suggest a magical relationship between Torah-study and the maintenance of

---

45. *Ma'or va-shemesh*, III, 19b.

the world, lacks a middle factor, namely our more direct efforts to preserve and repair the world in light of some of the Torah's directives and implications. Considering a more modern mindset, perhaps that direct, middle factor should substitute for the more magical relationship which the master's words would appear to convey.

4

On the Fourth Book of the Torah (*B'midbar* / Numbers)

B'midbar
The Need for Both Torah-Study and Prayer[1]

It is known that we are unable to attain a stage of illumination in our thinking and understanding (*he'erat ha-mohin*) through engaging in Torah-study alone. For along with Torah-study, it is necessary to engage in (sacrificial) worship through which our forefathers made connection with the higher realms of existence, enabling them to illuminate the holy *mohin* (higher mental capacity) in a way to cast light on the *midot* (ethical and spiritual qualities). *'Avodah* (originally, sacrificial worship) takes on the form of prayer (*t'filah*), which now comes in place of the sacrifices. And only through engaging in both Torah and prayer is it possible to attain the goal of wholeness in illuminating one's thought.

The Tabernacle was the scene of engagement with both Torah and worship. The priests found it necessary to occupy themselves with Torah-learning in order to know the laws of the sacrificial offerings. But Torah-study without serious effort and intent in prayer, just like prayer alone without Torah-study, does not enable one to come to that goal of illumination of understanding concerning *midot*.

Comment: This comment, with its dual-emphasis, reflects a criticism, on the part of the early followers of Hasidism, of a one-sided emphasis upon Torah-study that failed to give emphasis also to the more devotional dimension of religious life. In the eyes of the pietist critics, such over-emphasis upon talmudic learning to the exclusion of devotional experience permeated the official rabbinic leadership and institutions of learning, a criticism that, in turn, evoked counter-accusations voiced by the more conventional

---

1. *Ma'or va-shemesh*, IV, 1b.

religious camp.[2] Actually, the criticism expressed in this passage is not, however, a Hasidic innovation. As evidence, one might note a somewhat earlier tale from the kabbalistic ethical literature, "The Failing of Torah Without Prayer,"[3] voicing, indeed quite harshly, that very same criticism.

This passage from *Ma'or va-shemesh* goes out of its way to achieve a sense of balance: it is not uni-directional, but is directed against neglect either of Torah-study or prayer, a stance appropriate for the Kraków master who, aware of tensions between conflicting emphases, frequently sought a mediating position accommodating both and, in some significant sense, critical of both polarities.

---

2. Note Wilensky, Mordecai, *Ḥasidim umitnagdim*.
3. Kaidanover, *Qav ha-yashar*, VIII:7–8; Wineman, *Beyond Appearances*, 31–33.

Naso

Blessing Requires Love[4]

> "The Lord spoke to Moses: Speak to Aaron and his sons: Thus shall you bless the people of Israel. Say to them: The Lord bless you and protect you. The Lord deal kindly and graciously with you! The Lord bestow His favor upon you and grant you peace." (Num 6:22–26)

Rashi *z'l* interpreted the words, "bless you," to indicate that they will be blessed with possessions, and he explained the words, "and protect you," as indicating that bandits will not attack you to take your money. And according to the Midrash, "the Lord deal kindly with you" [more literally, "cause His face to shine upon you"] refers to the light of the Torah, that He will enlighten your eyes and your heart in the Torah.[5]

The interpreters of the Torah have already noted and asked, "Why is it not written, '*speak* to them,' but rather, '*say* to them?'" And it seems to me that the wording suggests that one who comes to bless the Israelites must have in his spirit and heart a strong love for them, to the extent that he will love even the least of the least of Israel as himself. And through this he glorifies them before their supernal Father with various meritorious qualities, awakening compassion and great mercy toward them, and extending to them various kinds of blessings.

And this is alluded in the word *'emor* ("say"), the word relating to the verse, "You have affirmed (*he'emartem*) this day that the Lord is your God . . ." (Deut 26:17), meaning that the blessed Holy One commanded the priests, "So (with this quality) you shall bless the people of Israel"—that you love them. Then you will be worthy to bless Israel. . . .

---

4. *Ma'or va-shemesh*, IV, 8a.
5. *Midr. Num.* 11:13.

Comment: According to an opinion preserved in a midrashic source, prior to blessing the Israelites, the priest is to recite his own blessing, praising God "who hallowed us with the holiness of Aaron and commanded us to bless Your people Israel *with love*."[6] The tenor of that statement resembles various Hasidic statements concerning the relationship between the *tzaddik*, the Hasidic holy man, and his followers.

Again, Kalonymus Kalman tended to read the Torah-text essentially in terms of the religious or spiritual landscape of his own time, as the Hasidic masters and homilists generally tended to view the biblical priesthood as a mirror-image of themselves. Hence, what is emphasized concerning the *kohen* in such homilies may have little real connection with the specific duties and roles of the ancient priest or priesthood as noted in the Torah. Such homilies tended to recreate the biblical priest in the model of the Hasidic *tzaddik*, thought to have the capacity to influence even his erring followers through a loving relationship and to connect the souls of his followers with their higher, divine Root, and hence with their truer selves. In fact, the preacher went on (in the following passage) to exclaim very clearly that "the *tzaddik* is called *kohen*," the term *kohen* (priest) simply being a name once given to the *tzaddikim* in an earlier time. It follows that the priests' act of reciting a blessing in God's name (Num 6:22–27) would, in the eyes of Kalonymus Kalman, be an empty gesture without a relationship of love for the recipients of that blessing.

---

6. *Midr. Num.* 11:4.

B'ha'alotkha

Sadness and the Craving for Food[7]

Why does the passage concerning Aaron's lighting the menorah (Num 8:1–4) follow the dedication ceremony of the Tabernacle and the gifts of the tribal princes (Num 7)? In that ceremony, the princes of the tribes participated, while neither Aaron as priest nor his tribe were included. Aaron felt himself irrelevant, but the blessed Holy One told him that "your portion is greater than theirs." Aaron and his sons are to kindle the lights of the menorah and attend to the flames, "raising up the lights" (*b'ha'alotkha et ha-nerot*): the very wording conveying ascent, for they are required to kindle the lights until the flame ascends by itself....

There is a principle that "envy among scribes increases wisdom."[8] The proper envy in this regard would be an envy of the deeds of *tzaddikim* and the desire to be able to act as they do and to walk in their paths. While any person might envy the deeds of the *tzaddikim* and wish to do as they do, one will also realize that theirs is a divine gift, for a *tzaddik* has the capacity to draw the souls of Israelites closer to God, and they themselves are ignited to a degree that they can utter words of Torah and of prayer like flames of fire. And such utterances on their part, conveying awe and trembling, can enflame the hearts. That, however, is a gift from God and is not within everyone's reach. Only a humble *tzaddik* who is as nothing in his own eyes, even belittling and treating himself with scorn, can be so gifted.

... "The lampstand was a hammered work of gold, hammered from base to petal" (Num 8:4). All its parts, from the smallest to the largest, were made of one solid piece of gold (Exod 25:31). For Aaron was himself

---

7. *Ma'or va-shemesh*, IV, 8b–9b.
8. *b. Bat.* 21a.

devoid of any element of self-importance.... In his eyes, every Israelite, from the least significant to the greatest, was beloved, and he loved all of them "from base to petal," with a complete love, suggesting that all the people of Israel should themselves unite and become one through complete love and oneness.

Aaron was commanded to kindle the flame until the flame comes up by itself.

For the *tzaddik*, who here is called *kohen* (priest), elevates the souls of all the Israelites, attaching them to the blessed *'Ein-sof* (the infinite state of the Divine). When the Israelites gather together in a true gathering to come to the *tzaddik*, he ignites their hearts for the worship of God; after their departure from the *tzaddik*, however, the burning enthusiasm that they experienced in his presence is extinguished. Rashi explained that Aaron's task was greater than all the sacrificial offerings of the tribal princes, for he must enflame their hearts in a way that they would experience the same inner enthusiasm even after they depart from him and are no longer in his proximity. Even when they are separated by physical distance, he nevertheless continues to enflame their hearts, as conveyed by the words, "Aaron did so" (Num. 8:3)....

An important principle of worship consists of a person's distancing himself from sadness and depression—God spare us from them—to the furthest possible extent.[9] The holy Zohar teaches that sadness is a speck of idolatry, insofar as idolatrous thoughts circulate in the brain of a depressed person. [The Zohar emphasizes the role of joy in serving God; see *Sh'mot*: "True worship requires joy," and note #1 on that homily.] And it is crucial to distance oneself from sadness, which can bring a person to all kinds of transgressions. The initial signs of such sadness become evident when the appetite for food grows within him and takes over, as a person experiencing depression—God forbid—eats with a ravenous appetite, eating very rapidly and desiring to eat without ceasing, along with other desires such as continuous sexual activity. And without such a person's attaching himself to the *tzaddikim* and learning from them a path of life, it is impossible to advise him to prevail over his Evil Inclination and its appetites.

Such a person, immersed in appetite, however, is unable to learn from a *tzaddik* who is already purified in every way and who has brought all aspects of his life to a state of holiness. Such a *tzaddik* eats and drinks oils and wine, wears lovely clothes and lives in beautiful dwellings, and in

---

9. Note *b. Ber.* 31a.

all of these things he serves and worships on a high level, raising up holy Sparks (imprisoned within material things) and bringing them within what is holy. But how can one in need learn from such a person?

Instead, he must attach himself to a *tzaddik* who has not yet reached such a high level, one who is still engaged in the process of purification and worshipful behavior. Only then might the person be open to change to some small degree. In order to adequately purify himself, such a *tzaddik* builds a fence around his own behavior and guards himself even from what is permitted. And from him the person in lowly straits is able to learn to establish such limitations for himself and to prevail over his Evil Inclination.

In regard to this, our Sages said that a community cannot appoint a *parnas* (community administrator) unless that person has a basket of impure, crawling things on his back,[10] indicating that he still has in himself something requiring repair. [In that talmudic source, it is said that Saul, the first king of Israel, was himself beyond reproach as was his family, but as a result he could become arrogant.] Through his own engaging in further repair and repentance, he also enables others to repent and repair themselves. And we can understand that Aaron was chosen for his role precisely because he still had a stain on his character, something he had in common with others whom he could then bring to repentance.

"The people took to complaining bitterly before the Lord . . ." (Num 11:1), meaning that they fell into a state of sadness. [The homily relates the word *mit'on'nim* ("complaining") to the word *'onein*, one cast into grief immediately after a death in the family up to the time of burial.] And "a fire of the Lord broke out against them" (Num 11:1). Depression is detestable insofar as it contains an element of idolatry. For this reason they were punished, and though Moses prayed and the fire subsided (and the manna, wondrous food, was given to them), the strength of their appetite nevertheless continued due to their sadness and they clamored, "If only we had meat to eat!" (Num 11:4). And Moses, who was completely purified of material desire, asked how he could possibly repair others, since he shared nothing of their condition. . . .

"Then the Lord said to Moses, 'Gather for Me seventy of Israel's elders . . .'" (Num 11:16), meaning such elders who were still striving toward their own purification, for from such people others would be able to

---

10. *b. Yoma* 22b.

learn. And God proceeded to provide them with food in such abundance that it became utterly detestable in their eyes. . . .

Moses did not comprehend God's intent. . . . But immediately as they began to consume the meat given to them, they felt that it was too disgusting to eat. . . . Therefore that place is called *kivrot ha-ta'avah* ("the graves of appetite," Num 22:34), for in this way their appetites were demolished, and neither were they drawn now to other lustful desires . . . though they did retain something of the desire for *lashon hara*, gossip and evil speech. [In this way the episode centering upon appetite and complaints concerning food connects with the criticism of Moses by his own brother and sister which follows (Num 12).]

Comment: The above passages illustrate how Kalonymus Kalman Epstein, among other Hasidic preachers, sought to read the laws and narratives found in the Torah concerning the priests (*kohanim*), Aaron and his sons, in a way that reflects the *tzaddikim*, the charismatic mystics who served as the central figures of the emerging Hasidic communities in Eastern Europe. Quite amazingly, the reader will find virtually nothing in these homilies in line with the basic biblical conception of the priesthood as a class set apart through heredity from father to son. Nor does one find any emphasis upon the more comprehensive cultic duties of the ancient priests beyond the homiletical effort to distill from those duties some allusion to and insight into the role of the Hasidic *tzaddik* of a much later time.

While not explicitly mentioned in the homily, perhaps underlying Kalonymus Kalman's discussion of Aaron's appointment to kindle the lights of the menorah in the Tabernacle is that verse from Proverbs which metaphorically likens the human soul to a candle, "The lifebreath [soul] of man is the lamp of the Lord" (Prov 20:27). This homiletical exercise, masterful in character, read the role of the priests and the very wording of the command given to Aaron in a way to suggest the charismatic gifts of a Hasidic holy man, thought to be capable of kindling a flame in the hearts of those drawn to him.

In comparing the biblical priestly texts with their interpretation in the Hasidic homilies, the reader realizes that the biblical cult could not speak to the Hasidic preachers in its own terms. Many centuries and changes in religious expression and mindset separated the one from the other, and for this reason, the words relating to the priestly cult were read as allusions to a very different religious landscape which emerged over time.

The reading of this episode in *Ma'or va-shemesh* connects also with another tendency noted previously. In the master's rendition of the episode of the splitting of the Reed-Sea (on *parashat B'shallaḥ*), that episode was retold in a way that provided no active role for God in the fate of the Egyptians. God is not thought of as the perpetrator of punishment, neither in that episode concerning the fate of the Egyptians, nor in this episode of the ungrateful Israelites bitterly lamenting what they felt to be a lack of food. The homilist simply ignored, in effect erased, God's sending a plague to punish the complainers, and he explained the name of that particular site in the desert, *Kivrot ha-ta'avah* (the graves of desire) to refer not to the death of the complaining mob, but rather to the healing of their insatiable appetites and cravings which are then explained as due to a sadness within themselves.

The homiletical comments transformed an emphasis upon punishment to an accent upon healing.

Sh'laḥ l'kha

God's Mercy Overrides His Anger[11]

God created the worlds in order to benefit those whom He would then bring into being. He gave humans free choice and will in order to allow for reward and punishment along with the counsel to "choose life" (Deut 30:19). And if not for His patience (tolerance of evil over an extended time), man would lack any real choice. For otherwise, if a person would sin, he would immediately be punished, something that would force someone, against his own will, to turn from his evil way due not to his own choice but to his fear of punishment at God's hands.

Wishing to grant merit to Israel, the blessed Holy One gave them freedom of choice in regard to *yir'at shamayim* (one's fear of or obedience to God) even while all else might be determined from above.[12] And all this is possible precisely because of God's patience. The righteous choose the good and say, "Let us search and examine our ways, and turn back to the Lord" (Lam 3:40), for perhaps we have sinned and God refrained from punishing us due to His patience, while the wicked have a space to err as they observe that the way of the wicked prospers, as they maintain, "I will be safe, though I follow my own willful heart" (Deut 29:18).

We might understand that all this might be the case prior to the disclosure of God and of His long-patient forbearance [God's refraining from exerting His power of punishment during the early generations]. But after God's reality was revealed for all to witness, as in the generation of the wilderness, one might easily think that God would no longer be patient in the face of sin. But the Holy One wished to make known to His creatures that even with that disclosure of His Divinity, His patience endures. . . .

11. *Ma'or va-shemesh*, IV, 10b-11a.
12. *m. 'Abot* 3:15.

Sh'lah l'kha

And when God forgave the generation of the wilderness, all would know that His patience is ongoing, even after His Divinity became known.

When God created the worlds to benefit those whom He would create and who would receive the manifestations of His lovingkindness, if with creation, God's brightness lacked garments and constrictions (*tzimtzumim*), His brightness would be too overbearing to experience. What did He do? He clad Himself with garments emanating from His brightness, which itself would be beyond what any person could mentally conceive. . . . And He created worlds and creatures and constricted His brightness to a point allowing His creatures to be able to bear the experience of His lovingkindness.

And should there be any accusation on the part of the *Sitra 'Ahra* (evil, demonic force) against the Israelites, then the holy man of that generation (*tzaddik ha-dor*)—and there is such a person in every generation—, through his prayer, stands in the breach to counter the force of that accusation and sweetens the force of punishment at its root. He sweetens the very divine Name from *'Adonai* to *Havayah* [the latter name underlies the former name and connotes the more ultimate nature of the Divine], "sweetening the judgments" with mercy, as explained in the Zohar,[13] allowing punishment only through the fourth generation (Exod 20:5).

If they repent, those garments then attach themselves to the thirteen expressions of mercy (Num. 14:18) with which God created the world. In this way, God encompasses the forces of judgment and includes them in His all-encompassing Mercy, for it is God's will to benefit His creations with His lovingkindness rather than to awaken Judgment and punishment. . . .

The very essence of the act of bringing a sacrificial offering is *t'shuvah* (repentance). Prior to the episode of the spies (Num 13–14) the Israelites mistakenly thought that in bringing an offering they could automatically be graced with atonement even without *t'shuvah*. But they misjudged, for the essential element in bringing a sacrifice is precisely *t'shuvah*. So God taught them, at this point, that such atonement does not depend simply on the bringing of an offering, but rather upon the person's complete repentance accompanying the offering. . . . *T'shuvah* requires a person's annulling all externality from one's very self and his turning away

---

13. Zohar, III, 76a.

from the *k'lipot* (Shells of evil and impurity), so that one might remain clear and pure.

In *t'shuvah*, the repentant must, at the very least, connect with three basic levels of the soul, *nefesh, ru'aḥ* and *n'shamah*, and repair their lack of wholeness. And he must confess his sins to God in prayer (*t'filah*) which, in the bitterness of exile, substitutes for the sacrificial rites that took place in the Temple. In this manner, even in this bitter exile, we shall offer "the bullocks of our lips" (Hos 14:3) with *t'filah* and *t'shuvah* to enable us to ascend to the higher levels.

Comment: The real thrust of this somewhat complicated homiletical discourse emerges only when comparing it with the Torah-portion to which it refers. The episode of the spies in *Sh'laḥ l'kha* (Num 13–14) bears a tone of grave disappointment both with that delegation of scouts which Moses had sent out to bring back a report on the land of Canaan and with the Israelites-at-large who responded sympathetically to their discouraging report. That report portrayed a rich land with mighty people who could easily overcome the Israelites were they to invade the Land. The ambience of the chapters comprising this portion is one of divine wrath upon both the spies and the Israelites in the desert who were so ready to desert their collective project. The people-at-large reacted with nostalgia even for their lot in bondage where they lived with a certain degree of security, knowing at least where their next meal was coming from.

God's initial reaction, according to the toraitic account, was to contemplate abandoning the Israelites to their destruction in the desert, and later, even with His forgiveness, that generation, except for the two members of the delegation of spies who differed from the "majority report," was sentenced to die in the desert and never live to enter the Land.

While the tone of that episode as a whole is largely one of wrath and sharp criticism, in his homilies on that same portion, Kalonymus Kalman focused instead on the theme of forgiveness. Even in the face of the very Torah-reading serving as the basis of his discourse, the Kraków master displayed an insistence upon associating God with mercy, compassion, and forgiveness, rather than with wrath and punishment.

Koraḥ

Aaron, as High Priest, Maintains His Humility[14]

It is known that the blessed Holy One said, "I dwell . . . with the contrite and the lowly in spirit" (Isa 57:15) and that the holy *Sh'khinah* is able to rest and reside only with the person who is especially humble in spirit. Mount Sinai itself proves the point, and furthermore our Sages said that the blessed Holy One elevates the person who lowers himself.[15]

For the essential principle is a humility of spirit, a person's being as nothing in his own eyes and his constant searching, at every time and season, every hour and minute, to learn how to serve God, as it is written, "Seek His presence constantly" (Ps 105:4). And the person who, in his own eyes, more closely approaches the Gate of Nothingness is more able to serve as a chariot for the holy *Sh'khinah* (divine Presence). He is the greatest in his generation and becomes the head of the generation. . . .

The penitent must always say, "I will serve God truthfully, and though I have not yet attained any experience of Divinity, I simply accept upon myself that role of being a servant of God." Repentance (*t'shuvah*) belongs to what is concealed, for the forty-nine Gates of Repentance are drawn from forty-nine Gates of Understanding, which are within the concealed world. And God has found the *tzaddik* of the generation deserving of a place of honor due to his continual attachment to repentance at its higher level.

. . . (Upon his being anointed high priest) Aaron still worried, "Perhaps I have found pleasure in the anointing oil," and a *bat-kol* (heavenly voice) was heard saying, "How good and pleasant it is that brothers dwell

---

14. *Ma'or va-shemesh*, IV, 13b–14a.
15. *b. Sotah* 5a.

together" (Ps 133:1).¹⁶ [That verse is followed by that brief psalm's second and last verse, which begins, "It is like fine oil on the head running down onto the beard, the beard of Aaron . . . ."]

Elimelekh (of Lyhzansk), the rabbi of all the exiles, explained that it is the way of the *tzaddikim* who truthfully serve God to worry at all times, suspecting themselves of having taken pleasure in this world even while all they do is for the sake of God. Such a person is given to self-examination, feeling that perhaps he might be doing everything for the sake of material benefit and delight, seeking greatness for himself and the like. Aaron the priest was himself troubled by the fear that perhaps, when he was anointed as high priest, he had experienced some personally pleasurable feeling, some sense of self-glorification and in his own high position, feelings that were not for the sake of God . . . .

At times the *tzaddik* estimates in his own mind that all that he does is solely for the sake of God and not for any personal satisfaction. Nevertheless, he must not allow that claim itself to bring him to a sense of his own position and status as towering over others. Responding to the promptings of his own heart in realizing that his actions are truly of the nature of holy worship, he must nevertheless grasp also that he has achieved these good deeds not through his own self-purification but as a gift from God.

. . . And even those who are completely righteous may not ascribe what they have attained to their own good actions, but must rather view those attainments as a free gift that the blessed Creator brings about for the benefit of those He brought into being. That realization is true not only in regard to worldly delights, for even the *tzaddik* of the generation, who serves God and attains a sense of His Divinity, needs to know that this too is a gift. . . .

Even though Aaron the priest was the *tzaddik* of his generation, nevertheless he could not ascribe his attaining that level to himself. For even what he attained in the realm of the holy was due not to his own deeds and accomplishments, but rather to God.

Comment: While in some instances the homilist referred to Moses as a *tzaddik*, more broadly this identification was made in relation to the biblical *kohanim*, "the descendents of Aaron" as a whole. Moses stood alone in his own category, whereas Aaron represented a class as his direct descendents

16. b. ʿErub. 13b.

became the priests. And as we have noted, Hasidic homily-texts repeatedly read the references to the *kohanim* in the Torah as allusions to the *Tzaddikim*, the Hasidic masters and preachers themselves, bypassing much of the biblical conception of the priesthood.

In this portion, Korah, from the tribe of Levi, led a revolt against the authority of his cousins, Moses and Aaron, claiming that the latter wished only to hold onto their own power and positions to the exclusion of others. While the preacher's comments in defense of Moses and Aaron do not directly relate to the episode of that revolt, they are valuable in reference to themes heard more generally throughout the homilies.

In the Torah, God refers to Moses as the most humble of people (Num 12:3), and Kalonymus Kalman established a claim also for the humility of Moses' brother Aaron, as well as for the importance of humility itself. He refers to Mount Sinai, which rabbinic sources describe as a lowly mountain. In those sources, not only did God ignore the higher mountains while choosing Sinai, but also ignored the tall trees and chose, instead, a small thorn-bush as the setting for his addressing Moses, the shepherd.[17]

In any sphere of activity in life, no person can claim to have created his or her own abilities and capabilities; no one creates his or her own mind or body. One might only develop such capabilities which are, in themselves, gifts that a person cannot ascribe to himself or to his own doings. That realization is crucial to the quality of humility (*'anavah*) so emphasized and treasured in Hasidic teaching as a whole.

---

17. *b. Hor.* 12a.

Ḥukkat
To Each His Own: The Uniqueness of Each Person[18]

Every single *tzaddik* has his own root. And so Moses, our Teacher, wished to bring forth water from a rock connected with his own root rather than from the rock connected with the root of Miriam. But the people all assembled together near Miriam's rock, for in their minds it made sense to seek water precisely from that particular rock insofar as it had already once opened miraculously for them, providing them with water. It would seem, therefore, to be a simple matter to obtain water from the same rock.

But the bent of mind of Moses, our Teacher, may he rest in peace, pointed in a different direction. He had sought to open for them a rock connected to his own soul-root and to that of his brother, Aaron. For every *tzaddik* has a unique root, and even if he is able to bring about a miracle that a previous *tzaddik* performed, he does not bring it about through the same root and manner as the prior *tzaddik*.

Had the Israelites agreed with Moses, it would then have been an easy matter to bring forth water at a time of need.... But their difference of opinion concerning the water made it difficult to obtain water when it was needed.... To the rebels he wished to explain, "You think that I am of the root of my sister, Miriam?" and so he asked "... Shall we get water for you out of this rock?" (Num 20:10)—meaning from the same rock from which Miriam produced water. "But I am not of her root," he explained, and for this reason he sought to obtain for them water from another rock.

In this regard, however, he acted incorrectly. He should not have overruled the will of his people in a way that brought them to complain that, God forbid, God has the power to bring forth water from one particular rock, but is powerless to bring forth water from another rock. And

---

18. *Ma'or va-shemesh*, IV, 17a.

so God said... "Because you did not trust Me enough to affirm My holiness (in the sight of the Israelite people, therefore you shall not lead this congregation into the land that I have given them," Num 20:12).

Comment: The above excerpt is part of a much larger passage relating to the episode of Moses' striking the rock with the intent of obtaining water from the rock for his people in the desert (Num 20:1–13). Its context is found in later Jewish lore as Miriam, Moses' sister, came to be associated with a moving well of water that followed the path of the Israelites through the dry desert but which, with her death, ceased to provide water.[19] Though the excerpt itself is quite unrelated to what directly precedes and follows it in the preacher's discourse on that episode and is also quite unrelated to the biblical account of that episode, it voices, in an interesting way, a significant thrust of Hasidic teaching and one unmistakably present also in other homilies within *Ma'or va-shemesh*.

Kalonymus Kalman Epstein was particularly sensitive to the uniqueness of each person, a uniqueness which, in his thinking, radiated from a deep place within the self and from that person's own higher root. Each person has such a higher root, and one person's root is not the same as another's. And as is borne out in the above passage, this is true even concerning siblings within the same family. Such sensitivity to the essential uniqueness of each person, expressed in various Hasidic sources, is clearly voiced already in the Mishna in the warning given to witnesses prior to their testimony in a case involving potential capital punishment. "Unlike identical coins produced from a single mold, though God created all humans from a single mold, that of the First Man, no person is really similar to another."[20]

The same passage points also to the complexity of Moses' role as an educator. He sought to teach what his following would fail to understand and as a result, even in the face of his insightful wisdom, Moses is assigned a share in the guilt concerning the consequences of his disagreement with his people.

In this excerpt, the Kraków master related to the theme of the uniqueness of each individual specifically in connection with the individuality of each holy man. Elsewhere, however, the ramifications extend to the folly of one's followers who hold up their *tzaddik* as a model even to the point of imitating particular mannerisms of the holy man in the way he performs

---

19. *b. Ta'an.* 9a.
20. *m. Sanh.* 4:5.

holy deeds. Precisely such shallow imitation, making for a questionable, lower-level expression of identity with the *tzaddik*, may likely have impressed upon the Kraków master the importance of conveying a sense of that distinct uniqueness of each person.

In addition, perhaps the Kraków master sought to convey that the living cannot seek to emulate those who are no longer living. Miriam had died; Aaron and Moses were still living. For all the virtues of those no longer living, each generation must seek its own deeper root and way of understanding. Imitation of the past cannot serve as an authentic path for those living in the present without negating an important part of who and what we are. That very individuality of each generation is voiced in a particularly interesting way in a homiletical comment of Efrayim of Sydelikov on the first official *mitzvah* in the Torah.[21]

The Significance of Song[22]

> "Then Israel sang this song: 'Spring up, O well—sing to it—.'"
> (Num 21:17)

It seems that the import of these words can be understood on the basis of what is found in the Gemara, where the verse, "Moreover, I gave them laws that were not good . . . " (Ezek 20:25), is said to apply to "whoever recites without melody, and whoever reviews his study-lesson without song."[23] [This saying, stated by Rabbi Shefatiah in the name of Rabbi Yohanan, refers to reciting the Torah without cantillation and to reciting the Mishna without a melody to aid memorization.]

The essence and purpose of the worship of the Lord is that one might grasp the innerness of the Torah and attach himself to the blessed *Ein-sof*. However it is not possible for a person to comprehend the innerness of the Torah without his first clearly learning the plain (surface) meanings of the Torah-text. And as "not study but deeds are the essential"[24] [a saying which came down in the name of Rabban Shim'on ben Gamliel], so one must learn in order to teach and observe and fulfill (the Torah),

---

21. *Degel maḥaneh 'Efrayim* (Bo).
22. *Ma'or va-shemesh*, IV, 19ab.
23. *b. Meg.* 32a.
24. *m. 'Abot* 1:17.

whereas if one studies for the purpose of gaining a laudable reputation, he will not attain any true understanding of the *halakhah* (law).

For this reason, the following counsel is given to the person seeking a true grasp of the *halakhah*: immediately upon awakening in the middle of the night, he should pour forth *t'ḥinot* (prayers for forgiveness) and *bakashot* (prayerful requests) before the blessed God, and he should examine his deeds and repent concerning them. And afterward, he should sing songs and praises before the King to Whom praises are due—all prior to studying. After all these, he will be able to study with a powerful intent to observe and to fulfill (the Torah's words). And only then will he attain a clear and true understanding of the law, as it was given to Moses at Sinai.

Concerning King David, it is written "And the Lord is with him" (1 Sam 16:18), words which our Sages interpreted as indicating that the *halakhah* concerning every matter was in agreement with his understanding.[25] How did David come to deserve that?—because he was "the sweet singer of Israel" (2 Sam 23:1) and would awaken in the middle of the night to accept upon himself the yoke of the Kingship of God, singing songs and praises to his Maker without end. [David, it is said, would awaken at the end of the second of four watches (*mishmarot*) comprising the night; according to a rabbinic agada evoked by the verse, "I will wake the dawn" (Ps 108:3), David hung his harp above his bed so that the north wind might strike its strings in the middle of the night, at which time he would awaken and study Torah.[26]] Then afterward when he would begin to study, he was able to arrive at a clear and true grasp of the *halakhah* as it was given at Sinai.

But regrettably, one who does not engage in repentance and who fails to recite songs and praises prior to his study is injurious both to himself and to his act of worship. . . .

The Israelites, unlike Moses himself who naturally retained a clear and precise sense of the law even without song, had to awaken themselves with song in order that the law, truthfully formulated, might be disclosed to them.

Comment: Kalonymus Kalman viewed song as an indispensable feature of prayer. While words alone often lack that power of expression, song

25. *b. Sanh.* 93b.
26. *b. Ber.* 3b; also *Midr. Lam.* 2:22.

draws from a deeper level of the self with which the worshipper then connects. For this reason, song is an indispensable element in one's preparation for prayer. But proceeding beyond extolling the power of song to open the inner reaches of the self in a way that enables a person to pray, the preacher claimed that song is necessary also to enable one to study with focus, drive and concentration. And certainly some people have experienced that music contributes to putting the mind at ease so that it can function better in the course of serious mental pursuits.

Again, one cannot ponder these statements concerning song without thinking of the place of the *niggun* in Hasidic life and experience. The *niggun*, a melody without words, testifies in a special way to the power of song to forge a person's connection with a deeper part of himself where, in turn, one connects with his divine Root. That very depth, not contradicting but rather situated beyond the province of the cognitive mind, can function as a gateway to allow a sense of connection with what is higher than ourselves.

The passage in the Torah telling about the digging of a well accompanied by song (Num 21:16–18) consists of but three brief verses. But the Kraków master utilized that brief passage to define what might be considered a cultural definition of Hasidism. In contrast with *lamdanut*, the ideology of talmudic study which held up mental activity of that nature as the highest level and expression of religious living, Hasidism joined Torah-study to an activity intrinsically more emotional and devotional in character, namely song. That view does not negate the life of the mind, but rather allows for another type of engagement that, in turn, becomes an actual prerequisite for study with true comprehension.

Balak

The Danger in One's Imitating Another's Path[27]

> "As Bilaam looked up and saw Israel encamped tribe-by-tribe, the spirit of God came upon him." (Num 24:2)

Rashi, may his memory be a blessing, explained the words, "And Bilaam looked up," to suggest that he sought to infect the Israelites with his envious eyes. . . . He saw each tribe encamped symmetrically in its own space. He saw that their tent-openings were not opposite one another, and "the spirit of God came upon him." The Zohar understood the word *'alav* (upon him) as meaning that because the divine Presence settled upon the Israelites, the envious Bilaam was unable to curse them.[28]

And it would seem to be a case of correspondences (*midah k'neged midah*): Just as the Israelites organized themselves in an arrangement by which no one could gaze into his neighbor's tent and look through the tent-opening to see his neighbor's actions, hence not allowing for envious eyes, correspondingly God mercifully protected them from the envious eye of the wicked Bilaam, may his name be blotted out.

One might also suggest that their tent-openings, which were not situated one opposite the other, allude to the principle that each *tzaddik* (holy man) must hold onto his own path to holiness, discovering his own path, rather than their imitating one another. Such imitation, for example one's doing what he had seen his rabbi doing, repeating his behaviorisms and motions, would make for a situation in which one performs a *mitzvah* (a holy deed) as something simply learned from other people [rather than flowing from one's own spiritual insight and depth of feeling].

That is not the way; instead, each one, acting alone, must find for himself his own gates of holiness. That is the meaning of the tent-openings

---

27. *Ma'or va-shemesh*, IV, 21b–22a.
28. Zohar, III, 211b.

not being situated one in view of the other: that one person not walk in the path to holiness that his fellow opened, but rather he must walk in the path that he himself opened. And in that sense, "the spirit of God was upon them."

One can go further, understanding Rashi's comment concerning the privacy of each tent as an allusion to the realization that the *Sitra 'aḥra* ("the Other Side," the cosmic evil force) always stands opposite holiness, confronting it like a monkey with a human face. When a person wishes to enter into holiness and to accept upon himself a commitment of serving God's Kingship, the Evil Force fortifies itself against that person to fight against him and confuse him. And consequently, a person must make himself aware of the strategies of the Evil Force, for when the Accusers (demonic agents of the *Sitra 'aḥra*) know that person's path in serving God, they are then prepared to engage in combat with him.

To avert that kind of circumstance, it is necessary for one to create a new opening, a path that the Accusers will not know. In this way the person can be spared from the hands of the Accusers and can ascend successively from one level to a higher level as the spirit of God comes upon him.

The way is not the same for all persons, for each person must walk in life according to the root of his own holy soul and his own intelligence.

Comment: While the text in the Torah speaks of the orderly encampment of the tribes around the Tabernacle, each in its own designated space, Kalonymus Kalman related, rather, to Rashi's comment that the orderly arrangement of the tents, set up in such a way that the opening of one tent was not opposite that of another tent, allowed for privacy, thus avoiding the very possibility of envy. The Kraków master went further and proceeded to read Rashi's comment in a way that suggested a further, quite different thought. He read it symbolically as indicating that each *tzaddik* must fashion his own path and gateway to holiness, rather than his relying on the paths that others have forged, and certainly not imitating the ways of others. We note, again, a strong emphasis upon the uniqueness of each person and a criticism of imitation in the realm of the spiritual.

While the passage refers to each *tzaddik* having his own path to God, the concluding sentence in the same passage broadens that conception into an assertion that every person has his own gateway to God and to the service and worship of God.

The same essential note was sounded by some other important figures in Polish Hasidism. Simhah Bunam of Przysucha (1765–1827) related an often-repeated parable conveying that "the real treasure is found within oneself."[29] That parable about a treasure which, on the basis of a dream, was thought to be buried beneath a bridge, is found also in the *Masnavi* of Rumi, who lived some five-hundred years earlier.[30] And later, the name of Menahem Mendel of Kotsk (1787–1859) is associated with a fierce diatribe against imitation of any sort including even a person's imitating himself. A person who repeats even his own practice succumbs to routine as his practice disconnects from its original spiritual force.[31]

Those two figures felt the need to confront the tendency which is perhaps inevitable in any group that holds up its leaders and teachers with special and holy esteem, namely the tendency to look upon the ideas and even the mannerisms of the master in his fulfilling holy deeds as any kind of precise model for his followers. Kalonymus Kalman was adamant in his criticism of such imitation of the master. Not only is the individuality of the followers sacrificed, but their relationship to the master assumes a very superficial expression. In other places in his homilies (note for example "The basis of Moses' hesitation" on *parashat Va'era*), he forcefully argued that each person is unique and, furthermore, that a person's very conception of Divinity defies communication insofar as it is necessarily grounded in the very uniqueness of the individual at its deepest place.

And we recall from his comments on the promise to Abraham that his seed will be countless just like the stars of the heavens (Gen 15:5) Kolonymus Kalman's suggestion that the stars are specifically mentioned as a model insofar as "each star shines by its own light" ("As the stars that shine by their own light," on *parashat Lekh l'kha*).

---

29. *Sefer Simḥat Yisra'el*, 47a. Tr. Wineman, *The Hasidic Parable*, 172–74.
30. See Wineman, *The Hasidic Parable*, 176.
31. Heschel, *A Passion for Truth*, 140–45.

Pinḥas

The Longing for the Sublime Light That Can Be Fulfilled Only with Death[32]

The blessed Holy One created all the worlds to benefit His creatures in order that they might know the sweetness of His friendship and love. And for this purpose He repeatedly contracted His Divinity until this world of *'Asiyah* was created in which it would be possible to err—God save us—due to the nature of free will and choice, all in order that man might choose the good and detest evil.

And in the process, holy Sparks of holy souls fell bringing about a confusing fusion of good and evil. There is nothing in the world, even in inert matter, which does not have within it a holy Spark, though such a Spark might be covered and concealed by numerous garments along with the falling of the Sparks from the seven Primeval Kings, as is known to people of knowledge. [The Primordial Kings of Edom, based on Gen 36:31—forces representing strict judgment—came into being and then died during the process of Emanation, giving rise to a more merciful world-order.]

The essence of the service and worship of God aims at separating out the scattered Sparks of one's soul and lifting them up to the place from which the soul is hewn. When the holy Sparks are raised up, the *k'lipa*h ("Shell") is left devoid of any life-force, as the Shells fall into the deep abyss where they are powerless to lead man to sin. And how can a person sift out the Sparks of his soul? This is accomplished by devoting both his body and his spirit to God at all times, whether through fulfilling the *mitzvot* or Torah-learning or prayer, and especially in affirming God's

---

32. *Ma'or va-shemesh*, IV, 22ab.

Oneness twice daily in reciting the *Sh'ma* [three passages from the Torah prefaced with a statement proclaiming the Oneness of God, Deut 6:4].

As long as a person is alive, one is in need of food and drink and shelter and clothing along with other similar needs. But in meeting all these needs, one's real motivation must be solely for the sake of God, as his soul thirsts with longing to taste the sweetness of God's love. And all the days of one's life a person should long to experience the Light of the countenance of the King of Life. As a person turns his thought from this world and its needs, his aspiration in prayer is for the soul to experience, even to some small degree, that sweetness of the sublime Light. In such moments, the soul is moved by a constant longing to connect with the sublime Lights.

And when this desire overpowers him, that person comes even to detest his life, and were it possible he would prefer to sever his spirit from his body and simply and joyously attach himself to the sublime Light. For it is painful to him that his spirit remains attached to the body, as precisely his attachment to the body prevents him from ascending and cleaving completely to the sublime Light. But at a time of peak spiritual experience, his very body is purified due to his tremendous longing to be likened to higher worlds, a longing that burns within him like a fiery torch. And even his body ascends above.

That spiritual sensation is beneficial to him even following his prayer. And even though the desire itself is no longer as powerful as before, nevertheless his body ceases to seek anything of a material nature but desires only that he engage in holy worship in all his deeds and all the aspects of his life. In eating and drinking and tending to other needs, in everything that he does he engages in the worship of God, lifting up the scattered Sparks of his soul. And should his longing to attach himself to God further intensify, his body becomes purified to such an extent that the very matter of his body is transformed to what is soul-like in nature.

The initial example of a person of such longing is Enoch, who so intensely longed to cleave to the sublime Light that he could no longer tolerate his body. Due to the intensity of his longing, his body became purified and he became spiritual to the point that "he was no more, for God took him" (Gen 5:24) to serve before Him on high. Consequently, all the ascents of the worlds occur through him, for he had been in this world and ascended from it.[33]

33. For background, note Ginzberg, *Legends*, 5:156–64; Zohar I, 55b, 157a and 172b, and Zohar, tr. Matt, 1:313, 321.

And the same is true concerning Elijah—may his memory be a blessing. Due to the strength of his longing, his body became purified to such an extent that rather than undergoing death and burial he ascended above in a storm. For this reason he constantly serves as a messenger of the Merciful One, helping persons when they are performing a *mitzvah* and protecting them from the power of the *Sitra 'aḥra* which conspires to confuse them. And this is especially the case in connection with the *mitzvah* of circumcision, which is not dependent upon the infant's choice but is an act in which his father rejoices; there Elijah is always to be found. [In Jewish lore, Elijah is thought to come to every circumcision ceremony (*b'rit*), where a special chair is set aside for him at the ceremony, a practice relating to the period of the Hadrianic persecutions when Roman edicts forbade the rite of circumcision along with other Jewish practices.] And he always speaks on behalf of the people Israel, to draw down upon them beneficial influences and to cease the efforts of the Accusers who rise against them.

Elijah alone merited that distinction of his body becoming so thoroughly purified. However, in the moment of one's action and longing to cleave to the sublime Light, anyone who does any *mitzvah* or good deed with a depth of devotion and longing along these lines would rejoice if it were possible for him to leave this world and ascend to the higher world, because it is for this that he yearns. At the very hour of his deed his body is purified, and Elijah clads himself in it; his efforts are achieved through miracles and wonders, and such a person has the power to separate out and elevate holy Sparks.

And at the very moment that *Pinḥas*/Phineas acted zealously for the Lord of Hosts (Num 25:1–15), a tremendous desire to cleave to the sublime Light seized him to such an extent that his soul virtually departed from his body. And due to the intensity of his longing, his body itself was purified and the aspect of Elijah clad itself in him. He became as an angel, and the men of the tribe of Simeon could not see him as he approached Zimri, and many miraculous happenings came to his aid. And in this worshipful deed, he lifted up (fallen) Sparks that had been scattered among the Shells.

Out of the vastness of his longing, God promised that he would be attached to the sublime Light and would resemble an angel of the God of Hosts, as it says, "An angel of the Lord came up from Gilgal" (Judg 2:1), an angel that our Sages interpreted in reference to Phineas.[34] In this way he acted out of his zeal, atoning for the generations, as Elijah was clad in him.

Comment: The action performed by Phineas/*Pinḥas* (Num 25:1–9) in which his zeal for God found expression in violent action on his part bears similarity to the account of Elijah as found in a later part of the Hebrew Bible (1 Kgs 17–2 Kgs 2).

Both figures were determined and relentless and also merciless in serving their cause. Phineas slew Cozbi, the Midianite woman who successfully tempted the Israelite men-folk including Zimri who succumbed to her sexual enticement, and Elijah appears as a kind of utterly iconoclast warrior in Israelite monotheism's struggle with Canaanite and Phoenician pagan belief and the immoral acts associated with it. Violent behavior motivated by religious zeal is attributed both to Phineas and to Elijah who, at Mt. Carmel, is said to have slaughtered four-hundred-fifty prophets of Baal (1 Kgs, 18:19, 40; 19:1). Rabbinic sources did not overlook that degree of similarity between them, and the Pseudo-Jonathan Targum (Aramaic translation) goes further and actually identifies the two figures as one.[35] Also the *haftarah* (reading from the Prophets) assigned to the portion, *Pinḥas*, when that Shabbat does not fall within the three-week period preceding the Ninth of ʾAv, is taken from the biblical account of Elijah.

In a vast number of folktales from a later period, the figure of Elijah, who avoided the experience of dying and instead ascended to the heavens in a whirlwind or in a fiery chariot (2 Kgs 2:11), returns to the world in various masks and guises, sometimes testing people but also mercifully helping unfortunate victims in difficult situations. It could be said that, over time, the biblical Elijah underwent a definite personality change. The Elijah of Jewish folk-culture is characterized not by vengeful acts in defense of the God of Israel, but rather by compassion. And in Hasidic tradition, Elijah is sometimes understood not as a person, but as a mindset, a way of thinking and relating to the world.[36]

While Kalonymus Kalman Epstein constructed his homiletical discourse upon that identity of Phineas (*Pinḥas*) and Elijah (ʾ*Eliyahu*), he radically altered the distinguishing features of that pair in a way that clearly goes beyond the biblical texts and downplays the violent expression of their

---

34. *Midr. Lev.* 1:1.
35. *Tg. Ps.-J*, Exod 6:18.
36. Wiener, *The Prophet Elijah*, 116–31.

religious zeal. In his homily, the two exemplify instead the full intensity of an attachment to God to the point that they desire the death of the body in order to free them to fulfill their insatiable spiritual longing.

The above passage is a window to highly ascetic expressions of Jewish mystic themes which identify the love of God and self-negation as an aspiration that is fulfilled in the soul's leaving the body for a continued existence within the divine realm. Michael Fishbane's *The Kiss of God* is devoted to tracing, through an array of sources, the theme of death as the ultimate spiritual aspiration. In *Ma'or va-shemesh*, the two biblical figures, Phineas and Elijah, along with Enoch, represent the extreme degree of asceticism in their will-for-death. Traces of this theme are not absent in Hasidic teaching, although more generally this tendency is neutralized in Hasidism's broader aspiration of cleaving to God not in death, but in every moment of life and within one's very pursuit of meeting all of life's needs.[37]

As stated in another homiletical discussion in *Ma'or va-shemesh*, "Indeed, the sublime Emanator, who so desired the service of the *tzaddik* in this world, shows that righteous person that "the earth is full of His Presence" (Isa 6:3), and so also in this world he will find the ineffable sweetness of God. And in this way he, once again, desires life in this world as he feels that in this world too he will find and experience that divine sweetness."[38]

---

37. Fishbane, *The Kiss of God*, 46.
38. *Ma'or va-shemesh*, IV, 5a (*Rimzei Shavu'ot*).

Mattot
Defining One's Motivation[39]

It is known that the Land which God bequeathed to our fathers is very holy. Abraham our father, may he rest in peace, longed very much for the land of Israel. . . . And Moses longed to come there. For there is no *torah* (learning) like that of the Land of Israel; its very atmosphere is one that fosters wisdom. . . .

Not all wars are entirely for the purpose of conquest. Even if they are *milḥamot mitzvah* (wars which we are commanded to fight), nevertheless they do not lack some measure of personal motivation and intent in line with some aspect of the Evil Inclination which mires the engagement in war. Moved by a desire for worldly delights, (our fathers) may have striven to possess the Land of Israel, a land of milk and honey, preferable to all other lands.

And the intent of the tribes of Gad and Reuven (who wished to settle not within the land of Israel itself but rather beyond the River Jordan) was that the war be solely for the sake of God without any other motivation coming into play. In the wars for the Land of Israel it was crucial that there be no place for extraneous motivations such as worldly delight and benefit, promptings of the Evil Inclination. And for this reason they wished to remain and receive their inheritance in the land of Sihon and Og (rulers in the area east of the River Jordan) and, afterward, to lead the fighters in the wars of the land of Canaan.

And it is clear, since they would not receive any inheritance within the Land of Israel, that their intent was that the war be solely for the sake of God. In their eyes, there could be no legitimate place for fighting motivated by a quest for worldly advantages. . . .

---

39. *Ma'or va-shemesh*, IV, 29a.

... The children of Gad and of Reuven said to Moses, "We will build here sheepfolds for our flocks and towns for our children" (Num 32:16). ... We will seclude ourselves (restrict ourselves to our own location) to connect ourselves to God, binding ourselves to Him, particularly at the time of going forth to war, when holiness and purity are especially required. ... And they said, (we will join our fellow-tribes in war) "until we have established them in their place" [*makom* (place), a word which in later sources came to refer to God],[40] hence meaning: to attach our very senses to a sublime place, to the blessed *'Ein-sof*. And understanding their words in that light, Moses told them, "If that be your intention ..."—he agreed with their words.

Comment: The Torah, it would appear, is highly critical of the two-and-a-half tribes that chose to remain in land which they acquired beyond the River. But as they were nevertheless willing to participate with their fellow-tribes in the conquest of the Land (Num 32:16–19), the Kraków master, in another master-stroke of transformation, painted them in thoroughly altruistic colors, ascribing to them the noblest of intentions, a willingness to serve with no element of personal reward or benefit. This remolding of the biblical text exemplifies that general tendency of Kalonymus Kalman, and often of the tradition in general, to depict various biblical figures and groups in a decidedly noble and ideal light. Those tribes were more than willing to join with their brethren in the war of conquest without their receiving any benefit from that action. Their motivation, hence, was pure, while it could always be said that the other tribes fought for what they expected to gain materially for themselves. In the very wording of the Kraków master's comments concerning the other tribes, one might note that he identified an element of self-serving motivations and expectations within the very actions that the Torah-text itself deemed holy and divinely ordained.

It would also appear that the words of the homilist are really intended to resonate not in the world of ancient warfare, but rather in the study of Torah. Repeatedly, Kalonymus Kalman, like somewhat earlier Hasidic preachers, voiced criticism of the world of *lamdanut* (an ideology of learning) and attributed personal and egotistical motivations to many adherents of that camp who pursued the paths of intense rabbinic learning. While in other areas as well, the teachers of Hasidism were aware of the danger of engaging in certain actions of a religious character out of impure motivations rather

---

40. *Midr. Gen* 68.9.

than "for the sake of God," they located that danger most intensely in the area of rabbinic learning. Already in the very first printed Hasidic text, *Tol'dot Ya'akov Yosef*, one finds very pointed criticism of the normative religious community and of its leaders for whom mastery of the Talmud and later legal sources could be the path to a rabbinic position or to marriage into a wealthy family or to be known in one's community and beyond. In that context, the preacher's reading the request of the two-and-a-half tribes as a model of integrity very likely echoed much closer to home.

Mas'ei

Cities of Refuge as Cities of Repentance[41]

Six cities of refuge, *'arei miklat*—a precise number, neither more nor less. [The setting aside of six cities to which one who inadvertently caused another's death might flee in order to save his life from vengeful attack, Num 35:6–34.]

One must ponder, how does a person come to commit murder—God forbid—even without intention? One might well presume that this is not that person's first transgression, as one doesn't suddenly come to commit such a grave transgression. Rather, "One transgression brings on another,"[42] and if the culprit wishes to engage in repentance, he must question himself and examine his deeds in order to grasp what kind of sin preceded and led up to his act of (unintentional) murder. He must seek to recall and clarify all his prior transgressions in which he blemished some basic moral quality or principle. For had he ever blemished any such quality, even a seemingly minor one, he could come, unfortunately, over the course of time, to murder, insofar as "one transgression brings on another."

And there are six such qualities concerning which a person must ponder. If, for example, one sinned through an evil love, loving what is not his, in this way he could come to murder, for by his loving what belongs to his fellow he could be drawn to murder him. Similarly through fear: if he fears someone, he could come to murder that person. And he could be influenced by his own egotistical thoughts, for his ego might never be satisfied, not even with all the expanse of the world, or he might wish to triumph over his fellow against that fellow's wishes. Or he might have

---

41. *Ma'or va-shemesh*, IV, 31b–32b.
42. *m. 'Abot* 4:2.

sought (sexual) delight, as the Midrash explains that an adulterer eventually becomes a murderer. [A talmudic statement claims that an adulterer comes to his act prepared either to kill or be killed.[43]] If he blemished any of those six qualities—love, fear, self-glorification, the will to triumph over others, honor, or sexual desire [understood as corresponding to six of the *s'firot*]—"one transgression brings on another" until it leads him to commit murder, God forbid. Therefore the penitent must reconstruct and ponder his acts and emotions until it becomes clear to him exactly which quality he had blemished.

And this is itself possible only if he goes to *tzaddikei ha-dor* (the righteous or holy men of the generation), as doing so allows for a considerable degree of solitude and seclusion together with prolonged attentiveness. For this reason he is unable to clarify his own life and actions and emotions until he goes to *tzaddikei ha-dor*, and even there it might require a very long time until the *tzaddik*, who serves God, is able, over the course of time, to bring the sinner to a state of repentance.

And just as a *tzaddik* serves God according to his own particular aspect, the heart of the sinner who desires to repent and change will direct him to that particular *tzaddik* who serves God according to that particular quality which the sinner himself had blemished. And then he will consider one quality after another until it becomes clear which quality he had blemished, and only then, will he be able to come to complete repentance.

And so six Cities of Refuge were designated, corresponding to those six qualities. . . . For the Levites were truly *tzaddikim*, who served God, each one according to his own aspect and emphasis, and when the thought of turning in repentance arises in the murderer, his heart will immediately direct him to the particular city where the *tzaddik* is located who serves God with that very quality which the murderer had blemished. [Aaron, who together with his male descendents comprised the priesthood, was himself from the tribe of Levi; in that sense, the priests (*kohanim*) were really a sub-division of that tribe.] And he would not necessarily go to the nearest city of refuge, which would be geographically accessible to him, but each one would be led to proceed to the place where he might be able to repair the particular quality in need of repair.

Comment: The above homiletical discourse relates to the provision (spelled out in Num 35:9–28) that upon the Israelites' settling in the land

43. *Midr. Num.* 9:12.

of Canaan, six cities be set aside as places of refuge for anyone who unintentionally caused the death of another person. If the fugitive can make his way to any one of those designated cities, he will be protected from "blood vengeance" on the part of the victim's family whose sense of family obligation would require their pursuing and killing the murderer. The fugitive must then remain in his place of refuge until the death of the current high priest.

It will be obvious to the reader that Kalonymus Kalman here viewed any action on the part of a person, even a seemingly unintentional act, as "Freudian" in nature, negating the possibility of anything being truly unintentional. Any such deed is somehow related to some deeper quality or blemish in the person. And in this homily, the preacher did not relate seriously to the role of the cities of refuge as a way to counter the pursuer's obligation of "blood vengeance" even in the case of unintentional killing.

The preacher's concern was very different, and in terms of that concern he treated the person making his way to a city of refuge as a culprit, even if he himself was not at all consciously aware of his acting with intent. As in other examples of interpretation, the preacher severed the institution of such cities of refuge from the very basic situation which, according to the biblical text, led to their establishment. And as the particular law is removed from a significant, even central element in its context, another context is then substituted for those six designated cities.

To the preacher's mind, the cities of refuge were to be established not to protect a person who accidentally caused another's death, but, rather, to provide for the person a process of *t'shuvah* (repentance). And what the master outlined for that kind of situation is hardly any recipe for easy or instantaneous repentance. He thought of a city of refuge as a setting in which, with help, the person could examine and re-examine what led him to cause a loss of life, namely some transgression far less grave in nature which, however, pointed to a basic blemish in the person which eventually, even without conscious intent, expressed itself in the taking of another's life. And in this passage, the homilist enumerated six potential qualities or blemishes and artfully drew a numerical correspondence of those six qualities with the six cities of refuge.

In the preacher's reconstruction of the cities of refuge, the person does not flee to such a city out of a desire to save his life from his pursuers, but because something within him awakens to seek the way of self-understanding and repentance, and he furthermore comes to a particular city of refuge due to the presence there of a *tzaddik* who serves God with a focus on the particular quality which the person fleeing had betrayed at some point in his earlier life. Only that particular *tzaddik* could hence direct him to be able to identify his own 'original sin' sometime in the past which set him in the direction that culminated in his causing another's death.

Despite their name, the cities of refuge served, in his thought, not as a place of refuge, but rather as the scene of a lengthy and arduous depth-introspection allowing, ultimately, for true self-understanding and the repair of a basic undiscerned blemish. The preacher creatively utilized, re-ordered, and re-interpreted the elements of the biblical legislation in order to address themes of significance in his own way of thinking, namely introspective understanding and the need for true repentance. The preacher's conception of the cities of refuge included a basis for the precise number (six) of cities of refuge as well as for the provision that the person seeking refuge remain there until the death of the high priest. And his providing a rationale for those details created a space for his listeners to accept the preacher's diverting from the very givens of the law as stated in the Torah-passages.

The significance of Kalonymus Kalman's homily stands out boldly when the reader considers that the Kraków preacher died almost thirty-five years before Sigmund Freud was born. Though the two thought in very different terms, they shared a realization that self-understanding, when bound up with an occurrence concealed from one's very memory, can be an exceedingly difficult process requiring a lengthy span of time.

5

On the Fifth Book of the Torah (*D'varim* / Deuteronomy)

D'varim

As the Stars of the Heavens [1]

> ("Thereupon I said to you, I cannot bear the burden of you by myself.) The Lord your God has multiplied you until you are today as numerous as the stars in the sky." (Deut 1:9–10)

... It is said in the Talmud that the moon complained to its Maker, "Two kings cannot possibly share a single crown," to which God responded, "Then go and make yourself smaller!"[2] [According to this agada, the sun and the moon were originally of equal size, and the moon complained that such a situation is untenable, thinking that God would respond by appointing the moon the larger of the two lights.] All the worlds and everything in the world both give and receive, receiving and being impacted by the next higher level of being, while giving to or effecting the next lower level; only the *Ein sof* (the infinite state of the Divine) is an exception in this respect. Hence, the sun is impacted beneficially from what is above it, even while it impacts the moon. God's response to the moon flows from the necessity that the one who receives is necessarily smaller than the one that influences and bestows power to it, and accordingly He told the moon, "Go and make yourself smaller."

It is also found in the Talmud that "one kingdom does not rule over its neighbor even to the extent of a hair-breadth,"[3] for they are separated by clear and defined borders. When the time comes for a *tzaddik* to become the influencing force in his generation, another must make way for him, for they are subject to borders, and one kingdom does not infringe upon its neighboring kingdom.

---

1. *Ma'or va-shemesh*, V, 3ab.
2. *b. Ḥul.* 60b and Rashi on Deut 1:10.
3. *b. Ber.* 48b and *Midr. Gen* 6:3.

This is not the case, though, when none of the *tzaddikim* of a generation wishes to occupy a commanding role but all prefer instead another pattern, that of a fellowship (*ḥevruta*) in which each serves God together with others as equals, as they encourage one another in the service and worship of God. In that case, it is unnecessary for one to make way for the other. And the stars provide a model of that arrangement: one star does not impact another as occurs with the sun and the moon. Each star is appointed for its own realm, in terms of its own uniqueness, and all the stars are friends (*ḥaverim*, fellow-peers) together in the service of God.

... A large number of *tzaddikim* in a generation, all capable of wondrous and miraculous deeds, is beneficial both for the entire world and for those *tzaddikim* themselves. For if there were but a single *tzaddik* at any time he might become proud, viewing himself as occupying a higher level than others. But when there are many such *tzaddikim* in the generation, then none will succumb to pride, for the reason that there are many others equally capable of attaining the same level. And furthermore, when there are several such *tzaddikim* in the generation, each one is humbled by his fellows, for each one of them has some quality that is not found in the others.

Unlike the case with the sun and the moon, among the stars one is not envious of the others and none belittles the others. . . . And for this reason Moses likened Israel to the stars, that the *tzaddikim* might similarly be numerous, so that none will succumb to arrogant pride over the others, as each is aware of his fellows' virtuous qualities.

Comment: It might seem, perhaps, that the preacher has offered a kind of midrash on Gen 1:16, the verse from the creation-account that, after mentioning the greater and smaller lights, adds the word, *v'et ha-kokhavim* ("and the stars"). A midrash[4] explains the stars, mentioned in that verse, as a consolation or compensation given to the moon after it was ordered to "make itself smaller." While the first part of the verse, relating to the two major lights, evoked in its midrashic reading issues of pride and competition, what followed enabled Kalonymus Kalman to hold up the stars as alluding to a different social dynamic, free of pride, rivalry, and hierarchy. The numerous stars allow for a different pattern and relationship, one applicable to humans as well.

4. *Midr. Gen* 6.4.

The preacher can be forgiven for not grasping the force of gravity and its impact even among the stars, for like his comments on Miriam's dance in *parashat B'shallaḥ*, the master aspired and struggled to establish an alternative to hierarchy. In this passage, however, that alternative, a conception of fellowship veering toward a distinctively democratic strain of sensitivity, is limited in that it would apply to the relationship among *tzaddikim* rather than to their relationship to their community of followers.

The implications of his analogy, however, are given broader scope elsewhere in this collection. One might recall that in the master's homiletical comments on *parashat Lekh l'kha* in which Abraham is told that his seed will be as numerous as the stars, they are likened specifically to the stars for the reason that "a star shines by its own light." There not only the holy men but all the descendents of Abraham are likened to the stars, each of which shines by its own light.

Va'ethannan
The Background of Moses' Death[5]

By means of the fusion of divine Names, it would be possible to unify all the worlds from the lowest point in the earth to the blessed Infinite. That fusion of Names would raise up all the forces of Judgment and evil to their higher Root, annulling the forces of evil and externality, and God's Divinity would then be made manifest in all the worlds. We lovingly hope for that time when all evil will be severed out from all the worlds by means of the name *AHYH* (a variation and higher state of the divine Name), for then "the Lord will be One and his Name One" (Zech 14:9).

And it was within the power of Moses to unify the Names, for Moses is *Da'at* ("knowledge" or more precisely: spiritual understanding), and when he prayed before God to be able to enter into the Land, with the very language of his prayer he could have accomplished that unification, for his intention in wishing to enter into the Land was to separate the worlds from all evil. But he did not proceed then to act out his prayer [and unify the Names and all existence], for such was not the Creator's Will for that time. Even so, the wording of his prayer and pleading serves as a guide to the *tzaddikim* of the generations that they might know how to perform unifications.... The verse indicates that Moses' intention was that *'Adonai* would be One and His Name One, and that we might be able to pronounce the Ineffable Name in its written form as will be the case in the future.[6] [This can occur only when all existence will be redeemed and free of evil. Until then, according to rabbinic tradition, the Ineffable Name is written in one way while it is pronounced differently, and the Name can be pronounced as written only at the designated Temple site].

5. *Ma'or va-shemesh*, V, 6ab.
6. *m. Sanh.* 11:1, *b. Sotah* 38a, and *b. Pesah.* 50a.

... The blessed Holy One created the worlds with all their creatures, creating everything so that His Glory might be praised and recounted and that His Divinity and His divine Presence (*Sh'khinah*) might be revealed in both the lower and upper worlds. But the wicked push away the feet of the divine Presence, and as their wickedness intensified, the divine Presence became more and more concealed until it acquired a pronounced state of hiddenness, as is known to Kabbalists. But at the same time God brought about a counter development, namely that there would be righteous ones (*tzaddikim*) in every generation who would extend and reveal the holiness of the divine Presence below.

Now how is it at all possible "to push away the feet of the divine Presence," considering that in truth, "His presence fills all the earth" (Isa 6:3) and "there is no place devoid of His Presence"? [The Aramaic statement, *leit 'atar panui minei*[7] echoes the midrashic statement, *'Ein makom belo Sh'khinah*, there is no place where the *Sh'khinah* is not present.[8]] However, people lacking a more developed understanding who are drawn solely to the natural state of the world, to eating and drinking, seeking pleasure and engaging in trade without being at all drawn to His Divinity, repel and thrust aside "the feet of the *Sh'khinah*." And in truth, God made everything that is in Nature, for Nature, too, is derived from the Creator who created everything with Wisdom. Hence, as long as people serve God properly there is no need for changes in the ways of nature (supernatural miracles altering the ways of Nature), for God directs His world through the wisdom of Nature, and at every single moment His Providence constantly guides all the worlds and its creatures, and all their power and life-force and energy are His....

But humans who are drawn only to Nature and devote all their days and years exclusively to natural activities bring about a separation between God's Divinity and Nature, "repelling the feet of the divine Presence," something that logically is impossible.

At the same time, the righteous of the generation do just the opposite: they extend the holiness of that Presence below, recognizing the holiness of the *Sh'khinah* within the Wisdom of Nature. Though they eat and drink, engaging in natural acts, they nevertheless immediately connect with God's Divinity in all the levels of their souls and attach themselves to

---

7. *Tikkunei Zohar*, ch. 57.
8. *Midr. Exod.* 2:9.

the Infinite One. In this way, they cause the divine Presence to be revealed in the lower realms after it had become hidden due to human iniquity.

. . . Our Sages correctly taught that Elijah the prophet [who taught the Oneness of God and unified the divine Names, 1 Kgs, 2:1] is to be found on the market-day,⁹—meaning that precisely on the market-day, when people follow their natural pursuits such as trade and commerce, buying and selling, and similar natural activities and endeavors, he comes and reminds them that *'Adonai* is *'Elohim* (1 Kgs 18:39) extending the holiness of the *Sh'khinah* to the very sphere of natural activity.

Rather than opening a chasm between God and Nature, in the very wording of his prayer and pleading, Moses, our Teacher, alluded to the importance of unifying the divine Names, restoring [within human consciousness] the holiness of God's Divinity within the Wisdom of Nature and thus making a revelation of God's Divinity possible in the lower worlds. And understand!

Comment: This discourse can be understood within the context of a series of homilies by different Hasidic homilists who located the core-motivation of Moses' request and insistence that he be allowed to the enter into the Land in his determination to bring about a total redemption and unification of all existence including an absolute end of all exile. This lofty aspiration would be realized, according to the various renditions, had Moses been able to be joined by the original generation that had left Egypt, or through Moses' performing certain *mitzvot* that apply and are possible only within the Land of Israel (*Mitzvot ha-tluyot ba'aretz*), or if Moses could have entered the Land and, at the designated Temple site, pronounce the Ineffable Name there in its written form, or if such was God's will.

Moses wished to bring about, within his own lifespan, a messianic culmination of the struggle between good and evil, and Kalonymus Kalman seemed, in this homily, to assume that Moses would have had that capacity had he been allowed to enter the Land.

But such was not God's Will for that time. The passage then goes on to explain that refusal, offering a more comprehensive reason, namely that Moses failed to grasp the nature of the real obstacle standing in the way of such total unification. Cosmic exile, as a state of being, cannot easily be altered in some symbolic way by fusing together divine Names, for the obstacle to total unification and redemption is the disconnect, in people's

---

9. *b. Ta'an.* 22a.

minds and consciousness, between God and Nature —or perhaps more precisely, between God and the conduct of all aspects of a person's life.

The homily grasps the natural course of life and of the world as related to God in all its aspects. The homilist set forth the interesting position that ideally there would be no place for any divine miracles contradicting the orderly conduct of nature; it is only in response to the wicked that miracles occur and are necessary. Nature and God themselves are not contradictory propositions, and the Kraków preacher, it would appear, experienced the miraculous precisely within the natural.

But the real thrust of this homily lies in the errant belief that the pursuit of natural actions in the world is in no way related to God. A person's meeting one's natural, physical needs is too often regarded, in people's minds, as having no connection with the Divine, and to the mind of the Kraków master, precisely that disconnect is the great heretical divide in people's thinking and the major obstacle in the way of redemption.

Kalonymus Kalman maintained that such a crucial disconnect cannot be remedied by certain cultic actions such as were intended by Moses. It can be remedied and repaired only by reconnecting the entire scene of human life with Divinity, for God's Presence is everywhere including the entire scene of life. A repair of that disconnect in human consciousness, the Kraków master was insisting, cannot take place in a single act in the space of a few moments or hours. Rather it requires generations and is the task and role of the righteous (*tzaddikim*) of the generations to reify the faith in the Oneness of God.

Moses himself erred in his conception of the way to bring redemption to his people and to all existence. What is required is not a cultic act or a series of acts that Moses himself might have accomplished were he allowed to enter the Land, but rather a transformation of consciousness, requiring an ongoing devotion, encompassing generations, to the task of hallowing all of life.[10]

Prayer in Community and Solitude[11]

> "But if you (pl.) search there for the Lord your God, you will find Him, if only you (sg.) seek Him with all your heart and soul . . . ." (Deut 4:29)

10. See Wineman, "A Hasidic Myth of the Death of Moses."
11. *Ma'or va-shemesh*, V, 7b.

Note that the verse opens in the plural, "If you (plural) search there," and concludes in the singular, "if only you (singular) seek him with all your (singular) heart and soul." That verse appears to me to obligate a person to purify himself to great length, and the essential element in that purification is prayer with inner intent (*kavanah*), engaging in prayer with reverence and love. . . .

But the essential point is precisely to pray with a congregation. Even if those constituting the congregation pray rapidly or in a drawn-out manner, one is obligated to forego one's own considerations in order to pray with a congregation rather than alone, and then one will be able to attain significant spiritual levels. Even if a thousand people are praying together in a single prayer-assembly, the prayer of any one person among them is not similar to that of the next person. For even in such a scene, every person finds God according to his own inner intent and his preparation prior to the actual event of praying.

Comment: Returning to a theme with which the master frequently engaged, he once again appears to be pulling the same rope from both ends. His words emphasize both inner intent on a personal level and the importance of praying with a congregation, even assigning priority to the latter. As he emphasizes the spiritual ethic involved in prayer within a community of worshippers, even one with definite shortcomings, the preacher, however, brings the two ends of the rope together. The polarity and tension sounded in this homily are, at least on the surface, resolved with the recognition that even in an exceedingly large assembly of prayer, each person is nevertheless praying as an individual in that he is building upon the spiritual capital of his own inner work preceding the actual reciting of prayer.

Jewish practice traditionally situates prayer within a group context, but at the same time, prayer itself is not a group-activity but one that is ignited within the inner depth of a person.

ʿEikev

The Nature of Manna[12]

When the intention of our holy fathers found favor in God's eyes, He promised to give to their posterity the Land of Holiness, where the fallen worlds did not descend but only the aspect of souls, as is known, (a land free of all that is evil or unholy). . . . It is called the Land of Israel because even its earthiness is purified of all dross and base matter, and for this reason its very air and atmosphere breed wisdom and aid in elevating all the worlds. It is clearly different in character from all land beyond it where the Sparks are clad in an external garment.

One who comes to serve God and to gather the Sparks and uplift the worlds must be determined to prevent that externality, cladding the Sparks, from inflicting damage upon him. For if he is unable to raise up the Spark, bringing it forth from its imprisoning Shells, not only does he not assist the process at all, but the Spark itself will effect him adversely, casting him, God forbid, into the hands of the very Evil that clads that very Spark.

But that is not the case in the Land of Israel where the earthiness is itself purified. And hence there one can more easily locate the innerness of food, so that the external aspect of the act of eating will not inflict damage upon him.

Similarly, also the manna (though eaten in the wilderness, outside the Land) represents food that is highly purified in that sense. The manna exemplified the situation that existed prior to the sin of the First Man, when he was still clad in a garment of Light [ʾor with an ʾalef, in contrast to a garment of skin, ʿor, spelled with an ʿayin][13] so that even his

---

12. *Maʾor va-shemesh*, V, 11b-12a.
13. Based on *Midr. Gen*, 20:12.

external aspect cladding his innerness was also in an iridescent, purified state. And similarly the external aspect of the manna was so purified that it was digested into the body's limbs without producing the waste and filth which exemplifies the *Sitra 'aḥra* (the Evil Force). In the case of the manna, its innerness was more accessible, as the Sparks that fell with the shattering of the vessels (*sh'virat ha-kelim*) nevertheless retained the character of the higher holiness.

... And so by means of the manna, realizing that the physical aspect of food in itself does not constitute the life-energy of man, you will grasp "that man does not live on bread alone." Rather, man lives on "anything that the Lord decrees" (Deut 8:3, literally, "from all that proceeds from the mouth of God"), identifying the very essence of his own life-energy as the Spark that is of the very essence of God who is present within the food.

Comment: In his approach to the subject of manna, Kalonymus Kalman again exemplified the tendency of the Hasidic masters in their homilies to focus on an element in the biblical account quite independently of its actual narrative context. In the above passage, the meaning of manna is not bound up with the hardships of journeying through the desert or with the complaints of the Israelites concerning their lack of food. It acquires, instead, a very different meaning, one that suggests an insight into the nature and meaning of food itself and its place in life.

While in thinking about food, people tend to focus upon its external sense and benefit, food, like everything else, is here felt to have an internal dimension that is holy. Something of the Divine is present within everything and is therefore present within the very food we eat.

While conveying that we are to eat for the purpose of maintaining our health and our very lives, at the same time the Kraków master did not view food simply as a means of life. Rather, like everything else, food (symbolized by bread) contains an inner spiritual meaning and presence and serves as a connection with the holy and with God.

That realization is captured in a startling manner in the words of Moshe of Kobrin who, it is reported, once lifted up a piece of bread and exclaimed, "God is in this piece of bread," (as in all else that exists).[14] (Note also "The meaning of manna," on *parashat B'shallaḥ*).

---

14. *'Or y'sharim*, 87.

R'eih

Fellowship as the Path to God[15]

> "See, this day I set before you (*lifneikhem*, the plural object) blessing and curse: blessing, if you obey the commandments of the Lord your God which I enjoin upon you this day; and curse, if you do not obey the commandments of the Lord your God, but turn away from the path which I enjoin upon you this day . . . ." (Deut 11:26–28)

It is clear to everyone's eyes that these words are addressed not to a single person but to a plural addressee. The general principle is that one really comes to the way of God by means of *dibbuk ḥaverim* (fellowship in which members are attached to one another). . . .

By means of the journey to the *tzaddik* of the generation, in which people gather together as a holy flock of sheep, each person annuls his own sense of self (and his own righteous self-estimation) in the presence of his fellow. As one sees the higher level of his fellow in Torah-study and in *mitzvot* and good deeds, that person consequently lowers himself in his own eyes. And he then responds lovingly to every single person and identifies with them joyfully and lovingly.

And that is precisely the principle: that each one recognize the (higher) level of his fellow and feel his own inadequacy in the other's presence, whereas in his own home each might tend to be upright in his own eyes and to consider himself a great Torah-student and a devout person of good qualities, failing to detect in himself even any particle pointing to the contrary. And then his Evil Inclination [here: in the form of egotism] prevails over him, and he emerges greater and greater in his own eyes.

---

15. *Ma'or va-shemesh*, V, 13b.

That is not the case, however, when people gather together to go to the *tzaddik*. There, a person's egotism vanishes as he finds there people living with an awe of God and wholly devoted and accomplished in Torah-learning and in *mitzvot*. One finds there among them both people much younger than himself and also people much older than him who are, nevertheless, energetic in the worship of God. And they all extol the *tzaddik* over their own accomplishments and yearn for a life of still greater devotion to God. And one finds there both rich people, who nevertheless do not pursue worldly desires but treasure the way of serving God and wholeheartedly respect the *tzaddik*, along with poor people who, even in their poverty and distress, turn away from their own concerns and seek to serve God joyously and lovingly. And upon seeing all these people with open eyes, then even if one's heart were like a heart of stone, it would melt within him and disintegrate in the presence of every single person there. And that is *dibbuk ḥaverim*.

. . . And as each person annuls his own self-esteem, that person is more apt to acquire intelligence and wisdom and learn how to study Torah and to obey God with awe. . . .

Comment: The observation that the language of the biblical verse (Deut 11:26) signifies a collective rather than a single individual addressee serves as a jumping-off point for the preacher's discussion. He went on to reflect upon the specific type and scene of fellowship consisting of the followers of a *tzaddik* on their coming together to be in the presence of the *rebbe* and of one another.

More specifically, the passage speaks of the kind of fellowship that can draw each participant to a deeper devotional life. This requires, to his mind, a fellowship involving various spiritual models who have the potential to challenge each individual in the group to aspire to a deeper level of spirituality.

Readers may have noted that Kalonymus Kalman could also be quite critical of the followers of Hasidic leaders. He was not blind to the pitfalls of that kind of group in terms of how its members grasp their relationship to the holy man. In this homily, he describes an ideal picture of such a community.

The Need to Overcome, and Sometimes to Strengthen, a Sense of Self[16]

"See, this day I set before you blessing and curse." (Deut 11:26)

Why (in the Hebrew text) does the verse (following the directive, *R'eih*, "See") begin precisely with the word *'anokhi* (a rarer and particularly strong word when there are also other ways of expressing "I")?

... I had heard from the holy Maggid, Yehiel Mikhel of Zlozetch, concerning the verse, "I (*'anokhi*) stood between the Lord and you..." (Deut 5:5), that one who is significant in his own eyes and feels pride in having attained a certain level of learning or deeds in effect constructs a partition separating himself from God and, consequently, is incapable of experiencing even any sense of the pleasantness of God. And that is the nuance of the word *'anokhi* (I): that a person's sense of his own significance serves as such a screen standing between himself and God.[17]

... But not all times are identical. For when a person is about to pour his thoughts and feelings before God in prayer, if at that moment he asks himself, "Who am I to approach the King of kings, the blessed Holy One?" he will feel ashamed to pray enthusiastically, attaching himself to God. He will be unable to bring himself near to the service of God and, instead, will simply desist from prayer. For this reason, in approaching prayer, he must strengthen his resolve. Even if he feels weak he must say, "I am strong enough even to come to the palace of the King." For this reason the verse reads, "See I (*'anokhi*)," for depending upon the circumstance, a person's fortifying his sense of self can evoke either a blessing or a curse.

Should he be in need of strengthening himself to bless the King, the King of kings, the blessed Holy One, he might need to strengthen his own sense of self in order not to be ashamed to speak to God. In that situation, he will find blessing, while if he exalts himself unnecessarily, he will be cursed...

Comment: Humility (*'anavah*) is a core-value in Hasidic teaching, but it is also clear that humility is not a simple concept, and Hasidic texts sometimes include a rather intricate analysis of different kinds of humility along

---

16. *Ma'or va-shemesh*, V, 14ab.
17. *Mayyim rabbim*, 52ab.

with the problematics of that value. The varied moments and circumstances of a person's life call for varied ways of a person's relating to oneself. Some moments call for greater humility and a rejection of any exaggerated sense of self, while others require greater self-esteem and a realization of one's worth and capability. This difference is voiced also elsewhere in Hasidic teaching, as in the oft-quoted counsel of Simhah Bunam of Pryzucha, that "A person must have two pockets. In one is written, 'I who am but dust and ashes' (the words of Abraham in pleading before God on behalf of the inhabitants of the cities of the plains, Gen 18:27), and in the other, 'For me was the world created.'"[18]

A similar distinction between positive and negative humility is voiced in *Likkutei t'filot*, a collection of prayers composed by Natan of Nimerov, based on the teachings of Rabbi Nahman of Bratzlav. Natan, in that reflection, distinguished between true humility and a blemished humility in which a person feels himself too weak and debased to be able to engage in serving God.[19]

The Call to Unseat Pride within the Self[20]

> "You must destroy all the sites at which the nations you are to dispossess worshipped their gods, whether on lofty mountains and on hills, or under any luxuriant tree." (Deut 12:2)

What difference should it make whether the pagan altars were situated on high mountains and hills or on low mountains? . . . And can one really entertain the notion that the Israelites actually smashed altars?

. . . This wording, however, seems to exemplify a broader pattern. In *Mishna Avot* we read, "Be exceedingly humble."[21] And in addition, "Moses received the Torah from Sinai,"[22] meaning that he received the Torah due to the character and quality of Mount Sinai, the lowest of all the mountains, upon which God gave the Torah. God called to all the mountains, to Mount Carmel and Mount Tabor, which however were disqualified

---

18. *m. Sanh.* 4:5. Yoetz Kim Kaddish Rakatz, *Siah sarfei kodesh*, III, 149, #29; Buber, *'Or ha-gannuz*, 414.
19. *Likkutei t'filot*, II, #35.
20. *Ma'or va-shemesh*, V, 15ab.
21. *m. 'Abot* 4:4.
22. *m. 'Abot* 1:1.

precisely due to their grandeur and their pride.[23] And from Sinai, Moses our Teacher learned humility. Similarly we read, "It is not because you are the most numerous of peoples that the Lord set His heart on you and chose you—indeed, you are the smallest of peoples . . . " (Deut 7:7). On the basis of the Midrash,[24] Rashi commented on that verse that it was "because you make yourselves small" rather than exulting yourselves when God bestows good upon you. While the nations of the world exult themselves and choose the high mountains and hills, Abraham said of himself, ". . . I who am but dust and ashes . . . " (Gen 18:27).

. . . The verse can be read as an allusion: "the high places" signify haughtiness which itself must be destroyed, the qualities of those who conduct themselves with an eye to their own grandeur. (In Deut 12:2), the repetition of the root 'a-v-d ("destroy") points to a still deeper meaning, namely that the very essence of idolatry is precisely such haughtiness of spirit which must be thoroughly destroyed, as our Sages said, "Be exceedingly humble."[25] And the same verse which speaks of destroying the high places continues, "Do not worship the Lord your God in like manner" (Deut 12:4), for God detests pride. "But look only to the site that the Lord your God will choose amidst all your tribes as His habitation, to establish His name there" (Deut 12:5)—this refers to Moses our Teacher, chosen out of all the tribes, for from him you shall learn; just as he was humble, so you too shall be humble. And it is for this reason that the Temple, the place where God caused His presence to dwell, was in the portion of Benjamin, the youngest of all the tribes. . . .

The words, "you shall seek His dwelling-place and come there" (Deut 12:5), refer also to the place where the divine Presence dwelt, namely Mount Sinai which was the lowest of all the mountains. For the Presence of 'Adonai rested on Mount Sinai even while He detested all the high mountains, as the blessed Holy One dwells "with the contrite and lowly of spirit" (Isa 57:15). There, in every generation, you shall seek Him.

Comment: While building upon a number of earlier texts and interpretations, the above passage offers a brilliant reading of a biblical verse in a way that transcends and completely transforms the plain sense of the original text.

23. *Midr. Pss.* 68:9.
24. *b. Ḥul.* 89b, also *Yalqut Shimoni*, I, #845.
25. *m. 'Abot* 4:4.

In his discussion, the Kraków master explicitly discounts the verse's literal meaning, namely that the Israelites should actually and utterly destroy the pagan places of worship in the land of Canaan. The key to his reinterpretation revolves around the stated location of the pagan altars upon "the high mountains and hills," the kind of terrain which he read as alluding to human qualities: pride, haughtiness, self-exultation, and by implication, egotism itself which, in the framework of Hasidic teaching, is an utter failure to see oneself and the world accurately. Reading these verses in a way to reflect Hasidism's basic focus on interiority, Kalonymus Kalman concluded that it is not the altars on the high terrain but rather qualities within the self that must be challenged, negated, and demolished.

While midrashic readings convey the tradition that Sinai was a lowly mountain which was divinely chosen for that reason, the master went further and took the liberty to interpret the mention of the site of God's dwelling (in Deut 12:5) as referring not only to the Temple-site in Jerusalem but also to Mt. Sinai itself. And he brought together the figures of Abraham and Moses, viewed as exemplars of humility, with God's choice of Sinai to comprise a triad antithetical to the "high places." This reading in *Ma'or va-shemesh* grasps the liability of the "high places" not in their more obvious association with pagan belief and practice, but rather in their symbolic relationship to egotism and arrogance.

In this homily, the master and preacher wove together earlier strands and themes in a way to suggest an identification of pride and arrogance as the very core and essence of idolatry, the idolatry that all too easily can acquire a home within any person or group or ideology.

Shoftim

To Judge Oneself: Internal Judges[26]

> "You shall appoint judges and officials for your tribes, in all the settlements ('gates') that the Lord your God is giving you, and they shall judge the people with due justice." (Deut 16:18)

One who wishes to serve God in truth is obligated at all times to inspect his deeds, meaning, not only that one refrain from any deed that is not good, but that a person should carefully inspect even his good deeds and his study and prayer to ascertain whether he engaged in them in a spirit of reverence and awe as is necessary, and whether they are pure, devoid of any blemishing thought or self-centered motivation. That is the intent of the statement in the Gemara that a person should "inspect his deeds."[27] As further clarified, one must thoroughly inspect his deeds to determine whether he transgressed any positive or negative law and, in addition, he must also inspect his good deeds as to whether he did them in a spirit of reverence, free of any blemishing thought or motivation. . . .

We find an allusion to this in the rabbinic saying, "In the case of the righteous, their Good Inclination judges them."[28] The righteous judge themselves: they judge their Good Inclination and their own Torah-study and good deeds, evaluating them afterward as to whether they are truly worthy. And if they should find in their good deeds any speck that is even somewhat blemishing, then they afflict themselves, accepting upon themselves some discomfort and punishment. The righteous who hold their deeds up to inspection to know if they are pure then go on to engage in *t'shuvah* when necessary. And *tzaddikim* of that nature have the capacity to sweeten the Judgments (punishments) at their root and to draw

---

26. *Ma'or va-shemesh*, V, 17b.
27. *b. Ber.* 5b.
28. *b. Ber.* 61b.

down unqualified compassion, goodness, and lovingkindness upon the Assembly of Israel.

In this way we can comprehend the verse mentioned above more clearly as declaring: you, yourself, must assign for yourself judges! For a *tzaddik* must both provide for himself judges to judge his own Good Inclination and also officials to criticize himself and to engage in repentance "in all your gates (*she'arim*) which the Lord your God gives you,"— in all the measures (*shi'urim*) that are determined with the wisdom that is God's gift to you . . . .

Comment: Though hardly unique in the classical Hasidic homily-collections—the same general interpretation is found in *No'am 'Elimelekh*, containing the homiletical comments of Elimelekh of Lyzhansk, on the very same verse—this homily in *Ma'or va-shemesh* illustrates with utter clarity the Hasidic emphasis on interiority. The homily interprets a passage from the Torah relating to the organization of society and its system of justice in a way to relate to a person's own capacity for self-judgment and self-criticism. A prescription bearing an external, social meaning is read as expressing a meaning oriented to what occurs or fails to occur within one's inner self.

The judges mentioned in the text are read to refer not to those who sit in a court of law but rather to the self-critical role of the mind and conscience of the individual himself. And the need to judge one's Good Inclination (*yeitzer tov*), mentioned in the passage, goes even further: the Kraków master speaks of the need not only for an examination of one's deeds, but also of the need to examine the self-critical apparatus within one's psyche to ascertain its objectivity in the way it views the person's own actions.

Altars of Pride and Routine[29]

> "You shall not set up a sacred post ['*asherah*, a tree or tree-like structure, associated with pagan Canaanite practice]—any kind of pole beside the altar of the Lord your God that you may make . . . ." (Deut 16:21)

---

29. *Ma'or va-shemesh*, V, 18ab.

... ʾ*Asherah* recalls the word ʾ*ashrei* ("happy, blessed"), suggesting praise and glory, and in this vein the verse intimates that no sense of glory or pride shall enter within your consciousness regarding your religious devotion. You should not consider yourself a *tzaddik*!

And this is the meaning of ʾ*asherah*: the verse reads, "... beside the altar of the Lord your God that you may make," meaning that if you make for yourself an altar, whether of Torah-learning or of prayer or of hospitality, all of which can be types of altars, just as a person's eating-table is considered an altar,[30] what you are doing shall not promote your self-glorification, thinking that you have done something outstanding. And any person who engages in religious devotion to any degree out of a sense of self-aggrandizement is being tested, for he has not yet approached his religious devotion in the proper spirit.

And the very next verse adds, "... or erect a stone pillar, *matzeivah* [similarly associated with Canaanite religious practices], for such the Lord your God detests" (16:22), intimating to us still another matter: in a person's devotional life, it is only fitting that one ascend to ever-higher levels, each day adding thought and energy that fuels his worship. One who remains standing on the same level, one whose prayer today is simply like his prayer yesterday and the day before, without adding (any spiritual fuel to his prayer), is characterized by laziness and tiredness as he remains on a lower level without experiencing the pleasantness of the Light of God and of his worship. And this is what is meant in the words which immediately follow, "or erect a stone pillar (*matzeivah*)"—you shall not remain standing (*nitzav*) on the same level, "for such the Lord your God detests." [A stone pillar is, by nature, something standing and immobile, something that connects, in the preacher's mind, with a person's remaining on the same level, never progressing to a higher level in one's spiritual life.]

Worship of that nature is not desirable in God's eyes.

Comment: The more direct meaning of the prohibitions stated in this biblical verse applies to practices that are pagan in character or association. The preacher would be aware of this even from the wording in the Torah. The ʾ*asherah* and the *matzeivah* are reported there as objects that God hates (*sanei*)—nothing less! Beyond the more normal force of a prohibition, the text employs a highly emotional term, something that would be applicable

---

30. b. Ber. 55a, based on the wording in Ezek 41:22.

in a particular way to pagan beliefs and practices. In addition, Rashi, in his comments upon those two verses associates them, even defines them, in terms of Canaanite law or practice. (Note Rashi's comment on Deut 16:21–22; in addition, the same are referred to in the same context in Exod 23:24 and Deut 7:5.)

The preacher, however, heard or overheard in the wording of the Torah-text intimations that lead far from that plain and generally assumed understanding of the text. In this passage, Kalonymus Kalman not only reiterates his concern with the temptations of pride that are present within religious endeavor as in any other kind of endeavor, but points to an additional theme, namely *the imperative to grow through time*. Religious and devotional life are accompanied by the danger of stagnation, of one's standing on the same rung of the ladder without any improvement or deepening of one's inner self and one's consequent ascent to a higher level of devotion.

The homilist employs both the connection and the sound-similarity between the word *matzeivah* (a stone pillar) and *nitzav* (standing) very creatively in order to read the mention of the prohibited stone-pillar as referring to one's standing spiritually in one place even while going through the motions of devotion and deeds of kindness. The prohibition hence, he maintained, is understood as referring not to an actual stone-pillar, but to a person's being spiritually stagnant. Through the lens of his homily, the verse relating to features of ancient pagan worship is read as alluding to a person's inability to grow. And the implication emerges that precisely that inability to grow and deepen one's spiritual life is itself a definition of paganism.

Ki tetzei

The Beginning of the Year: *Rosh Ha-Shanah*[31]

The Jerusalem *Targum* (Aramaic translation, "Pseudo-Jonathan") read the opening verse of the Torah (Gen 1:1) as "With and through Wisdom the blessed Holy One created (heaven and earth)," and our Sages explained further, "With the Torah, the blessed Holy One created the world."[32] This idea is further clarified in the *Tikkunim* in that the letters of the Torah comprise the *nefesh* (the lowest strata of soul) of the worlds, while the vowels are the *ru'aḥ* (the next higher level), and the cantellation-signs are the *n'shamah* (the still higher lever of soulness) of the worlds, insofar as the cantellation-marks serve as the key to the intention of the word and of the particular subject-matter of a verse.[33]

On the basis of this pattern, the external reality (*ḥitzoni'ut*) of the worlds functions through their innerness, through the very soul of the worlds. And the entire purpose of *Rosh ha-shanah* [the fall holy day that came to mark the beginning of the year], expressed through prayer and the sounding of the shofar, is to extend the worlds' innerness to the lights of their externality in order that they, too, might glisten and become whole. In this way the hostile forces (*ḥitzonim*, "forces of externality") will be annulled.

This, however, is contingent upon *t'shuvah* (involving self-examination and contrition), and when Israel engages in a true, complete and whole-hearted *t'shuvah*, then they enter the World of Thought which is the World of *T'shuvah* and are no longer visible to the Accusing forces.

---

31. *Ma'or va-shemesh*, V, 23b.

32. *Midr. Gen* 1:1.

33. *Tikkunim, Zohar ḥadash*, 103c, 104b, 105c, 106b, 107d. Note also Giller, *The Enlightened Will Shine*, 11 and 24.

Then all the worlds ascend, from this lower world to the higher realms of being, and the Light of the soul of the worlds glistens even within the external aspects of the worlds as a higher spiritual understanding reaches and effects them. Through this process, all decrees of punishment are cancelled. It is for this reason that we observe *Rosh ha-shanah* over two days, as within the course of a single day we lack the power to actually lift up the world (to its higher plane). And this process is referred to as the act of enlarging the worlds.

But when we fail in this endeavor, God forbid, the worlds remain on the level of their lower character.

. . . We find truth expressed in the verse, "Happy is he whose transgression is forgiven, whose sin is covered over . . ." (Ps 32:1). Blessed is the person who engages in *t'shuvah* at its highest level, elevating and connecting the forces of Judgment at their root.

. . . But there are those people who simply follow what they see the *tzaddikim* do and never shatter their own hearts of stone, healing them and transforming them to become a heart of flesh (Ezek 36:26) and they accomplish nothing at all. They go through the motions as though simply following directions that they have learned from others and believe that such empty motions comprise awe (*yir'ah*). They engage in fasting and cause themselves hardships, while never impacting the hardness of their hearts. Their pretense of *t'shuvah* lacks all substance until they truly shatter their hearts (and their pride and self-satisfaction) to the point of experiencing awe and fear before the blessed God. . . . For fasting and similar self-imposed privations are merely secondary, and their purpose is but to prepare them to acquire a broken and contrite heart.

Comment: The real connection between the homily and the Torah-portion has less to do with the content of the Torah-portion in this case, than with the point in the year at which it came to be read. The portion, *Ki tetzei*, is read during the weeks approaching *Rosh ha-shanah*, within the season centered around the theme of *t'shuvah* (repentance) which begins with the beginning of the month of *'Elul*, a full month prior to the holy day itself. And the text in *Ma'or va-shemesh* goes on, in fact, to examine certain seemingly unrelated laws which follow, reading them as allusions to the nature of *t'shuvah*.

The act of *t'shuvah*, sincere self-examination followed by a purging of one's negative actions and qualities, is presented here in terms of cosmic effects consisting of an elevation of all the worlds. But underlying that rather mythic, kabbalistic world-picture presented in this homily is the Jew's distancing himself from all that is external in nature and attaching himself instead to the inner dimension of all experience and of all existence. *T'shuvah*, closely bound up with introspection, can be understood in this light as re-orienting and attuning one's very consciousness from what is external to what is internal to the person himself and his own life and deeds.

The preacher confronts the danger lurking in all forms of ritual, namely a tendency to allow the form to take precedence over the inner meaning of the ritual act. And we note, moreover, his even more specific concern with those who imitate the external behaviorisms of the *tzaddik* rather than reflect upon true introspection and *t'shuvah*. The preacher drew upon the words from Ezekiel, "And I will give you a new heart and put a new spirit into you; I will remove the heart of stone from your body, and give you a heart of flesh" (Ezek 36:26), but what the biblical prophet presented as a change to occur at a particular point in history following the Babylonian Exile, the homilist understood in terms of the ongoing practice of *t'shuvah*.

The reader might also note the concept, referred to in the homily, that the letters of the Torah—not the words themselves but the very letters—comprise the soul of the worlds, a conception found in the writings of Moses Cordovero and in even earlier texts.[34] Beyond the level of words is that of the letters, denoting a deeper, more abstract and luminous character. In this vein, the view, attributed to the *Besht*—and discussed in the introduction to this work—speaks of an inner attachment to the letters of the Torah.[35] The letters come together to form words, even as they are never completely subsumed by the words or their meaning, but serve as the innerness of all that exists.

Amalek[36]

> "Remember what Amalek did to you on your journey, after you left Egypt—how, undeterred by fear of God, he surprised you on the march, when you were famished and weary—, and cut

---

34. Idel, *Hasidism—Between Ecstasy and Magic*, 58.

35. *Tol'dot Ya'akov Yosef*, Int. Also Scholem, *On the Kabbalah and its Symbolism*, 71, and Etkes, *The Besht—Magician, Mystic, and Leader*, 148–50.

36. *Ma'or va-shemesh*, II, 29a.

down all the stragglers in your rear. Therefore, when the Lord your God grants you safety from all your enemies around you, in the land that the Lord your God is giving you as a hereditary portion, you shall blot out the memory of Amalek from under heaven. Do not forget!" (Deut 25:17-19)

The Midrash interpreted the phrase *'asher korkha ba-derekh* as "(Amalek) surprised (or met up with) you on the march . . ." (Deut 25:18), reading the verb *korkha* as an expression of *k'rirut* ("cooling"), similar to the cooling of a boiling element.[37] And we might understand these same words as referring to a cooling and extinguishing of the fire of the Israelites' love for one another. Initially the Israelites exemplified a warmth and enthusiastic mindset in which they truly felt love for one another, and Amalek brought them to cool off their love to the point of leaving a person incapable of loving his fellow.

. . . Amalek brought them to that cooling process by means of pride and arrogance, for *'Amalek* in *g'matria* is equivalent to 240 (*ram*, high up, exalted), an expression of lordship and arrogance. It is through a lowliness of spirit (humility) that each person comes to note his own shortcomings and his need to correct his own actions, while he sees the righteousness and worthiness of his fellow's deeds. And these aspects of humility bring him to love his fellow and allow a sense of oneness to develop. But if a person is exulted in his own eyes, then he sees (only) the blemishes of his fellow and hence comes to hate him. . . .

'Amalek (in *g'matria*) has the numerical value of 240 (*ram*, high), and while formerly the Israelites were able to love one another, the impact of the Amelekites cooled off the Israelites' warmth and enthusiasm.

. . . "You shall blot out the memory (*zeikher*) of *'Amalek* from under heaven" (Deut 25:19): if you erase the word *zeikher* (227) from the name *'Amalek* (240), you are left with thirteen which, in *g'matria*, is equivalent to love (*'ahavah*) and also to One (*'eḥad*), representing the Ineffable Name. And so in the process of erasing (the *zeikher*, the very remembrance of *'Amalek* which symbolizes haughtiness), the Name will be whole, and we are left with love. [From comments on *T'tzavveh ufarashat Zakhor*, the Torah-reading for the Shabbat immediately preceding *Purim*.]

---

37. *Tanḥ.* (*Ki tetzei*), # 9.

Ki tetzei

Comment: The concluding verses of this Torah-portion refer to Amalek, described as a wild and cruel desert tribe which attacked those at the rear of the line, the very weakest among the Israelite population who could not keep up with the others during the course of their journey through the desert.

This brief section has proved to be a highly problematic passage in which, it would seem, the Israelites are commanded to utterly destroy the Amalekites, wiping out an entire desert tribe. Of course, the Amalekites have vanished from history, and one cannot destroy a population that no longer exists! Many texts, however, including legal texts, have wrestled with that command, which, in the process, came to be interpreted in various ways. A tradition in Hasidic interpretation explained Amalek as the Evil Inclination, the negative propensities which each person must seek to annul within himself.[38]

In reading this homily from *Ma'or va-shemesh*, the reader meets with a mathematical game in which a commandment, seemingly amounting to genocide, is radically and beautifully transformed, as arrogance and its fruits are reduced to love and Oneness. Utilizing one of a whole bag of traditional interpretative tricks, the preacher bequeathed to us a reading that is nothing less than a gem of moral re-interpretation, a unique reading of what is morally a totally problematic command.

---

38. *No'am 'Elimelekh* 148 (*B'shallaḥ*, end).

Ki Tavo

The Bringing of the First-fruits: Thanksgiving Must Precede Fulfillment of Appetite[39]

The *mitzvah* of bringing the first-fruits (*bikkurim*) of the new season (Deut 26:1–11) has to do with the nature of man in relation to his materialistic impulse and his animal-soul.

When a person sees growing things ripening when it is still early in the summer, with his desire gravitating around his appetite, he would immediately consume them just as soon as they are accessible to him. And the blessed God was apprehensive that in (the Israelites') coming to the beloved Land with its grapes and figs and pomegranates, things that by nature a person treasures, the people's appetite might lead them down the path to degeneration, God forbid.

God therefore decreed that they rein in their appetites, and so when the first fruits, figs and pomegranates ripen, a person may not immediately eat them. Precisely at the time when the produce is in the process of ripening and one's appetite is burning with delight, a person is commanded to prevail over his spirit and over the pull of his appetite and subdue his desire and inclination. He is to hold off from eating that fruit until he first utilizes it in connection with a divine purpose by bringing it to the place which God has chosen and to the priest who serves there . . . who knows how to lift up the holy Sparks.

And our Sages intimated this when they said, "When a man goes down into the midst of his field and sees a fig ripening, he should tie it with a reed-rope (*gumi*)."[40] I seem to recall hearing the explanation from Elimelekh (of Lyzhansk) that when a man goes down into his field and

---

39. *Ma'or va-shemesh*, 24b–25a.
40. *m. Bikk.* 3:1.

sees a fig that has ripened, and his appetite is burning within him, then he ties it with a rope of grass as a sign that he is reining in his appetite by remembering that he is flesh and that tomorrow people will bring up grass to his pallet. And for this reason it is decreed that the body waste away in the dust—if it is not decreed due to the sin of the First Man who acquiesced to desire and so caused the impurity of the primeval serpent to cleave to him and to his posterity.

. . . And due to that reason, our fathers were required to go down to Egypt to purify their materialistic impulse and to bring forth the holy Sparks which had fallen there. . . . And for the same reason we were commanded concerning the *mitzvah* of the first-fruits in order that we not be drawn after the lustful desires of our hearts, lest the dross of material desire be part of what we are.

Comment: In his homily on the bringing of *bikkurim* (first-fruits of the harvest) prescribed in *parashat Ki Tavo*, Kalonymus Kalman went beyond a celebration of the harvest itself to propose a meaning and need for the bringing of the first-fruits to the Temple-site within a much broader context, namely the danger of repeating and intensifying the sin of the First Man. He read the practice of bringing the first fruits of the harvest season as a way of actually repairing that primordial spiritual failing and surrender to appetite. In sharp contrast with the First Man's failure, the bringing of the *bikkurim* is seen as a human triumph over a lustful appetite to eat immediately of the very first fruits of the harvest.

In a considerably briefer and less dramatic situation, one might extend this same principle to the practice of reciting a blessing (*b'rakhah*) prior to beginning a meal or to tasting any kind of food or drink.

And extending the same basic pattern, though Kalonymus Kalman could hardly be aware of the ecological knowledge with which we are familiar in our own time, we might imagine his insistence, were he living today, that we not continue to burn the world's energy-sources without first giving careful thought to their effect upon the atmosphere and upon the very scene of life.

Nitzavim

What Comprises a Community in Its Entirety?[41]

> "You (pl.) stand this day, all of you, before the Lord, your God—your tribal heads, your elders and your officials, all the men of Israel, your children, your wives, even the stranger within your camp, from woodchopper to waterdrawer—to enter into the covenant of the Lord your (sg.) God . . . ." (Deut 29:9–11)

A number of points regarding the wording in these verses are worthy of consideration. First, we read, "You stand . . . all of you," and after that, it says, "your tribal heads . . . ," which would appear to be superfluous, as they would all be included in the words, "all of you." And for the same reason, the words, "all the men of Israel," would similarly appear to be superfluous. And we might also consider the question, why does the passage begin employing the plural form while then going on to conclude with the singular (*'elohekha,* "*your* God, with a singular suffix")?

The grammar would seem to convey that, as is known, religious devotion and repentance require that we become one, uniting together as one person. It is essential that we be inter-connected by bonds of love for one's fellows, with each one able to see in his fellow that person's virtuous qualities and his devotion to his Creator, without one's considering his fellow's negative or questionable facets. For in this way we will desire to become like that other person in terms of his good deeds. It means that one person will not direct his attention to his fellow's limitations in *mitzvot* and good deeds, holding these against him and not seeking the other's good, but will rather note the ways in which his fellow's worship and deeds go beyond his own. When such an attitude of love is prevalent, the hateful Accuser has no power over either of them. . . . And then, rather than to call the people of Israel to account for their transgressions,

---

41. *Ma'or ha-shemesh,* V, 28b–29a.

the blessed God will relate mercifully toward them, awakening the divine quality of forgiveness.

In this vein, the text reads, "You *stand* this day"—you will then have the power of endurance in the presence of the Lord because "your tribal leaders and elders ... all the men in Israel" will together be as one person with one heart, relating to one another with love and brotherly feeling and friendship. The word *kol* ("all, every") alludes to the *tzaddik* who is referred to as *kol*, in that through his followers' joining together with the *tzaddikim* of the generation who connect their souls to their Root, they become as one person. ... God will then be forgiving of their wrongs, the judgments (potential punishments) will be sweetened, and compassion will be awakened.

... Even if their worship and religious life are not entirely pure, nevertheless all of them are included, from those of lowly position even to those of the highest rank. Through their purification in the furnace of affliction (based on Deut 4:20) and in the difficult experience of servitude, they all bring about the revelation of Divinity as they participate in purifying the worlds to the point that God's true Kingship may be disclosed and fulfilled in us. "For the land shall be filled with devotion to *Adonai* as water covers the sea" (Isa 11:9). The wise and learned ones are like the fruit of the tree, while the unlearned are like the leaves. And concerning the ʿamei ha'aretz (the unlearned members of the Israelite community), our Sages said, "If not for the leaves, the fruit of the tree would never develop and ripen."[42]

By means of their connecting themselves in bonds of love, evoking a sense of oneness among them, the unlearned both rely upon and assist those of learning and wisdom. In this way they render possible the Sh'khinah's dwelling among them, hence preventing any evil force of judgment to exercise power over them .... And in this matter our Sages said (that even if, God forbid, they turn to idolatrous worship but peace reigns among them), no punishment can prevail over them.[43] ... It becomes apparent that every single Israelite is a handle and a utensil rendering possible the Sh'khinah's dwelling within the world. And may His Kingship soon be revealed.

---

42. b. Ḥul. 92a.
43. *Midr. Gen* 38:6.

Comment: Though the preacher's interpretive methods might be less than convincing, in reading those verses from this Torah-portion, his thought turned to the social reality in which he himself participated and which he sought to develop, a community consisting of all kinds of Jews, both learned and unlearned. That kind of community becomes real through the love and acceptance of and by each of its members. Only when that kind of group truly becomes "like one person with one heart," is the intent and promise of such a circle realized. Echoing rabbinic comments relating to the Israelites' coming to Sinai "with one heart," having overcome a past of dissension and division,[44] the master turns to the need of such a community in his own time and place.

The Paradox of Religious Expression[45]

> "Concealed acts concern the Lord our God; but with overt acts, it is for us and our children ever to apply all the provisions of this Teaching." (Deut 29:28)

The explanation of this verse can be found in the name of the 'Ar'i on the verse, "Silence befits You … all mankind comes to You, You who hears prayer" (Ps 65:2). The explanation of that verse that "were our mouths full of song as the sea … we would still be unable to give thanks to You for even one infinitesimal fraction of Your constant blessings," *Nishmat* [a reflection included in the Shabbat morning prayer-service and based upon a talmudic prayer[46]], is known to every one who prays to God. Even those angelic beings serving above and having a number of heads and in each head a thousand mouths, etc., as is found in the Midrash, are able to utter but a small fraction of His praises.[47]

The essence of prayer is located in the heart, for the thoughts of the heart exceed what the mouth is able to express. And the Lord knows the innermost thoughts of a person. However, there is still a need to formulate an order of praises in order to be able to teach those who come after

---

44. Mek. 62a, *Baḥodesh*, end of *parashah* #1, on Exod 19:2.
45. *Ma'or va-shemesh*, V, 30a.
46. *b. Ber.* 59b.
47. See *Gedulat Moshe* in Wertheimer, *Batei Midrashot*, IV, 22ff; Ginzberg, *Legends*, 2:307; 5:416–18, n. 117.

us to pray. For if there were no prayers and praises to God other than what is in the heart, one person could never recognize another's prayer or be able to learn from it. For this reason there is need to study aloud and also to pray aloud so that those who hear might, in this way, acquire instruction as they hear things that proceed from the heart with great love and awe before God and are then able to do likewise.

. . . Prayer, by its intrinsic nature, should rightfully be secret, having a place only in the realm of one's own thought where it is hidden from others. But the revealed forms of Torah-study and prayer have the purpose of communicating to our children, so that they might fulfill all the words of this Torah, worshipping God and performing His *mitzvot* and engaging in His Torah. For it is not possible to learn these, simply and directly, from the heart of another person. . . .

. . . The essence of the *mitzvah* (commanded deed and holy act) is its innerness, the awe that one experiences in engaging in the *mitzvah*. At the same time, however, one cannot fulfill the *mitzvah* without doing (*ma'aseh*), as the *mitzvah* is actually fulfilled through the limbs of one's body. In one respect, a *mitzvah* is not fulfilled simply on the level of intention in heart and mind without a person's actual action, even while at the very same time, by their very nature, love and awe exist in the mind and heart, in what the mind thinks and the heart understands concerning the greatness of the One who forms creation. Through these the person loves God and lives with an awe of God . . . .

Comment: While providing a thoughtful rational for liturgy, an official and shared body of prayer, within the same homily the Kraków master has also revealed a sense of the basic paradox involved in liturgy.

An order of prayer consists of words, whereas the impulse to pray—he insisted—is rooted in something deeper than language and words. If the essence of prayer is located within the heart, it might follow that, ideally, one's heart would be the true location of prayer. And since that language of the heart, just like one's conception of Divinity, transcends any attempt to translate it into words, one could easily maintain that liturgy itself, a shared and standardized order of prayer employed by a community, or even by Jewry as a whole, is necessarily and intrinsically a failure. (Of course, the preacher was utilizing the medium of language to express the very limitations and failure of language.)

At the same time, however, Kalonymus Kalman introduced a pressing consideration pointing in the opposite direction. Even granting their inherent limitations, we nevertheless remain dependent upon language and upon words. There is a need precisely for shared expression, for without the use of words and an order of words, such as liturgy, one generation would be completely unable to transmit or even to communicate its faith, even imperfectly, to the next generation or to others of the same generation. Prayer would be reduced to its own intrinsic innerness, with no possibility of communication. One cannot even begin to convey what is within the heart—he explained—other than through the use of words, however limited words might be in serving that purpose. In this way, the Kraków sage explained the need for an accepted order of prayer in the form of a collective liturgical tradition to convey, paradoxically, what really cannot be conveyed or shared.

Though much has changed, the unresolved tension in the mind of the Kraków master and preacher between the primacy of the individual and that of the community—one might suggest—continues in an ongoing conversation to this very day, a conversation in which some voices place the emphasis upon roots and institutional or traditional forms, which are shared, while others accentuate the importance of wings, seeking to express that innerness of the individual person. And perhaps that tension within the mind of Kalonymus Kalman was never resolved due to a basic recognition on his part of the interdependence of roots and wings, in that sense granting primacy both to the individual and to the community.

Vayeilekh
The Limits of Relying upon One's Leader[48]

> "And (Moses) said unto them, 'I can no longer be active (literally, "come and go")'. . . . The Lord your God Himself will cross over at your head . . . .'" (Deut 31:1–3)

On the basis of the plain meaning one would explain that this instruction was given to us in order to awaken the hearts of the Israelites during these approaching days, the Days of Awe. On those days, a time of judgment by the God of Jacob, it is important that one's heart not rely upon the prayer of the *tzaddik*, the holy man in whose shadow one takes refuge and who might plead one's case, or that one might place his trust in some *mitzvah* that the holy man has done that will allow for acquittal of his followers. This matter of judgment depends, rather, solely upon the individual himself. Only the person himself can turn in a wholeness of *t'shuvah* and voice his own case in prayer and pleading before the Master of Mercy that God, whose hand is stretched out to accept penitents, might be compassionate with him and accept his repentance.

This interpretation is expressed in a lovely parable, found in the Midrash,[49] concerning the lion, the king of the beasts, who was angry with all the other beasts who then crawled, trembling in fear of that anger. They themselves did not know how they could find the courage to come before the king to plead before him to remove his anger toward them. Then the fox, the brightest of the beasts, offered to go before them to appease the king on behalf of all the others, for he knew three hundred parables with which he could appease the lion-king.

The beasts trusted his words and followed the fox who led them all. After walking a certain distance, however, he turned around to them

---

48. *Ma'or va-shemesh*, V, 36a.
49. *Midr. Gen* 78.7.

and told them that he had forgotten one-hundred of the parables. They answered him saying that they would suffice with the other two hundred parables which he still remembered. A little further on he told them that he had forgotten another hundred, and again they responded that the remaining hundred parables would suffice. And as they were approaching the king's court, he informed them that he had forgotten all the parables, and now they must help themselves, each one standing and pleading for his life before the king who might perhaps be moved by compassion toward them, for "you can't rely upon me now."

The meaning of the parable is obvious. Though the *tzaddik* stands in the breach on behalf of the Israelites and brings them near to finding shelter beneath the wings of the *Sh'khinah* and leads them to the vicinity of the King's court, nevertheless, as they approach the King's court, he informs them that the real matter depends solely upon themselves. Only they can appease the King of the kings of kings through a whole and honest repentance and through prayer and pleading.

And similarly, after leading them during all his days and bringing them near to the blessed God, in the end Moses our Teacher, may he rest in peace, warned them not to rely upon his praying on their behalf. Don't think—he told them—that he has appeased God for them and that they themselves therefore have no need to seek forgiveness and plead before Him. For essentially everything depends upon one's own praying and pleading before God, seeking forgiveness for one's iniquities, that God might forgive them in His great mercy.

And this is the meaning of what he told them, "I am unable to be active"—I am no longer able to bring you within the palace of the King, and from now on, do not depend upon me. For only God can forgive you. . . .

Comment: In his reading of a verse which, in the Torah, is connected with the very last days of Moses, the preacher—as we have already observed—sometimes read those portions in relation to the time of the year in which they came to be read, as the *Days of Awe*, days of judgment, were approaching. And in addition, the context of Moses' words are given a different meaning as the homily understands them not in reference to Moses' approaching the end of his life, but rather that as a leader, irrespective of age, he is unable to plead for his followers. Each person must plead for himself and personally engage in repentance for his own failings.

The message of the Kraków master in this homily is a stark contrast with that of Rebbe Nahman of Bratzlav who assured his followers that he would make every effort to assist each and every one of them upon their being judged in the Afterlife. Should any of his followers lack a garment to cover one's spiritual nakedness in the World-to-Come, he told them that they can then come to the *tzaddik* and receive a garment from him, and he himself would bring to each such person a garment for the soul.[50] In contrast, employing this much older parable of the fox and the lion-king, Kalonymus Kalman insisted that ultimately each person must plead his own case and cannot rely upon his *tzaddik* to come to his aid.

While praising the role of the holy man in a Hasidic community, the preacher also made a point of rejecting and reacting against popular conceptions of the role of the *tzaddik,* just as he criticized patterns of behavior in which the followers of a *tzaddik* tended to imitate the latter's actions and mannerisms. And as evident in this homily, he was particularly critical of conceptions that violated the individuality, the responsibility, and the active spiritual role of each and every one of the followers in such a community.

---

50. *Siḥot haRan,* #23. *Shivḥe haRan, Siḥot haRan,* 14.

Ha ʾazinu

Fallen, Unripe Fruit of a Tree[51]

"They are a folk void of sense." (Deut 32:28)

... God established the earth and heavens and all the worlds with wisdom and understanding. The wise men of truth (kabbalists) ... wished to express the view that God is the Intelligence hidden beyond the reach or grasp of any idea, and that our holy Torah makes man intelligent, teaching him to cleave to that hidden Intelligence, that being the true and worthy intention in Torah-study. Acquiring intelligent and enlightened understanding requires one's turning to God in repentance both before study and at the time of study, and also following one's study, as a person removes his iniquities which serve as a screen separating him from the higher Light.

This is the intent of the words, *ʿam naval ve-lo ḥakham* ("They are a folk void of sense," lacking in all discernment, Deut 32:28; the word *naval* meaning "foolish"). The revealed Torah consists of "unripe higher wisdom" which is accessible to us, for by means of the revealed Torah, one can ultimately be able to grasp the higher Wisdom itself and to attach oneself to the hidden Intelligence. However, one who possesses only the unripe wisdom and lacks any understanding of what is of a still higher nature fails to attach himself to that Intelligence. [The analogy of fruit falling from a tree before it is fully ripened occurs in the Midrash where the Torah (in its revealed form) is likened to *novlot ha-ḥokhmah ha ʿila ʾit*, "the unripe fruit of the more sublime Wisdom," or perhaps fallen leaves from such a tree.[52]]

And this is the meaning of that verse [which more literally translates as "a foolish and unwise people"] as it refers to one whose study consists only of that unripe fruit and lacks all desire to go beyond it to acquire

---

51. *Maʾor va-shemesh*, V, 40b.
52. *Midr. Gen* 17.5.

the higher wisdom. At the same time, a person can acquire that higher wisdom only through his studying the revealed Torah through which he can find his way to cleave to the higher Wisdom. That is the meaning of the assertion that the Torah, God, and Israel are one, and whoever studies Torah in this way, accepting upon himself the Kingship of God with fear and awe and with his whole heart and soul, will have the strength and the power to expel the external agents (agents of the *Sitra ʾaḥra,*) the antithesis of the holy) to the wasteland of the desert, where no human has trod.

Comment: Utilizing word-play and alliteration, the above homily relates the word *naval* (foolish) to that reference in the midrashic literature likening the Torah in its revealed form to the unripe fruit that falls (*novlot*) from the tree of a higher, more sublime Wisdom. In addition, the homily's mention of the desert devoid of humans echoes, inversely, the image of Torah as rainfall present in the very opening verses of this portion ("May my discourse come down as the rain, my speech distill as the dew, like showers on young growth, like droplets on the grass," Deut 32:2). The desert, antithesis of a scene of life and rainfall, signifies here not only a hopelessly forlorn space beyond human habitation, but also suggests its use as a metaphor for a way of studying Torah that fails to lead one to a greater depth of understanding.

The homilist's mention of the *ḥitzonim* ("external" agents of the demonic) acquires meaning in terms of an external mode of study which, by nature, does not allow one to discover within the revealed Torah a pathway that transcends it. A focus limited to the revealed text and its implications fails to reach upward to a higher grasp of being and a depth-level of understanding. Instead, it views the plain, surface meaning and its implications as the end-product of study rather than locating within it a gateway to the very innerness of the Torah.

In this homiletical excerpt, the preacher located within the revealed text itself a presumed road sign indicating a higher truth to which that text, and our engaging with it, is to lead us. Again, Kalonymus Kalman made it clear that he viewed the revealed tradition to be a necessary road, even *the* necessary road which one must travel in order to seek a deeper dimension of spiritual truth.

With a more comprehensive historical perspective, one might conclude that even the formulations of mystic teaching must themselves be viewed as such "unripe fruit" of a sublime Wisdom that transcends all such formulations. And various passages in the literature of Jewish mysticism provide the same signal.

Zot ha-b'rakhah and Rimzei Simḥat-Torah
Our Torah is Copied from a Supernal Torah[53]

The Torah preceded the world by two-thousand years.[54] [Another tradition states the same general thought in that the Torah was hidden for 974 generations prior to the creation of the world.[55]] And all that is written in our Torah, given to us from Sinai, was written also in that higher place in the primordial Torah (*torah k'dumah*). However, we understand its words below as relating to physical matters, while above there was then nothing material at all; only the mysteries existed.

    Moses, who wrote the Torah with all its happenings which we grasp as narratives and occurrences, wrote the Torah as though copying from one book to another. In that earlier book transmitted to Moses, the same matters do not relate to what is material in character, as at that level only spiritual intelligences existed. And even details, such as "And his concubine whose name was Re'umah . . ." (Gen 22:24), which appear simply as having to do with episodes of a physical nature, bear meaning concerning the innerness of the same tales, an inner meaning that is spiritual and immaterial and deep, far beyond one's ability to grasp and decipher. . . . [The quoted verse appears in the aftermath of the binding of Isaac (*'Akedah*) when Abraham received details concerning his brother's family which remained in Haran; perhaps the preacher was referring to the Besht's interpretation of her name as indicating that false humility is even worse than pride.[56]]

    53. *Ma'or va-shemesh*, V, 51b–52a.
    54. *Abot R. Nat.*, Rendition 'Alef, ch. 31
    55. b. *Šabb.* 88b. Note also *Midr. Gen* 8:2, and *Midr. Pss.* 105:3, transmitting midrashic readings of Prov 8:22 and 30 and Ps 105:8.
    56. *Ba'al Shem Tov al ha-Torah*, 1:231–32.

Moses, who copied our Torah from a Torah that preceded the world, grasped the innerness of the things themselves, for there at the time of his writing, he was in the higher sphere where there was no separation or indentation among the words. And in this way while the Torah begins with the account of creation, the ending is fastened to the beginning, conveying that all was in writing from the hand of God on the basis of the higher Torah. [On *Simḥat-Torah*, both the concluding and the opening parts of the Torah are read, and the very last letter in the Torah combines with its very first letter to form a single word, *lev*, meaning "heart."]

Comment: The master grasped the Torah-reading on *Simḥat-Torah*, consisting of the concluding portion of the Torah immediately followed by the very first chapter of the scroll—the death of Moses followed by creation—as alluding to a conception of the Torah as coming from a realm above time and its structure and order. That practice symbolizes an assertion that the Torah comes from a higher realm and is copied from a higher Torah transcending and preceding the very material nature of our world including time itself. While our reading and understanding of the Torah is mandated by the kind of reality to which we must necessarily relate, the Torah, in that sense, is copied from a higher manifestation or expression of itself. While this view was mentioned in the earlier homilies of this collection, the preacher's mystic bent and orientation is conveyed more emphatically as the collection of homilies approached the very celebration of the Torah itself and of its reading.

While guiding us in the way we are to live in this world and mode of being, the Torah, to the master's mind, has its roots in an understanding of reality that transcends our own experience.

Continuity Transcending Death[57]

> "The period of wailing and mourning for Moses came to an end. Now Joshua, son of Nun, was filled with the spirit of wisdom because Moses had laid his hands upon him; and the Israelites heeded him, doing as the Lord had commanded Moses." (Deut 34:8–9)

---

57. *Ma'or va-shemesh*, V, 53a.

Why was the discussion of Moses interrupted with mention of Joshua, which logically should have occurred only at the very end, following the concluding words, *le'einei kol yisra'el* ("in the sight of all Israel," Deut 34:12)?

... While Moses was still alive, through him the Israelites were capable of experiencing the fear and awe of God. Consequently, when Moses our Teacher departed, they would cry and groan day and night, asking, "Who will stand in the breach before us, and who will direct us in the way of the service of *Adonai*? For who is so great that he can occupy the place of Moses? And even if so, there could not possibly be a rabbi like Moses." And they cried, for they had lost such a great Light, and they will never be able again to ascend to the service of God as they did during his lifetime, for never again would they have another rabbi like Moses.

That mood of fear continued until they perceived that, through Moses' placing his hands upon Joshua, son of Nun, the spirit of wisdom permeated Joshua. The people then wished to say that he was a pupil of Moses, and anyone who leaves behind a worthy son or pupil is considered as though he had not died; they were comforted, believing that the spiritual intelligence of Moses would appear in Joshua insofar as he was his pupil. [The wording recalls both a saying from the Midrash, "One who does not have a son is considered as though he were dead,"[58] and a talmudic saying, "One who teaches Torah to someone, it is as though he fathered him."[59]] ... And Joshua, in their eyes, was now like Moses himself, and they would be able to continue their spiritual attainments also through Joshua just as they did previously through Moses.

And with that thought they were comforted and ceased from their crying.

In recognizing that Joshua was Moses' pupil, it is as though Moses did not die. With that realization, they no longer wept over Moses' departure. Knowing that he will be with them even after his death, they ceased to mourn.

---

58. *Midr. Gen* 45:2 on the basis of Gen 30:1.

59. *b. Sanh.* 19b.

Glossary

'agada—story or folktale, lore. The word, in its broader sense, applies to everything in the Talmud that is not strictly legal in character (halakhah).

'avodah—worship, service, ranging from cultic worship to serving God in every aspect of one's life.

'Ar"i—acronym signifying Rabbi Isaac Luria (1534–72).

'Asiyah—our own world and realm-of-being, the lowest of the four kabbalistic worlds.

'Atzilut—the highest and most sublime of the four worlds or realms of being in the kabbalistic world-picture.

'Ayin—literally, "Nothingness," or more precisely, that which is considered as non-existence from a material vantage-point but what is actually the one true reality, the Divine as present within everything, giving existence to all that is.

Ba'al Shem Tov—Yisra'el ben Eliezer (c. 1698–1760), the central figure in the emergence of eighteenth-century Hasidism; often referred to by the acronym, the Besh't.

B'ri'ah—one of the intermediate kabbalistic worlds, higher than our own, and hence of a more spiritual character than our own.

Chariots—based upon Ezekiel, chapter 1, and its image of the divine Chariot borne by four living beings; to be a bearer of the Chariot is to be a true servant and worshipper of God.

'Ein-sof—the Divine in its infinite state, beyond all ideas, associations, or conceptual descriptions; the Divine Infinity is ultimately the one sole reality, just as it was prior to its desire to bring about a world.

'*Emek ha-melekh*—a seventeenth-century work based upon Lurianic Kabbalah, written by Naftali Bacharach and printed in Frankfurt in 1648.

'*Etz ha-hayyim*—a compendium of the teachings of Rabbi Isaac Luria, composed by Hayyim Vital (1543–1620) after Luria's death in 1572.

Gemara—the larger part of the text of the Talmud, consisting of oral discussions of the Rabbis on the Mishna.

g'matria—a strategy of interpretation, found in rabbinic texts, consisting of reading a word according to the numerical value of the letters comprising it and then equating the total with that of other words to suggest an equivalence of meaning.

Halakhah—Jewish law, based upon Talmudic tradition.

ḥasid / pl., *ḥasidim* ("pietist(s)")—the word is applied to various groups from early post-biblical times, including the stream that goes back to the Baal Shem Tov and those inspired by him.

Haggadah shel Pesaḥ—the text read at the Seder at the first evening(s) of the *Pesaḥ* festival.

hitbod'dut—prayerful solitude.

Isaac Luria (1534–72)—whose teaching and interpretation of Jewish mystic thought came to typify kabblistic teaching. Referred to by his acronym, the '*Ar"i*.

kavanah—inner intent, devotion.

k'dushah—holiness

kohen, pl. *kohanim*—the biblical priests and their descendents.

Men of the Great Assembly ('*anshei k'neset hag'dolah*)—a council of rabbis which was thought to function during the Second Temple period.

minyan—prayer-quorum consisting of ten or more Jews.

Mishna—a codification of the "Oral Torah," rabbinic law, edited by Rabbi Yehudah haNasi in the early third century, C.E., including Avot, a collection of sayings of the earlier rabbinic sages in five chapters which, with the addition of a later sixth chapter, is referred to as *Pirkei avot* and is read in the synagogue on the afternoon of the Shabbat during the weeks between *Pesaḥ* and *Rosh Ha-shanah*.

Mitnagdim ("Opponents")—the word used specifically for the Opponents of the Hasidim representing the more conventional rabbinic establishment and its followers.

mitzvah, pl. *mitzvot*—commanded deed; holy act.

Glossary

Moses Cordovero (the *Rama'k*)—the foremost kabbalistic thinker in Safed until his death which roughly coincided with the coming of Isaac Luria to Safed in 1570.

Onkolos—a second-century translation of the Torah (Pentateuch) into Aramaic.

'Or Ḥayyim—commentary on the Torah by Hayyim ben-Atar (1696–1742), a Sefardic rabbi who influenced Hasidism.

parashah—weekly Torah-portion, based upon the Babylonian tradition of Torah-reading in which the entire Torah is read over the course a single year.

Pesaḥ ("Passover")—the festival associated with the exodus from Egypt (*Mitzrayim*).

Rashi—acronym for Rabbi Shlomo ben Yitshak (d. 1105), who lived much of his life in Troyes, France, and composed what became the most popular commentary on the Torah and other parts of the Hebrew Bible and also commented on almost the entire Babylonian Talmud.

S'firot—ten manifestations of Divine being, underlying all reality including the human psyche, that came into being as separate, but integrating, manifestations as part of the attempt to reconstruct existence itself following the *Sh'virah*.

Sh'khinah—the immanence of the Divine; the name became the tenth or lowest of the *s'firot* (manifestations of Divine being, in kabbalistic thinking) and was considered the sole feminine *s'firah*, also called *Malkhut* (Rule or Kingship).

Shabbat—Seventh day of the week, "Sabbath," which begins with sundown on Friday and concludes with darkness the following night.

Sh'virah—"Catastrophe." In Lurianic teaching, the cataclysm occurring after the *Tzimtzum* in which the vessels containing the Light were unable to contain the Light.

Sitra 'aḥra— "The other side," the demonic or unholy reality that came into being as a consequence of the *Sh'virah* ("Cataclysmic Shattering"); the anti-Divine force.

Sparks (*nitzotzot*)—of the Divine that fell with the *Sh'virah* and are to be found within everything, including evil; the Israelite, in particular, has the task of cosmic repair by redeeming the hidden, fallen Sparks by restoring them to their holy source.

Talmud—the Mishna and Gemara (collection of conversations on the Mishna).

Two Talmuds were composed, known as the Babylonian Talmud [b.] and the Jerusalem Talmud [y.]

tanna—Rabbinic sages of the period prior to the editing of the Mishna in the early third century, C.E.

t'shuvah—Repentance; in pietistic literature, a continuous process of self-questioning and a deepening of spirituality accompanied by inner change.

Tikkun— "correction, improvement." In Lurianic Kabbalah, a re-ordering of existence following the *Sh'virah* and its cataclysmic effects.

Torah lishmah—engaging in the study of Torah for its own sake, rather than for any considerations of personal reward or benefit, including prestige. Torah-study motivated by such personal considerations is termed *Torah she-lo lishmah*.

tzaddik / tzaddikim—"Righteous." The word, however, came to suggest a "holy man," and in this light, the leader (and center) of a hasidic community came to be referred to by this title.

Tzimtzum— "Contraction" of the *'Ein-sof* and its Light; in Lurianic Kabbalah, a retreat from part of itself for the purpose of creating a space in which the worlds could come into bring. Hasidic teaching, however, understood *tzimtzum* more as a cladding of God's holiness and of the Torah necessary for the purposes of our realm of existence and its physical character.

Y'sod—"Foundation," the supremely masculine *s'firah* which engages in union with *Malkhut* (the *Sh'khinah*), its feminine counterpart.

yiḥuddim—(Unifications). Actions, often of a contemplative nature, which are believed to effect a unification of the *s'firot*, the spiritual reality underlying existence itself.

z"l—May his/her memory be a blessing.

Bibliography

The translation of all biblical passages is based upon *Tanakh, A New Translation of The Holy Scriptures according to the Traditional Hebrew Text*. Philadelphia, New York, Jerusalem: The Jewish Publication Society of America, 1985. The translations are reproduced by permission of University of Nebraska Press.

Rabbinic Texts

'*Avot deRabbi Natan*. Edited by Solomon Schechter. New York: Feldheim, 1945.
Babylonian Talmud. *Talmud Bavli* as printed in Vilna Ram edition. 16 vols. Jerusalem: El haMekorot, 1948.
M'khilta deRabbi Yishma'el. Edited by Ish-Shalom. New York: OM, 1948.
Midrash hagadol al ḥamishah ḥumshei torah.
    Vol. 1. *Genesis*. Edited by Mordecai Margoliot. Jerusalem: Mosad haRav Kook, 1947;
    Vol. 2. *Exodus*. Edited by Mordecai Margoliot. Jerusalem: Mosad haRav Kook, 1967.
    Vol. 3. *Leviticus*. Edited by N. E. Rabinowitz. New York: Jewish Theological Seminary, 1932;
    Vol. 4. *Numbers*. Edited by Zvi Meir Rabinowitz. Jerusalem: Mosad haRav Kook, 1967;
    Vol. .5 *Deuteronomy*. Edited by Solomon Fisch, Jerusalem: Mosad haRav Kook, 1972.
Midrash rabbah al haTorah veḤamesh haM'gilot. Sudlikov, 1819. 2 vols. [Includes *B'rei'shit rabbah, Sh'mot rabbah, Vayikra rabbah, B'midbar rabbah, D'varim rabbah, Shir haShirim rabbah, Rut rabbah, 'Ekha rabbah, Kohelet rabbah* and '*Ester rabbah*.] Also *Midrash rabbah*. Edited by M. A. Minkin. 11 Vols. Tel Aviv: Hotza'at Yavneh, 1974–81; and *Midrash rabbah* (English translation). 10 vols. New York: Soncino, 1983.
Midrash Tanḥuma. Edited by Solomon Buber. New York: Hotsa'at Sefer, 1946.
Midrash Tanḥuma HaKadum V'haYashan. Edited by Solomn Buber. Jerusalem: Urtzal, 1964.

Midrash Tanḥuma-Yelammdenu. Translated by Samuel A. Berman. New York: KTAV, 1996.
Midrash T'hillim. New York: OM, 1948. *The Midrash on Psalms*. Translated by William G. Braude. New Haven: Yale University Press, 1959.
Mishna. 2 vols. New York: Ha'Ahim Schlesinger, 1948.
Sifra. Jerusalem: Sifriyah toranit, 1991.
Sifre. New York: OM, 1948.
Pesikta deRav Kahana. Edited by S. Buber. New York: OM, 1949.
Pirke deRabbi Eliezer. Warsaw, 1812; Jerusalem: Shmuel Luria, 1963. English translation by Gerald Friedlander. New York: Sepher Hermon, 1981.

Christian Texts

The Apostolic Fathers. Translated by Kirsopp Lake. 2 vols. Matrix: The Loeb Classical Library, vols. 24–25. London: Heinemann, 1914.

Medieval Texts

Baḥya ben Asher. *Midrash Rabenu Baḥya 'al Ḥamishah Ḥumshei ha-torah*. Warsaw, 1878.
Baḥya Ibn Pekuda (Rabbenu Baḥya b'rabbi Yosef). *Sefer Ḥovot hal'vavot*. Hebrew translation from Arabic by Yehudah Ibn Tibbon. Jerusalem: Eshkol, 1969.
Batei midrashot, Esrim ve ḥamishah midrashe Ḥazal 'al pi kitve yad mi-genizot Yerushalayim uMitzrayim. Edited by Abraham Joseph Wertheimer and Solomon Aaron Wertheimer. 4 Vols. Jerusalem: *Ketav vaSefer*, 1968.
Maimonides, Moses. *Mishneh-torah*. 6 vols. New York: Rambam, 1957.
Perush Rashi al ha-torah. Jerusalem: Makor, 1969. Also, *The Metsudah Chumash/ Rashi. A New Linear Translation*. 3 vols. Hoboken, NJ: KTAV, 1991; and Art Scroll Saperstein edition, translated by Zvi Herczeg. Brooklyn, NY: Mesorah, 1994.
Sefer ha-yashar. Edited by Joseph Dan. Jerusalem: Mosad Bialik, *Sifriat Dorot*, 1986.

Kabbalistic Texts

Alshekh, Moshe. *Torat Moshe*. Jerusalem: Makhon Lev Same'ah, 1990. Translated by Eliyahu Munk, 2 vols. Jerusalem: Rubin Mass, 1988.
Ben-Attar, Hayyim. *'Or haḥayyim* Translation by Eliyahu Munk. 5 vols. Brooklyn, NY: Hemed Books, 1995. (First printed, Venice, 1842. The Hebrew text is also included in many editions of *Mikra'ot g'dolot*.)
Ḥemdat yamim. 4 Vols. Leghorn, 1763. (First printed, Smyrna, 1731).
Kaidanover, Zvi Hirsch ben Aaron Samuel. *Kav hayashar*. Frankfurt, 1705; Vilna, 1888. Translated by Avrahom David. New York: Tetsudah, 2007.
Sefer b'rit m'nuḥah. Jerusalem: Makhon Ramhal, 1998.
Tikkunei Zohar. Edited by Reuven Margoliot. Jerusalem: Mosad haRav Kook, 1978.
Vital, Hayyim, *Sha'ar ha-gilgulim*. Safed: Birkat Or le'Tzion, 2004.

Zohar. Based on the Vilna Ram edition. 3 Vols. New York: Or haZohar, 1954. *The Zohar —Pritzker Edition*. Translated and edited by Daniel C. Matt. Multi-volume, in process. Stanford, CA: Stanford University Press, 2004–. Also, *The Zohar by Rav Shimon bar Yohai from the Book with the Sulam Commentary*. Edited by Yehudah Ashlag and revised by Michael Berg, 23 vols, including the index-volume (Vol. 23). Los Angeles: The Kabbalah Center, 2003.

Hasidic Texts

Ba'al shem tov 'al ha-torah. Edited by Shimon Menahem Mendel of Gavartshu. 2 vols. Jerusalem, ndp.

Degel mahaneh 'Efrayim (Moshe Hayyim Efrayim of Sedilikov). Jerusalem: Sifrei g'dolei ha-hasidut, 1963. (First printed, Koretz, 1810.)

Keter shem tov (Aharon of Apt). Lemberg, 1885. (First printed, Zholkva, 1794.)

Likkutei t'filot. Jerusalem: Hasidei Breslav, 1957. (First printed, Bratslav, 1827.)

Likkutim y'karim. Jerusalem: Yeshivat Toldot Aharon, 1974. (First printed, Lemberg, 1792.)

Ma'or 'einayim (Menahum Nahum of Chernobyl). npp 1984. (First printed, Bratslav, 1842.). Part 1 (*B'reishit*), translated by Arthur Green. *Menahem Nahum of Chernobyl: Upright Practices, The Light of the Eyes*. New York: Paulist, 1982.

Ma'or va-shemesh 'al hamishah humshei Torah (Kalonymus Kalman Epstein). Warsaw: B'nei Shmu'el Argelbrand, 1876–77. (First printed, Bratslav, 1842.) A more recent edition appeared: Jerusalem: Hotza'at Makhon Even Yisra'el, 1992, 2 vols., along with separate volumes on *B'reishit* and *Sh'mot*, edited by Menahem Avrohom Braun. Jerusalem: Or ha-Sefer, 1993.

Mayyim rabbim (a collection of teachings attributed to Yehiel Mikhel of Zlozetch). Warsaw: Shriftgissar, 1899.

No'am 'Elimelekh (Elimelekh of Lyzhansk). Jerusalem: Hotsa'at Ben Adam, 1992. (First printed, Lemberg, 1788.)

'Or y'sharim, edited by M. S. Kleinman. Pietrkov: Trybunalski, 1924.

'Or Yitzhak (Isaac of Radvil). Jerusalem: El he-harim, 1992. (First printed, Jerusalem, 1961.)

Sefer Simhat Yisra'el, (Simhah Bunam of Pryzucha). Jerusalem: Bet Hilel,, 1982. (First printed, Pietrekov: 1910.)

Shivhei ha-Besht. Edited by Sh. A. Horodetsky. Tel Aviv: Hotsa'at Devir, 1968. (First printed, Kopost, 1814–15.) *In Praise of the Baal Shem Tov*. Translated and edited by Dan Ben-Amos and Jerome R. Mintz. Bloomington, IN: Indiana University Press 1970.

Shivhei haRan (includes *Sihot haRan*) by Natan of Nimerov. Jerusalem: Beit midrash Breslov, 1961. (First printed, Ostrog, 1816.)

Si'ah sarfei kodesh (Yoatz Kaim Kadish). 5 vols. B'nai B'rak: Lev, 1989. (First printed, Pietrekov, 1922).

S'fat emet (Yehudah Aryeh Lev of Gur). 5 vols. Jerusalem, ndp. (First printed, Pietrkov, 1905–8.)

Toldot Ya'akov Yosef (Ya'akov Yosef of Polonnoye). 2 vols. Jerusalem: Agudat beit vialipali, 1973. (First printed, Koretz, 1780.)

Modern Texts, Studies and Literature

Agnon, Shmuel Yosef. '*Atem re'item*, Book One. Tel-Aviv: Schocken, 1962.
Altmann, Alexander. *Studies in Religious Philosophy and Mysticism*. Ithaca, NY: Cornell University Press, 1969.
Altman, Donald. *Art of the Inner Meal: Eating as a Spiritual Path*. New York: HarperSanFrancisco, 1999.
Armstrong, Karen. *The Bible: The Biography*. London: Atlantic, 2007.
Buber, Martin. '*Or haGanuz, Sippurei Ḥasidim*. Jerusalem: Schocken, 1958.
———. *The Origin and Meaning of Hasidism*. Edited and translated by Maurice Friedman. New York: Harper Torchbooks, 1966.
Dan, Joseph. *Sifrut ha-musar v'had'rush*. Jerusalem: Keter, 1975.
Dynner, Glenn, ed. *Holy Dissent: Jewish and Christian Mystics in Eastern Europe*. Detroit: Wayne State University Press, 2011.
———. *Men of Silk: The Hasidic Conquest of Polish Jewish Society*. Oxford: Oxford University Press, 2006.
———. *Yikhus and the Early Hasidic Movement: Principles and Practice in Eighteenth- and Early-Nineteenth-Century Eastern Europe*. MA thesis, McGill University, 1997.
Eliade, Mircea. *Myth and Reality*. Translated from the French by Williard R. Trask. New York: Harper and Row, 1963.
———. *The Sacred and the Profane: The Nature of Religion*. Translated from the French by William R. Trask. New York: Harcourt, Brace and World, 1957.
Emerson, Ralph Waldo. *The Complete Essays and Other Writings of Ralph Waldo Emerson*. Edited by Brooks Atkinson. New York: The Modern Library, 1940.
Etkes, Immanuel. *The Besht: Magician, Mystic, and Leader*. Waltham, MA: Brandeis University Press, 2005.
Fine, Lawrence. *Physician of the Soul, Healer of the Cosmos: Isaac Luria and His Kabbalistic Fellowship*. Stanford, CA: Stanford University Press, 2003.
Fishbane, Michael. *Biblical Myth and Rabbinic Mythmaking*. Oxford: Oxford University Press, 2003.
———. *The Kiss of God: Spiritual and Mystical Death in Judaism*. The Samuel and Althea Stroum Lectures in Jewish Studies. Seattle: University of Washington Press, 1994.
Gibran, Kahlil. *Secrets of the Heart*. Edited by Martin L. Wolf. Translated by Anthony Rizcallan Ferris. New York: Philosophical Library, 1947.
Giller, Pinchas. *The Enlightened Will Shine: Symbolization and Theurgy in the Later Strata of the Zohar*. Albany, NY: SUNY, 1993.
Ginzberg, Louis. *Legends of the Jews*. 7 vols. Philadelphia: Jewish Publication Society, 1954.
Green, Arthur. *Devotion and Commandment: The Faith of Abraham in the Hasidic Imagination*. Cincinnati: Hebrew Union College Press, 1989.
Gries, Ze'ev. *The Book in the Jewish World, 1700–1900*. Portland, OR: The Littman Library of Jewish Civilization, 2007.
———. *Sefer, sofer v'sippur b'rei'shit haḥasidut*. Tel Aviv: Ha-kibbutz hameu'had, 1992.

Gross, David. *Otzar ha'aggadah—mei-ha-mishnah, v'hatosefta, ha-talmuddim ve-ha-midrashim v'sifrei hazohar.* 3 vols. Jerusalem, Mosad haRav Kook, 1961.
Grozinger, Karl Erich. *Kafka and Kabbalah.* Translated by Susan Hecker Ray. New York: Continuum, 1994.
Heineman, Isaac. *Darkhei ha-'agada.* Jerusalem: Magnus, 1954.
Heschel, Abraham Joshua. *God in Search of Man: A Philosophy of Judaism.* Philadelphia: Jewish Publication Society, 1956.
———. *Man is Not Alone: A Philosophy of Religion.* Philadelphia: Jewish Publication Society, 1951.
———. *A Passion for Truth.* New York: Farrar, Straus & Giroux, 1973.
Hundert, Gershon David. *Jews in Poland-Lithuania in the Eighteenth Century: A Genealogy of Modernity.* Berkeley, CA: University of California Press, 2004.
Hyman, Aharon. *Sefer haktuvah v'ham'surah 'al torah, n'vi'im ukh'tuvim.* 3 vols. Tel Aviv: Dvir, 1979.
Idel, Moshe. *Hasidism: Between Ecstasy and Magic.* Albany, NY: SUNY, 1995.
Lobel, Diana. *A Sufi-Jewish Dialogue: Philosophy and Mysticism in Bahya ibn Paquda's Duties of the Heart.* Philadelphia: University of Pennsylvania Press, 2006.
Margolin, Ron. *Mikdash 'adam: ha-hafnamah ha-datit ve'itzum ḥayei ha-dat hapnimi'im b'rei'shit ha-ḥasidut.* Jerusalem: Magnes, 2005.
Matt, Daniel D. "*Ayin*: The Concept of Nothingness in Jewish Mysticism." In *The Problem of Pure Consciousness,* edited by Robert K. C. Forman, 121–59. Oxford: Oxford University Press, 1990. Reprinted in *Essential Papers on Kabbalah,* edited by Lawrence Fine, 67–108. New York: New York University Press, 1995.
Nigal, Gedaliya. "*Mishnat ha-ḥasidut b'sefer Ma'or va-shemesh*." *Sinai* 75.3–4 (Sivan-Tammuz, 1974) 144–68.
Polen, Nehemiah. "Miriam's Dance: Radical Egalitarianism in Hasidic Thought." *Modern Judaism* 12.1 (1992) 1–21.
Schechter, Solomon. "The Chassidim." In *Studies in Judaism,* 1–45. Philadelphia: Jewish Publication Society, 1896.
Schimmel, Annemarie. *Muhammad Is His Messenger: The Veneration of the Prophet in Islamic Piety.* Chapel Hill, NC: University of North Carolina Press, 1985.
———. *Mystic Dimensions of Islam.* Chapel Hill, NC: University of North Carolina Press, 1975.
Scholem, Gershom. *Major Trends of Jewish Mysticism.* New York: Schocken, 1961.
———. *On the Kabbalah and its Symbolism.* Translated by Ralph Manheim. New York: Schocken, 1985.
Schwartz, Howard. *Tree of Souls: The Mythology of Judaism.* Oxford: Oxford University Press, 2004.
Stoffler, F. E. *The Rise of Evangelical Pietism.* Leiden: Brill, 1965.
Tishby, Isaiah. *Mishnat haZohar.* Texts from the Book of Splendor. Jerusalem: Mosad Bialik, Vol. 1 (with F. Lachover) 1949; Vol. 2, 1961. (English translation by David Goldstein, *The Wisdom of the Zohar—An Anthology of Texts.* 3 vols. Littman Library. Oxford: Oxford University Press, 1989.)
Thompson, Stith. *Motif Index of Folk Literature.* 6 vols. Bloomington, IN: Indiana University Press, 1955–58.
Weiner, Aharon. *The Prophet Elijah in the Development of Judaism—A Depth-Psychological Study.* Littman Library of Jewish Civilization. London, Boston: Routledge and Kegan Paul, 1978.

Wilensky, Mordecai. *Ḥasidism umitnagdim l'tol'dot hapulmus beneihem 1772–1815*. Jerusalem: Mosad Bialik, 1970.

Wineman, Aryeh. *Beyond Appearances: Stories from the Kabbalistic Ethical Writings*. Philadelphia: Jewish Publication Society, 1988.

———. "The Exodus in the Lens of Hasidic Teaching." *Conservative Judaism* 70.3 (2000) 39–45.

———. "A Hasidic Myth of the Death of Moses and Its Later Metamorphosis." *Hebrew Studies* (NAPH) 54 (2013) 121–32.

———. *The Hasidic Parable: An Anthology with Commentary*. Philadelphia: Jewish Publication Society, 2001.

———. "Hewn from the Divine Quarry: An Examination of Isaac of Radvil's 'Or Yitshak." *Hebrew Union College Annual* 77 (2006) 179–207.

———. "How the Hasidic Masters Read the Torah." *Conservative Judaism* 60.1–2 (2007–8) 62–73.

———. "Mircea Eliade and the Jewish Holy Day." *Judaism* 33.4 (1984) 485–89.

———. *Mystic Tales from the Zohar*. Philadelphia: Jewish Publication Society, 1996; Princeton, NJ: Princeton University Press, 1997.

———. "Sufis in the Hasidic *Mishkan*." *Conservative Judaism* 64.4 (2013) 110–20.

———. "A Wrestling with Interpretation in a Classical Hasidic Text." *Conservative Judaism* 49.2 (1997) 68–74.

www.ingramcontent.com/pod-product-compliance
Lightning Source LLC
Chambersburg PA
CBHW070241230426
43664CB00014B/2372